PRAISE FOR THE GAME

"A first-rate discussion of hockey by one of hockey's first-rate players and first-rate minds.... Essential reading for anyone serious about hockey as an important part of Canadian life."
Hamilton Spectator

"*The Game* is a beautifully written, insightful, perceptive, revealing look at hockey."
Toronto Star

"We always wondered what he was thinking about whenever the play stopped and he struck his characteristic pose resting his chin on his goal stick. Now we know. He was composing one of the best hockey books ever written.... There is a 'you are there' quality to the prose as the author-goalie lets you see everything through his eyes, spicing his vivid descriptions with personal reflections and observations.... *The Game* succeeds both as an inside look at hockey and a portrait of an articulate athlete who knew when to quit."
Winnipeg Free Press

"*The Game* is a brilliant adventure into ourselves. It makes all other books about the sport look preliminary."
Calgary Herald

"A book about Ken Dryden, about Quebec, about the rest of Canada, and most of all, a loving book about a special sport."
New York Times

"The best Canadian sports book in years."
Calgary Sun

"An incredible memoir, a poetic journey through the life of Les Canadiens. It rises above being just a book about hockey. It's a book about people, the fragile, delicate moments on the edge of fame and glory, failure and disillusionment. Dryden's *The Game* is the complete hockey book."
Windsor Star

"As Dryden reminisces, we are presented with a portrait, in broad and vivid strokes, of the players who comprised the best team in professional hockey.... All the ingredients of a winner."
Victoria Times-Colonist

"No one has ever delivered an account of our national sport as deep as this. On a scale of 1 to 10, give the guy his sweater number—29."
Regina Leader-Post

THE
GAME

For Lynda, Sarah and Michael

THE GAME

3rd Edition

Ken Dryden

A reflective and thought-provoking look at life in hockey

Macmillan Canada
Toronto

Canadian Cataloguing in Publication Data

Dryden, Ken, 1947-

   The game : a reflective and thought-provoking look at a life in hockey

ISBN 0-7715-7673-0

1. Dryden, Ken, 1947-   .2. Montreal Canadiens (Hockey team).
3.National Hockey League.   4. Hockey players – Canada – Biography.
I. Title.

GV848.5.D7A3 1999   796.962'092   C99-9932227-3

This book is available at special discounts for bulk purchases by your group
or organization for sales promotions, premiums, fundraising and seminars.
For details, contact: CDG Books Canada Inc., 99 Yorkville Avenue, Suite
400, Toronto, On M5R 3K5.

We acknowledge the financial support of the Government of Canada through
the Book Publishing Industry Development Program for our publishing
activities.

0 1 2 3 4 5 TRI 03 02 01 00 99

Cover design by Counterpunch/Peter Ross
Front cover photo by Denis Brodeur
Back cover photo courtesy of the Toronto Maple Leaf Hockey Club
Special thanks to Phil Pritchard and the Hockey Hall of Fame

Cover quote from *Quill & Quire*

Macmillan Canada
An imprint of CDG Books Canada Inc.
Toronto
Printed in Canada

Foreword

IN MARCH 1996, I WAS INVITED TO GO BACK TO MONTREAL for the closing of the Forum. The building that was hockey's Yankee Stadium and Wembley Stadium, the building that was the one right place to watch and play the game, was about to stage its final contest. It had become financially obsolete, with too few corporate boxes and seats to support the demands of today's game. The Montreal public had known for years this day was coming and they were ready. Originally constructed in 1924, the arena had been renovated and changed over the years and entirely rebuilt in 1968, leaving us the building that everyone called lovingly "the old Forum." It wasn't really the old Forum, of course, but it had come to feel that way, and therein lay the opportunity for the new Molson Centre, which would open a week later. A cherished structure *was* replaceable. It all depended on what was put in its place.

I didn't want to go back for that game, but I knew I had to. I don't like reunions. The people I once liked, I had liked for reasons that had to do with a time in my life and a time in theirs, and I didn't know if I'd changed or they'd changed or if our lives were just different enough that things wouldn't feel like I wanted and needed them to feel. I have a big stake in Montreal, in the Canadiens, in my teammates and in the fans. All that was a time I never imagined would happen, and then it happened in a way that was so much bigger and richer and more complicated and special than I'd ever had the right to dream. But the story was written. It was done and over and safely put away, mine forever and ever. It had all turned out. It had had a happy ending. I didn't want to put that at risk.

But I couldn't not go. The people in Montreal wanted a chance to remember and celebrate, and none of us had the right to get in the way.

I don't remember much about the game. The fans watched, and the players seemed to play, just waiting for it to end and the ceremonies to begin. Then the fans stayed in their seats, the arena darkened, red carpets were rolled onto the ice. At either end of the ice surface, in tuxedos, Richard Garneau, in French, and Dick Irvin, in English, began to tell the story of the team and its home.

The Canadiens had invited back all the team's former players who had been inducted into the Hockey Hall of Fame. We had been brought to a corridor near the ice and given a Canadiens jersey to put on with our name and number on the back. We were arranged in a line in order of the year of our Hall of Fame inductions, the order in which we would be introduced. The line straggled, bunched and rearranged itself as we laughed and talked, the event organizers panicking. The team that rarely lost but could never do drills, still couldn't.

Beside us in the corridor, resting in a stand, was a large gilded torch that we knew somehow would be used in the ceremony. A central image of John McRae's poem "In Flanders Field," the words that ringed the ceiling of the team's dressing room, that symbol of triumph, tradition and responsibility, looked hokey, and we knew it was sure to have some hokey purpose. Gump Worsley couldn't hold himself back. We knew what would happen next and began to chuckle. Gump took out his lighter, turned on the gas for the torch, and lit it. The torch came to life. So too did a scurry of event organizers, who until this moment had been mostly invisible, but now were everywhere, who quickly extinguished the flame, then repositioned themselves nearby.

The roll call began. Garneau, then Irvin, gave the details of each player's career, images of that player in action flashing on the videoboard above. One by one we came out. For that moment, the focus was on us entirely. And the moment went on. We walked with limps that had been earned on the very ice that was beneath us; the carpeting had been arranged in long thin bands that led to most of the ice surface. The walk was long; aging solitary figures taking a final lap. Each player came to a stop at a designated point on the carpet, several feet away from the next nearest player. The image on the videoboard then went to an extreme close-up of the player's face. Hair had thinned and greyed, facial scars that had once almost faded to inconsequence now looked like fault lines cut into fleshy, craggy faces. Yet, as the fans had the chance to study them, these faces looked less old, and more well lived-in.

Then it was my turn. When you are walking that way, it feels dumb and exhilarating and embarrassing and wonderful. You have been given a right, this once, to show off. Time moves very, very slowly; the crowd is louder than you ever dared dream. Then you stop at your position, and the sound continues. You look around for the comfort of teammates who at moments like this are always nearby, to joke with, laugh with, to deflect and control and minimize the moment, to spread it around because you're not sure you can bear it yourself. Because you're not supposed to. But they are thirty feet away, and you have to feel the moment yourself. All of it. You have to look into the crowd, because there is nowhere else to look and nothing else to do. You see faces, you see hands coming together, maybe for the first time. Then, you were too busy. Then, there would always be another time. You played season after season, years that would never end, then suddenly you're gone, and you never had the chance to say goodbye, never had the chance to say "thank you," and they didn't either. Now you do. Now they do. Then the feeling of all those years came back to me.

Then the sound stops, but the feeling doesn't. Then you have a chance to do something else you've never had the chance to do before. You look around at former teammates standing proudly at other stations on the carpet. You see them at a distance, separate from each other; the way others see them. Lafleur, Lemaire, Lapointe—look at them—Gainey, Savard, Shutt. Look at all those great players. I played with them. *I* did. Look at all those Stanley Cup banners above us. We won those. All of them. We must have been good. Really good.

Some minutes later, it was the Rocket's turn. In the beauty of a midnight sky, you don't look to see which star is brightest. But you know. The applause began, then wouldn't stop. And the Rocket, being the Rocket, stood there unmoving. "You cannot get to me," he was saying to the crowd, as he had said to every player he had ever played against. "I am a hockey player. I score goals. I'm not any more than that, and don't try to make me." He didn't move, and they didn't stop applauding. The crowd sensed it before he did—it had become a contest of wills. On the videoboard was Rocket's face; the camera focused in closer and closer. It took about 5 minutes, then the first sign—a tiny embarrassed smile. The crowd saw it—they clapped louder. A few minutes later, Richard raised his hand for them to stop. They didn't. Then his eyes started to glisten, then to well up—they got him! It was great.

I arrived that night at the Forum with a stake in what had been, afraid of what I might find. I left with a gift. I felt *the game* again.

KEN DRYDEN
August 1999

Introduction

THIS BOOK WAS LIVED AND RESEARCHED OVER TWENTY-FIVE years, thought about consciously on and off for at least the last five of those years, and finally written. It began as a boxful of scrap paper—hotel stationery, backs of envelopes, torn pages from newspapers and magazines—random inspirations that came from sleepless postgame nights, from twenty-two miles of silent highway from home to the Forum and back ("When am I going to remember to put a pen in that glove compartment?"), from games behind a peerless defense that often left me with nothing else to do. I was sure that, clipped together, filed, laid end-to-end, they would become a book. They did not. Like most midnight thoughts, what I found in the morning looked disturbingly thin and incomplete, often contradictory, not at all the story that had seemed to me so different and untold. Yet each scrap would later become a useful trigger for recollections otherwise lost.

It was a book I couldn't have written while I played. It needed time. As it is with a game, I needed to wait for lifelong, career-long feelings to settle and sort themselves out. I needed to distance myself from things I had long since stopped seeing, to see them again. In the end, it turned out to be the kind of wonderful, awful, agonizing, boring, thrilling time others have described writing to be. One of those things we call "an experience."

There are many people responsible for this book, and to them I owe a great debt. To my parents, Murray and Margaret Dryden, who introduced me to a sporting life; to my brother, Dave, who showed me just how much fun it could be. To my early coaches— Ray Picard, Ross Johnstone, Fred Fess, Ken Pleasance, Ken Thom, Ned Harkness—who understood the game but never forgot the rest. And to my teammates then and now. It started out as my story, and became theirs. I hope I got it right.

I also owe much to ever-patient typists and friends too numerous to mention here, but most especially to Don Coles, David Fisher, David Harrop, Art Kaminsky, Red Fisher, Alan Williams, Ed Burlingame, Doug Fisher and Rick French, who read the manuscript in its various stages and forms and made me believe they were as interested in it as I was. The errors are mine; they may see as much of themselves in the rest as they wish. To Rick Salutin, for his special help and friendship. To Doug Gibson, for encouraging the project in the beginning, and being there all along the way. To Jon Segal, for making me finally understand that it was a story I was telling. And to Lynda, Sarah, and Michael. They made the bad days less bad, and the good days seem better. Without them, this book could not have been written.

KEN DRYDEN
Toronto, May 1983

Monday

MONTREAL

I HEAR SOMETHING AND STIR, THEN SQUINT OPEN MY EYES. The room is filled with the morning sun. Sarah, aged four, appears and quickly disappears, shuffling noisily from room to room in her snowsuit, looking for something, apparently with no success. Downstairs, in a whispered shout, my wife Lynda tells her to hurry up. I look at the clock in the alcove beside me. It is 8:51. I start to get up, then I hear Sarah going down the stairs. I yell goodbye to her, and she yells a reply. I lie back, close my eyes, but I don't sleep.

It has been a short, restless night, yet I feel wonderfully refreshed. The sun, the crisp white sheets, a quilt pulled up to my nose—I'm filled with an enormous sense of well-being and for several moments I don't know why. Then I remember. The game, last night's game in Buffalo. I must be tired—it's less than four hours since I went to bed—but that can wait. I want to be awake, I want to lie in my bed and feel the feeling I earned last night, to wrap my covers around it, to gather it up and hold it, to feel all of it *completely.* It is the morning after a special night, and everything out of reach, out of mind, a few hours ago now seems possible again.

An hour later, my ski jacket undone, I bound down the front steps two at a time as the mailman comes down the driveway. I smile at him, he hands me the mail, and smiles—*he* knows. I back the car onto the street. Across the road, a neighbor carries in her garbage pails. I wave. She waves back and smiles—*she* knows. I drive along Highway 40 to the city, passing the few cars in sight, the weather cold and blustery, my window down, my elbow out, rock music screaming from my radio.

The car turns off at Atwater and cuts through the late morning traffic. Stoplights blink amber, then red; the car stops. My head bobs from side to side at unseen passersby, my fingers drum out rhythms from the radio. The light changes and the car starts up. Past St. Catherine Street, past de Maisonneuve and Sherbrooke, moving as if by some mechanical memory of its own to the same street, the same parking spot, as every other day. I get out and walk, faster and faster, the air so crisp and cold it burns my lungs. I go to the bank. A teller turns and smiles—*she* knows. I go to a coffee shop, to a bookstore, to a newsstand, they all smile—*they all* know. I'm as good as my last game and no one can forget it.

Last night was the sixty-second game of my eighth season with the Montreal Canadiens. It was perhaps our best game in what, for us, has not been a good year. After a tie in Chicago and a Saturday loss at home to Minnesota, we continued the frustrating pattern of good and bad play that has characterized our season by coming up with a vintage Canadiens performance—explosive, unyielding, immensely varied—and in doing so, reminded ourselves excitedly that what we've been searching for during most of the year is still there. For me, it was a personal triumph of sorts. I played well in Buffalo where too often I haven't played well (until recently, where I haven't played at all). Replacing Michel "Bunny" Larocque, our team's other goalie, who is injured, I finally put aside the season-long doubts and thoughts of the future that have preoccupied me, and just played. Later, when I arrived home from Buffalo at 1:30 a.m., the house dark and quiet, I went to my office, turned on a light, and sat—excited, alert, unable to sleep, unwilling to sleep, wanting to feel then what I feel now. It is a rare feeling when expectations and hopes, when a team, a game, and I, come together. And now after eight years and nearly five hundred games, after those hopes and expectations have been battered and mocked, it is rarer still. So each time it happens, each time I get the feeling, I guard it and nourish it, feeling it for as long as I can.

I thought only good thoughts as I sat there: about a team, the best of its time; about Scotty Bowman and Claude Ruel; about Larry Robinson, Serge Savard, Doug Risebrough, Rick Chartraw, Doug Jarvis, Guy Lafleur; about Mario Tremblay, Yvan Cournoyer, Larocque, Pierre Larouche, Pierre Mondou; Jacques Lemaire, Yvon Lambert, Gilles Lupien, Pat Hughes. Flipping through images, hearing their voices, sometimes laughing out loud, feeling things I would never say, knowing that only good people can play the way they play. Bob Gainey, Réjean Houle, Steve Shutt, Guy Lapointe; Brian Engblom, Mark Napier, Rod Langway, Cam Connor; it has been the rare chance to play with the best to be the best; five Stanley Cups in seven years, three Stanley Cups in the last three years, a desperate fourth just three months away.

I also thought about me: a little wearied, a little worn, tormented by doubts and feelings and lifelong illusions I can no longer reconcile, yet still able to find joy in the game. It is a different game from the one I played on a driveway twenty-five years ago, grown cluttered and complicated by the life around it, but guileless at its core and still recoverable from time to time. I felt good about that as I did about a lot of things, and as the night went on, I leaned back further and further in my chair and closed my eyes, deeply content.

About 5:30 a.m., as the outside turned from black to gray, the feeling got tired, and I knew it was time to go to bed.

It has not been an easy year. Almost since last season ended, there has been disruption and confusion where, as a rule, there was none. The team was sold; Sam Pollock, general manager of this era's latest successes (nine Stanley Cups in his fourteen years), left and Scotty Bowman, Pollock's long-time protégé, was passed over for the job he thought properly his. Instead it went to Irving Grundman, who until last year ran the business operations of the Forum. The decision has left Bowman deeply hurt and, for much of the season, distracted and petulant. At training camp, Bill Nyrop, a skilled, useful defenseman, skated off the ice and later that day was driving home to Minnesota, retiring at twenty-six. Days before the season began, veteran defenseman Pierre Bouchard, the popular son of former Canadiens' captain "Butch" Bouchard, was left unprotected and claimed on waivers by Washington. A public outcry followed, and Bouchard was traded back. The trade was against waiver regulations, and was nullified; Bouchard retired. Early in the season, Guy Lafleur left our dressing room in Toronto a few minutes before the start of a game and conferred about his lagging contract renegotiations with his agent, his lawyer, and Grundman; only then did he play.

For a team already distracted by success, these incidents have given us the crutches we were looking for, and definitely do not need. It's Grundman's fault, we complain, or Bowman's, it's everyone's fault but our own, and our ultimate fall—this year, next year, some year—now cushioned and comfortable, is more likely. Yet we feel no comfort. The season is slipping away from us. The signs are everywhere—defensemen who push and shove in the corners, but don't hit; forwards who shoot from long range, safe from the punishment that goes with rebounds, deflections, screens, and goal-mouth tip-ins; Larocque and I tight in our nets, or running out erratically, content that goals appear as "good goals"; injuries and illness we always played with that now seem too much; winning three or four straight games, not five or six, losing two, not one; scoring in late-game flurries to tie or win; looking for, needing, a "big play"—a blocked shot, a big save, a spectacular goal—to turn around a game, a "big game" to turn around a season. We have won too often, for too long. We know every signal, every sign, we see our demise in everything we do. Like a starlet at the morning mirror, everything we see is a haunting omen of breakdown.

Off the ice, it is no different. Depending on its strength and resilience, we have left the team to care for itself. We go in more and different directions after practices and games, with new and interesting friends, pursuing the conglomerate of interests that three Stanley Cups have opened to us. Most road trips have been cut to same-day commutes; we leave in the morning, and return after a game at night, without the bonding that life on the road can bring. Then, when things go wrong, someone, usually Lapointe, decides that we should have a meeting to make everything right again. It never takes long, a little beer and beer-talk and our problems disappear; in three or four weeks, the same problems three or four weeks worse, we meet again.

Like a once-rich man desperate to be rich again, we have gotten impatient, spoiled by our own success. The relentless discipline that got us here now bores us; everything must happen fast. So we wait for a moment—one game, one play—to trigger the "roll" that will sweep us along and make the rest unnecessary. But it won't happen that way.

Several times this season, I have felt the same nagging twinge—*we're not going to win this year.* It happens usually after a bad game when signs and signals swarm at us with their unmistakable message, but not always. I have felt it before in other years, but never so often and never with the same feeling, that if we lose, it will be because of us, no one else. It is not fun to feel a team break down, to find weakness where I always found strength; to discover that discipline and desire can go soft and complacent; to discover that we are not so different as we once thought; to realize that winning is the central card in a house of cards, and that without it, or with less of it, motivations that seemed pure and clear go cloudy, and personal qualities once noble and abundant turn on end; to realize that I am a part of that breakdown. There is something remarkably strong about a team that wins; and something remarkably weak about that same team when it doesn't. The team that is "more than just a hockey team," the athletic, cultural, and political institution that inspires romance in more than its followers, is *just* a hockey team if it loses; and the romance disappears. The team that won together, our favorite metaphor for *sharing* and *cooperation*, loses as twenty separate guys, each running for his own lifeboat. The 40-goal scorer with only 22 goals, insisting he's a "better all-round player"; the 30-goal scorer with 20, a victim of goalposts and injuries; the all-star goalie who is "playing the same as he ever did"—covering their asses while all about them are having theirs burned. And in whispers loud enough that everyone can hear but you—"Old Reliable's had it," "Young Phenom's no good," and "What the hell's wrong with Bowman?" With the season in doubt, with less credit to share, as Serge Savard put it earlier, "Everybody's pulling on the blanket."

In the fourth season after three Stanley Cups, a team is changed. Sated by success, we have different expectations, and the motivation and feelings we get from a game have changed with them. Joy becomes obligation, satisfaction turns to relief, and the purpose of winning becomes less to win, and more not to lose.

Even the games we played with ourselves, when there seemed no other games to play, have changed. For three years, too good for the league, we competed against ourselves—most wins in a season, most points, fewest losses. We chased records and broke them, then chased our own records and broke them again. Then two years ago, we won sixty of our eighty games, lost eight and earned 132 points. Last year, we won one fewer game, lost two more, and earned three fewer points. This year we will do worse. Like long-jumper Bob Beamon, proud of our records, we have a feeling that we have gone too far. We have set a standard we cannot match, so, competing against ourselves, we lose. It would seem enough to win, to compete against the rest of the league as others do, but our cranky feelings tell us otherwise. There is a different quality about this team, a quality we might deny, one that oftentimes we wish we didn't have, one that in the inflated rhetoric of sports sounds inflated but is not. It is *excellence*. We are not a "money team" like the Leafs of the 1960s, aided and abetted by a generous playoff system.* We must win and play well *all* the time; we cannot wait for May. So unhappy with ourselves in the best of times, we play through a less than perfect season.

---

*In the 1930s, John Kieran, late columnist of *The New York Times*, noting that a full season of games had eliminated only two of the NHL's then eight teams, remarked, "For efficiency and net results, this is about the equivalent of burning down a house to get the flies out of the dining-room."

Yet there is time. In nine days, we will play the New York Islanders, our latest rivals. All season we have assured others, as we assured ourselves, that this was all we needed—the spark from an outstanding game like the Sabres' game, a sense of late-season urgency, and a target. Now that we have them, more than an opportunity, it becomes a test, one we cannot avoid.

We have played the Islanders twice this season and lost both times, once in the Montreal Forum. Bryan Trottier and Denis Potvin, their two excellent players, are finally playing as well against us as they play against the rest of the league. No longer underdogs, the Islanders are anxious to prove what they can now sense—that they are the best. For us, the test might seem the same, but it is not. In nine days, we will have a showdown with our-selves—individually, and as a team—one that we have put off for most of the season, one we can put off no longer. It is a game we must win, a game we have always won; the kind that in other years reminded us and others that we were a team of a different class. We must prove it again. So as we gear up for the Islanders in our next days and games, we compete, as always, against ourselves. The only thing different is that this year, we are no pushover.

It is an optional practice , but the dressing room is almost full. I walk in, pretending to be early, but no one is fooled. Larry Robinson, a large defenseman with a snarl of curly hair that has given him his nickname—"Big Bird"—looks up. "Tabernac!" he shouts. "Look who's here!" (Most French-Canadian swear words are derived from religion—*tabernac* means literally "tabernacle"; *câlisse*, another commonly used one, means "chalice.") I try to be surprised at his surprise, mumbling something about always com-ing to optional practices. There is scattered laughter. Mario Trem-blay, as usual, is unimpressed. He stops lacing his skates and looks up.

"Go home, Dryden," he says evenly. "We wanna shoot on the board." ("The board," a piece of plywood cut out at each corner and at its groin, is hung from a crossbar to cover a net when a goalie is absent.) A brief argument follows about goalies and boards until Tremblay, thinking it over, relents. "Naw, let him stay," he snarls, turning back to his skates. "Ya can't make the board scream."

It has the look and feel of a child's bedroom. Shin pads, shoulder pads, socks, jocks, gloves, skates, and sweaters lie in twenty little heaps on the floor. Players in various stages of dress move easily about, laughing and shouting in equal measure. It is too big to be intimate, about the size of a large living room, too antiseptic and bright to be cozy. In early morning or late afternoon, it appears quite ordinary—fluorescent lights, chrome equipment racks, a red indoor-outdoor carpet, concrete block walls painted white with red and blue trim, a wide gray bench that runs around its borders. Functional, attractive in an institutional sort of way, it is a room that needs people. Only higher, above the chrome racks and near the ceiling, is it clear that this is a dressing room unique to one team.

Along the west wall and along parts of two others, team plaques, dark brown and lettered in gold, hang in two rows, one plaque for each season from 1918 to the present. Each offers just bare-bones information—the year, the names of team owner(s), executives, coach(es), trainer(s), and players (in two columns), the regular-season place of finish, and "Stanley Cup Champions" or nothing at all. I often look at those plaques, to read their names— Georges Vézina, Aurèle Joliat, Howie Morenz—to see the name "Maurice Richard" appear suddenly in 1943; to follow it up the right-hand column season by season as it gained seniority, jumping to the left column until it reached the top, and disappeared in 1961. I like to spot the changes that have happened in more than fifty years: the names increasing from twelve to more than twenty as hockey became a free-substitution game; then, as entrepreneurs gave way to corporations, to see "Owner" become "Chairman," to see "Vice-President, Corporate Relations," "Executive Vice-President and Managing Director" appear. I like to look at my own name—fifth from the bottom in 1971, at the top of the right-hand column two years later, absent for a season, returning in 1975 fifth from the bottom again, now back at the top of the right-hand column—sharing the same plaques with Jean Béliveau, Henri Richard, Frank Mahovlich, Guy Lafleur, and other remarkable company.

Across the room, there is something else. For journalists, it is *la différence*, the glimpse that tells the story. Large, photoed heads of former Canadiens players now in the Hall of Fame gaze down at the room from a horizontal row, and beneath them, their words in French and English to each of us below:

NOS BRAS MEURTRIS VOUS TENDENT LE FLAMBEAU,
A VOUS TOUJOURS DE LE PORTER BIEN HAUT!

TO YOU FROM FAILING HANDS WE THROW THE TORCH,
BE YOURS TO HOLD IT HIGH!

But tradition and style are one thing, a live team is quite another. One head, the Geoffrion head, has a moustache inked in.

The room has no lockers, no cubicles or dividers, no names or numbers, nothing to tell us where we should be. I sit down at one end of the bench between Larocque and a short narrow corridor that leads through a door to the ice. It has been my seat for seven years. When I was first in this room, I was squeezed into a place that hadn't existed between Rogie Vachon and Phil Myre, then the team's two goalies. The following year, Vachon was traded to Los Angeles, I moved into his place, and Myre moved into mine and part of his. Seven months later, Myre went to Atlanta in an expansion draft and since that time his seat has been filled by Michel Plasse, by Wayne Thomas, and for the past five years by Larocque.

I take my equipment down from the chrome hooks and throw it onto the floor, then reach under the bench for my skates. The room gets suddenly quiet. I look at one pair of skates, then at the other, and before I can say anything, several voices chorus, "Hey, I tried to stop him," and there is laughter. The laces to my skates have been shredded into macaroni-size pieces too small for knots to hold together. I look up at a roomful of blank faces. Before I can say his name, Lapointe, who cuts my laces twenty or twenty-five times a year, though I have never seen him do it, gives me an injured look.

"Hey, get the right guy," he shouts, and there is more laughter. Suddenly proper, he goes on the offensive. "Hey, *câlisse*, you know the rules: 11:30 in the room for practice."

"Pointu," I say weakly, using Lapointe's nickname, "not for optionals. Not when we're coming back from the road."

Then, like a good routine that never gets tired, he looks at me apologetically. "Oh, hmm, sorry," he says, as he always does, and laughs.

The faces in the room are stubbled and drawn but the eyes are alive and the bodies move about with a quick jerky energy. Still filled with last night's game, voices blurt on top of each other, and everything is funny—things not funny when they happened, everything that earlier was too personal, too embarrassing, too important to be funny, today is torn laughingly apart. Though there are some players here because they were told to be here, and others because it is expected, today we are all here for the same reason. After more than five months of a season, we need a day off more than we need practice, but everywhere else, distracted by grocery shopping or traffic jams, by normal living that today seems out of place, last night cannot be shared or understood. So we come here, just for a few hours, to feel special; to be with people who know our same feeling and are as interested in it as we are.

Tying up his skates, Réjean Houle talks back and forth in quick animated bursts with Lemaire and Gainey on either side of him. A small, versatile winger, Houle has a wide-eyed boyishness about him that makes him the frequent target of good-natured abuse. Robinson suddenly looks up.

"Hey, Reggie," he shouts, "that was a helluva play ya made last night."

Houle goes silent; we begin to laugh.

"Yup," Robinson continues slowly, drawing out each word, "not often ya see a guy on a breakaway put it in the crowd." There are screams of laughter.

Lapointe snaps down his newspaper. "Don't let it bother ya, Reggie," he says sympathetically. "No harm done." Surprised, we all look up. "The goalie just woulda stopped ya anyway," he says, and we all laugh harder.

Bowman has left the practice to Ruel, something he does infrequently but with some delight, though more to exercise the privilege of a head coach than to enjoy the day off. Ruel, a squat, dwarf-like figure, stands in the southwest corner of the rink surrounded by fifty to sixty pucks. Treating him like a substitute teacher, we skate by, talking, passing pucks between ourselves, paying no attention to him. Every so often, Ruel shouts, "Dougie! Dougie!" or "C'mon, my Mario," and Risebrough and Tremblay, like Pavlov's dogs, break quickly to center, catch one of those pucks on their sticks, and curl back for a shot on Larocque in the net beside Ruel. I skate around, pretending to be a forward, dropping the puck into my skates, kicking it back to my stick, stickhandling triumphantly around and through players who ignore me, swinging in front of a net for a shot, always to a top corner, staying out of the net for as long as I can.

Finally Ruel blows his whistle and our unwanted drills begin. To the cadence of his relentless chatter, we sprint between the bluelines, coasting through the corners, then sprint again, continuing this way for several minutes. A whistle, more words of instruction, and we organize by the color of our practice sweaters into line rushes, into two-on-ones, and one-on-ones. But the energy of last night's game is beyond our control, and as each bad play becomes funnier than the last, everything breaks down. When Tremblay's pass to Lambert crashes against the underside of a seat five rows into the stands, an exasperated Ruel blows his whistle and calls for a scrimmage.

It goes no better. At first, he stops play with each mistake he sees, but soon he gives up. It becomes a game of breakaways and countless goals, added up until only the difference is remembered.

I enjoy it for a while, making saves that I never get to make in a game; then, as too many goals go by me, I start to sulk and lose interest—until I see Lapointe.

He races to the corner for the puck, pumping his legs with exaggerated enthusiasm, and bumps Lambert—whose back is turned—harder than anyone is bumped in practice. Lambert turns angrily to complain; Lapointe steals the puck and streaks up right wing. Houle breaks with him and cuts for an opening at center. Lapointe sees him and angles his body towards him as if to pass, then doesn't. Houle swings sharply to his left to stay onside, his skates chattering violently apart on either side of the blueline. Lapointe laughs, and continues on. Others make duck-call sounds to Houle, the *canard*. Lapointe moves against Robinson, one-on-one, exaggerating his fakes left and right, then, pretending to stumble, falls into Robinson, his head striking him in the stomach. They both fall down, Robinson laughing, Lapointe on top of him scrambling to his skates, his legs moving faster than he can control, falling on his knees, spinning up, falling down again. The puck rolls to Larocque, who covers it with his catching glove. Everyone stops, except for Lapointe. He races at Larocque, stopping inches from him, throwing up a spray of snow in his face, hacking at his glove again and again. Chartraw shoves him away, Larocque rolls the puck to Robinson; play starts back the other way. A quick pass to Tremblay, then to Lambert, and it's two-on-one at our blueline with only Savard back. Lambert winds up to shoot. Lapointe dives full out, his stick extended, and hooks the puck away. Lambert follows through onto bare ice.

It doesn't happen as often as it once did. Age, injuries, and vaguely disguised "personal problems" have complicated the game for Lapointe, robbing him of some of his zest for playing. But on those days when he isn't distracted by illness or injury, by the current state of his relationship with Bowman or Ruel, with the press or the fans, when the slate is clean and it is just him and the game, Pointu plays with the unrestrained joy of a boy on a river, uncomplicating the game for all of us.

After fifty minutes, Ruel blows his whistle and practice ends. A few stay on, more from habit than from commitment; I walk to the room, pick up some cans of soda, and sit down. Robinson walks by to the other end, stands on a bench, and turns on the TV. It comes on to *The Gong Show* and Gene Gene, the Dancing Machine is vibrating around on the floor. We let out a roar. The camera cuts to a laughing Chuck Barris wearing a Philadelphia Flyers sweater. Feeling slightly important, we let out another roar. Quickly undressed, Shutt and Larouche are in the shower. As soon as they leave the room, Tremblay drinks the Cokes they had carefully poured over ice to chill while they were showering. Then, with a wink for us, a laugh and a devil-may-care leap, he skips to the bathroom to shave. In the shower, Lambert is singing. Lapointe grabs a bucket and tiptoes to the bathroom sink like a cartoon spy. He fills the bucket with cold water, and peers around the corner of the shower. Lambert is still singing. Lapointe winds up; we hear a scream. Lapointe dashes back into the room and quickly out again, dropping his bucket. Lambert, still lathered up, races after him, screaming threats. Losing his trail, Lambert stops to pick up the bucket, fills it, and resumes his search. Finally, he finds Lapointe hiding in a toilet stall; he backs him into the room. Naked, sobbing, pleading pathetically, Lapointe falls to his knees, his hands clutched in front of him. Lambert winds up to throw the water, then stops: in Lapointe's hands are Lambert's clothes.

Some days, I arrive late to practice and leave as early as I can. Other days, like today, I like to linger here. I read my mail, I read newspapers and look at the plaques on the walls, but mostly I just linger. I am comfortable here. It is not only a place to dress and undress, to wind up for and wind down from games. It is a place to relax and get away. It is our refuge. When restaurants, sidewalks, and theaters are taken away, when planes and buses, even our charters, are cluttered with press and ubiquitous "friends of the team," when autograph seekers, phone calls from a friend of a friend of a friend, petty crooks armed with out-of-town schedules intrude on our homes, the dressing room remains something that is *ours*. For a half-hour before practice, an hour and a half before games, for a few minutes after each, there are no coaches, no press, no friends, no fans, no families. It is just us—sitting around, getting along, making something.

Houle and Lambert make plans for lunch at a pub across the street. They ask the rest of us to go, and today many join them. Often overlooked as players, Houle and Lambert are important to our team. Generous and friendly, they thrive on a team's easy, warm spirit, carrying it with them wherever they go. So when we get tired of going our separate ways and are looking for a team feeling, we look for them and find it. Today, I would like to go too, but I can't.

Their large group moves out noisily *en masse* as the trainers pick up the remaining vestiges of our practice. I stay behind. Some minutes later, I look at the clock behind me, and leave.

Along the east wall of the Forum, overlooking Rue Closse, are the corporate offices of Le Club de Hockey Canadien Inc., a small-to-medium-sized Quebec company owned since last summer by Molson Breweries of Canada Ltd. I walk upstairs to the second floor, and follow a wide corridor more than a third of the way around the building until I see a large unmarked blue door. I press the buzzer beside it. From inside, another buzzer is pressed, the door unlocks, and I walk in.

At the reception desk, I ask to see Mr. Courtois. I tell the receptionist that he is expecting me. E. Jacques Courtois, a courtly, aristocratic Montreal lawyer, about fifty-five, is president of the Canadiens. The receptionist returns in a few moments, and shows me into his office. With Courtois is Irving Grundman. I shake hands with both of them and sit down. Before we are quite comfortable, Grundman asks me about last night's game. I tell them that we played well, intending to leave it at that, but I keep talking, more and more involved in what I am saying, as they seem to be in listening. When finally I finish, there is a pause. I take a deep breath and begin. I tell them that I have thought over what we discussed in our previous meeting, but that my feelings have not changed. I tell them I will retire at the end of this season. There is another pause, longer this time. Finally Courtois smiles. "Naturally I'm disappointed," he says, "but I am not surprised."

I always knew that the time would come; I just never thought it would come this way. When I was young, I always assumed that hockey would just end. That some September, some coach would tell me I was no longer good enough, and it would all be over. Each year, in a new age group, it might have happened. But it never did. Eight years ago, I joined the Canadiens; I had run out of age groups. For the first time since I had started playing, it seemed that I might have many more years to play. For the first time, it seemed possible that the decision to stop might be my own.

Before my first season had ended, I was already being asked when I would retire. I was only twenty-three, but I was also in my second year of law school, and others knew that soon I would need to make a choice—a year of articling (like internship for a medical student, a law school graduate in Canada must work in a law office for up to a year before he can practice law), and six months of bar examinations, both done outside Quebec, or hockey.

And without exception, those who for years had written or dreamed the dream of sports assumed that I would retire and practice law. I told anyone who asked that I had no plans to retire, that I would continue to play as long as I enjoyed playing and enjoyed it more than anything else I might do. I couldn't be sure how long that would be, of course, but in my mind I thought it would be until I was thirty.

Two years ago, when I was twenty-nine years old, I decided to play one more season. Before I was entirely committed to my own plan, Sam Pollock, then general manager of the Canadiens, offered me a generous extension to my contract, which had one year left to run. The offer came after what had been for me a beleaguered season. While (in many ways, it was *because*) the team had lost only ten games (eight regular-season, two playoff games), I had felt under constant, almost angry pressure in Montreal to justify myself as the team's number one goalie. Outside Montreal, it was no easier. With Vachon playing well in Los Angeles, and Glenn Resch the same in New York, I kept hearing the same questions with the same harassing inferences. I took Pollock's offer as tangible encouragement and agreed to the new contract. It was for four years, but at any time during the contract I could give Pollock one year's notice of my decision to retire. I told him I thought I would play two more years. Last June, having played one more season, I told him I would retire at the end of this year.

I have not enjoyed this year very much. For nearly the first time in my career, for the first time in my life, I am feeling old. I am thirty-one years old. I feel good. I feel the same: no more aches than I ever had, no special diet to follow, no regimen of extra sleep. My body seems to move the way it always has, the game moves no faster for me than it did. But suddenly age is the dominant fact of my life. After years of ignoring time, I have become sensitive to it. I look around the dressing room at younger players who look like me and older ones who have aged. I slap my stomach and say, "Ahh, I feel great," and I never did that before. My weight remains what it always was, but it looks different. I look different. I was always the youngest in everything I did—in school, on hockey teams and baseball teams. Then on July 29, 1976, a reporter from *The Gazette* called me a "veteran goalie." I didn't feel like a veteran then, but I feel like one now.

I have a past I didn't have before, and now I wonder what comes next? I have discovered that I enjoy being good at something. I like the way it makes me feel, and the way it makes others treat me. It isn't the praise, or the generous perks of celebrity; it is the implicit, unstated respect it gives. It is a shared understanding that requires no fast talk, no big cars or flashy clothes, that needs not be argued or explained. It is simply there—*they know*. What will I be good at now? Without the precious safety net I have carried under me all my life—scholar-*athlete*, articulate *athlete*—without the athlete, what will I be? Where will I find the feelings I have come to need—the sense of common purpose, the spirit of doing something I believe in, the feeling of doing something right? What is *good enough* for me now? Like Eliza Doolittle, filled with new and omnivorous expectations, I wonder, "What is to become of me?"

Until now, life for me has been one long continuum, and hockey has been its link. From age six to age thirty-one, I have shared the same passion and preoccupation; I have had the same pattern to my years. But that will now change. If it is true that a sports career prolongs adolescence, it is also true that when that career ends, it deposits a player into premature middle age. For, while he was always older than he seemed, he is suddenly younger than he feels. He feels old. His illusions about himself, fuelled by a public life, sent soaring then crashing, have disappeared just as those of contemporaries have come to full bloom. He is left bitter, or jealous; or perhaps he just knows too much. It is a life that is lived in one-quarter time. "Boy wonder," "emerging star," "middle-age problem," "aging veteran," all in ten short years, and now in his thirties and still a young man, he feels too old to start again.

As I think about next year, I feel myself slowly turning inward and away from the game. I feel that absorbing commitment I always felt only occasionally now. My highs are not so high, my lows no longer so depressingly low. It comes with age and a broadened perspective, but it is an emotional fudge. I don't want to feel the same precarious swings any more. I want to feel comfortable and secure; I want to control what I do, and how I feel. I have become detached and incessantly analytical. From the referendum on Quebec's independence to the "Son of Sam" murders, I find almost everything "interesting," and if pressed for more, I offer *explanations*. I show that I "understand" how such things happen, and I go no further. But as I hold back, giving less of myself, I find that I'm losing my enthusiasm for the game. In an athlete, it is not the legs that go first, it is the enthusiasm that drives the legs. I go to optional practices, I work as hard as I ever did, but my motivation is different: where once I felt joy, now I feel joy mixed with grim desperation. I will not get any better. I must fight to keep what I have.

I have one goal left in hockey. Other people, sensing I might retire, have urged me to stay another year or more, to turn three (after this season perhaps four) consecutive Stanley Cups, Vézina Trophies, and first all-star teams into five or a record six. But there is achievement in having good seasons, and in not having bad. I just don't want to be bad.

I have always played hockey because I like to play, and true as that was when I was six years old, it is still true today. If I continue to play, it could only be for a different reason, and I won't let myself play that way. Two weeks ago, we had a game in Vancouver. The night before, I talked with my sister Judy and her husband on the phone and told them something they had probably already sensed—that this would be my last year. The next night, after the game, we went out for a late dinner. After some unusually strained minutes, Judy said that she hadn't enjoyed the game very much. She said that she couldn't help feeling sad, watching, knowing that this was the last time she would see me play. I said nothing. On the verge of tears, I felt touched but embarrassed; I could no longer feel what she was feeling.

I have not enjoyed this year very much, but it has been a necessary year. If I had retired a year ago, I would have left with doubts. I have none now.

Early this fall, I met with Grundman and told him what I had told Pollock in June. He said that he was aware of our conversation, and suggested we meet periodically through the season so that he could be kept informed of any changes in my plans. A short time later, he called and we met in his office. He said that he understood my reasons for retiring, but wondered if my contract was a problem, and offered to discuss a revision to it. I was surprised at first and a little angry, for it seemed he hadn't understood at all (then I realized he was only doing his general manager's job). I told him that that was not the problem. He suggested we meet again later.

He called again about a month ago, this time for a meeting that would include Courtois. Courtois said that he knew I was anxious to pursue another career, but wondered if some sort of special arrangement might be made that would allow me to contine to play. He made a suggestion: a slightly reduced game and practice schedule while working part-time as a lawyer with his law firm or in the legal department at Molson's. It was the kind of hockey-law arrangement that had brought me to Montreal in the first place eight years before, but it came as a great shock to me. We talked of the problems it might create (including the initial one, the six-month bar exams I would need to take in Ottawa, more than 100 miles away), and of how we would work them out. It seemed a wonderfully simple and obvious solution. I told them I would think about it, as they said they would, and we promised to meet again a few weeks later.

I called the director of the bar course in Ottawa and asked him if he thought such an arrangement could work; he assured me he thought it could. For several days I thought about this combination that seemed to offer everything. But as the final meeting with Courtois and Grundman approached, I began to change my mind. It wouldn't work. The team was already splitting apart from the success of three Stanley Cups—a fourth would make it one more year divided; a Stanley Cup defeat, and it would demand the kind of special commitment I could not give. And for me it would mean only more years dabbling at the edges of a law career, a part-timer in a full-timer's game. But much worse, I would become a part-time goalie again. I had been one once, with the Voyageurs, but what was right for that time and that stage in my career would not be right for this. I would be available to the team only on my time, not on the team's, giving it what I could give, not what it needed; giving up a goalie's joy and satisfaction, his *need* to feel linked with, and in some way responsible for, the fortunes of his team. I have played only four or five fewer games this year than in other years, yet I feel like a hired hand, in for a few games, out for a few games, interchangeable, unimportant, and not playing the way I can. Next year, I would play less often and, as I would be unable to be around all the times I was needed, the team could only look to someone else.

And as I thought about it, other things became clear. I realized that what had excited me most about the offer was the challenge of working two careers. It wasn't to practice law. I had known for some time that I had little interest in that. Indeed, I was looking for an excuse. I knew that otherwise I would never allow myself to play another season, that I would taunt and abuse myself—too weak, too comfortable, too willing to put off a time I knew was coming—if I tried. But if I practiced law while I played, maybe I would let myself go on. Just as the team was looking for a way, so was I. Then I realized something else. It came to me late last week as I sat alone in my office. Shocked and disappointed in myself, I realized that I didn't want to play hockey either.

After I had told Courtois and Grundman of my decision to retire, and after Courtois had replied, we sat silent a moment, all of us, I think, a little relieved.

A few hours later, I drove home—my elbow in, my window closed, my radio silent. When I walked in the front door, Lynda rushed from the kitchen to meet me. She asked me what Courtois and Grundman had said. I told her. We exchanged glances.

Tuesday

MONTREAL

LYNDA AND SARAH ARE IN THE KITCHEN; MICHAEL, AGED ONE, plays with his trucks in the hall. I walk downstairs, saying "Good morning" over the banister to them and continue to the front door for the newspaper.

"Good morning, you guys," I repeat affably, "didya have a good sleep? Good, good," I continue, not waiting for an answer. "Huh? Michael did?" suddenly hearing what Lynda has said. "You're kidding. I didn't hear you at all, Mikes. You okay now? Good, good."

Sarah and Michael run around the kitchen; Lynda is cleaning up. I drink my orange juice and read the paper. I start with the front page.

"Mommy, Mommy," Sarah screams triumphantly, "look what I can do," and as we watch, she somersaults down the hallway outside the kitchen door. I turn to the sports section for the scores. "Mommy, come quick," Sarah screams again, rushing into the kitchen. "Michael's trying to climb on the dining-room table."

Lynda runs out behind her.

Some minutes later, my juice finished, the paper read, I look up. "Well, what're you guys up to today?" I ask, and while Sarah is telling me, I interrupt, and with a laugh, threaten, "Hey, I'm gonna get you guys."

Sarah and Michael run off screaming with delight and I chase them into the living room. Like a favorite uncle, I lift them up and twirl them around. We roll on the carpet laughing and screaming. Soon, Lynda calls them to get ready to go.

"G'bye, Sari," I call to her, "have a good time at Mrs. Swan's [nursery school]."

"Daddy," she says with a four-year-old's exasperation, "I just told you, today I go to the library."

"Oh yeah, yeah," I say weakly, "have a good time. You too, Michael. See you guys later."

I feel good; like yesterday, like Sunday night, but with a certain solemnity that wasn't there before—*this is my last season.* But what pop in and out of mind, too often and too fast now, are thoughts of next year, and they unnerve me. I feel empty. Next year seemed a long way off until yesterday. Yesterday I only wanted *not* to play. Today I must think of what comes next. I have lived with this moment for many years, planned for it as others, thirty years older, plan for their retirements. Why don't I feel better? What will I do?

There are just three months to go. I know this is the time when I should dedicate myself to the rest of the season, to my last chance, but when I think of it, I feel no surge of commitment and I disappoint myself. Yet somewhere inside there is a quiet, penetrating feeling. It has nothing to do with "going out on top," as others often remind me to do; that is *their* pleasure. I simply want to do it right; I want to do it in such a way that years from now, when I forget it had nothing to do with going out on top, I will feel no regret and others will feel none for me.

There has always been next year, another chance to do and think and feel what today I had no time for. Suddenly there are so many things left to be done, so many unanswered questions, and so little time. What does Lapointe look like? How does a dressing room sound? How does it feel to make a save, to let in a goal, to hear the crowd? What does a game feel like? What about Lafleur, Robinson, Houle, Gainey? I want everything to stop. I want to remember.

The next time I think of it—my last season—I say something to myself, too fleeting, too much in passing to be a vow, as I do in a game when the moment is right but I can't quite feel it, just a quick "Okay, here we go"; and I embarrass myself when I do.

Breakfast done, the paper read, it is mid-morning and my day is finally beginning. Today is a "practice day," as yesterday was; tomorrow and the next day are "game days." Today, we are "at home," tomorrow we'll be "on the road." If someone were to ask me the day of the week, I would think for a moment and say it is Tuesday, though I wouldn't be sure. And if they wanted to know more, I would tell them it is February, but I don't know the date. I almost never know the date. And while sports life runs on time (and because it does, actually fifteen to thirty minutes *ahead* of time), I wear no watch. On "practice days" it is "before practice," "practice," or "after practice"; on "game days," "before the [team] meal," or "after the meal." Occasionally, usually travelling to or from the West Coast, we have a day with no game or practice, a "travel day." Less often, perhaps once a month, we have an "off-day," a day at home. This is the "hockey season"; three months from now, six months ago, it was the "off season"—these are the seasons of our year. While others live by a calendar and a clock, we live by a schedule.

For eight months in a year, our time is fragmented and turned upside-down. Awake half the night, asleep half the morning, with three hours until practice, then three hours until dinner; nighttime no different from daytime, weekends from weekdays. At home, in the rhythm of the road; on the road, needing to get home. Then home again, and wives, children, friends, lawyers, agents, eating, drinking, sleeping, competing in a kaleidoscopic time-sprint, for 36 hours, or 38 or 54—and we're on the road again. It is a high-energy life lived in two- or three-hour bursts, and now, after eight years, I don't know how to use more. I am not very good at off-days. Weekends, which I get only when injured, disorient me. I go to the store, make a few phone calls, take the kids to the park, and it is barely noon. I start on something that takes longer, and don't finish; tomorrow and the next day and the next few weeks, I have no time. Always rebounding from one thing to the next, I'm always on the way to some place else; in contact with families, friends, and outside interests, but never quite attaching onto any of them.

I will not retire "to spend more time with my family" (whenever Lynda reads that of an athlete or a politician, knowing better, she gets furious at the hypocrisy and self-promotion). But what I will enjoy is being around day-to-day while Sarah and Michael grow up.

The house is quiet. I don't like daytime solitude as I do the night. I wish the kids were here. I pick up the mail at the front door and go to my office. One letter is from the Ministère du Revenu du Québec, and I open it first. It is a notice stating that I owe a small additional amount on last year's taxes. Below, it gives an explanation, in French, which I can only partly understand. Before I remember that this is a French-speaking province, I get upset.

It is an uneasy place to live now. Soon—the newspapers

speculate it will be in late spring or early summer—a question will be put to Quebeckers by referendum and the answer they give will affect Quebec and Canada profoundly. No one yet knows what the precise question will be, though most now know their answer, and in the next few months, with these hearts won, the minds of the undecided will be fought for, in a paper war of studies, polls, and editorials, and finally with *the question*, the one the Parti Québécois (PQ) hopes will deliver the right answer. A few days ago, both the PQ government and the Opposition Liberals released their referendum position papers—the PQ *"D'égal à égal"* and the Liberal *"Choisir le Québec ET le Canada"*—and for the time being, there's a pause in the cycle of commentary, charge, and counter-charge that started three years ago. Yesterday, the front page of *The Gazette* told Montrealers that the price of beer is going up sixty-five cents a case. Today we learned that CTV has been enjoined from showing an interview with Margaret Trudeau until after her book, *Beyond Reason*, is published. Tomorrow or the next day, there will be a new study or a new poll, and referendum talk will take over again.

On November 15, 1976, the people of Quebec gave the PQ a majority of seats in the 110-member Quebec National Assembly. At a victory rally in Paul Sauvé Arena in the east end of Montreal, more than 8,000 "Péquistes" celebrated and welcomed their leader, René Lévesque, the new premier of Quebec. A few miles across town that same night, more than 16,000 people watched as the Montreal Canadiens beat the St. Louis Blues, 4-2.

There was a different atmosphere in the Forum that night. It was as if the crowd was watching with vacant eyes, their minds committed somewhere else. A near miss, a save, a goal, the kind of event normally anticipated then climaxed with a loud Forum roar, brought a muted and delayed reaction, and sometimes nothing at all. At first, we tried to ignore it, but as the crowd's distraction became our own, the game bogged down. Late in the first period, the message board flashed some early election returns—"Lib 8 . . . PQ 7"—but there was little reaction. Some minutes later, at a stoppage of play in the second period, the message board flashed again, slowly, each letter bouncing from the right side of the board to the left, one space at a time, in French and in English, so that before the message was complete, the puck had dropped and the game had begun again. I glanced back and forth between the game and the message board, until the board finally flashed to a stop—"PQ 15 . . . Lib 9." The rumble that had accompanied the first movement of letters turned to a silence deep and disturbed. Something was happening, and we were all beginning to know it.

Liberal supporters, too afraid to think of what that might be, sat silent; Péquistes, also silent, were too afraid to hope. Later in that period, there was one more message—"PQ 33...Lib 15." This time, the crowd reacted, not in large numbers, but like fans in another team's rink, with a loud and spirited roar.

In the dressing room between periods, we sat quietly at first, then hoping and pretending that nothing was as serious as it seemed, and the one-liners began in earnest; nothing very funny, but we laughed long and hard.

"Jean-Pierre Mahovlich, I'd like ya to meet Jacques Roberts."

"Hey Kenny, thanks for everything. It's all yours now, Bunny."

In the middle of the third period, the message board flashed again—"Un Nouveau Gouvernement." No longer afraid to hope, thousands stood up and cheered and the Forum organist played the PQ anthem. And when they stood and cheered, thousands of others who had always stood and cheered with them stayed seated and did not cheer. At that moment, people who had sat together for many years in the tight community of season-ticket holders learned something about each other that they had not known before. The last few minutes of the game were very difficult. The mood in the Forum had changed.

Since that night, Canada has been a battleground of emotions. Guilty, fearful of change, and suddenly aware of a feeling for Canada and its duality stronger and deeper than they had imagined, Canadians, especially English-speaking Canadians, have spent three busy years holding conferences, setting up cultural exchanges, sending telegrams of "love" to their Quebec brothers, desperate to affect the events they can feel affecting them. About a year ago, the pace of conferences and public hearings had clearly worn down as if suddenly there was nothing new to say, and first the academics took over, and now the politicians. In a few months, on referendum day, after an unofficial campaign longer than a U.S. presidential campaign, it will be up to the people of Quebec—the focus of all this attention—to say "yes" to a process which will create the momentum for independence, or to say "no" to stop it dead for a time. It may be a choice like other hard choices, one that most would prefer not to make, but it represents a chance to do what twentieth-century non-colonial societies can rarely do: decide democratically their own political and national future. To anyone who has asked me about Montreal for much of the near-decade I have lived here, I have always said the same thing: "There is no more interesting place to be." But that is only partly true.

I was twenty-one years old before I came to Montreal for the first time. It was summer 1968 and I came to visit Man and His World, which the year before as Expo 67 had helped give Canada in its centennial year the exciting spirit of a modern, bilingual, and unified country. A year later, I found an amusement park, a *big* amusement park, but with some of Expo's pavilions dismantled, and all of its spirit gone. I left the next day.

Two years later, Lynda and I stopped in Montreal on our way to Europe on our honeymoon. There I signed a contract with the Montreal (now Nova Scotia) Voyageurs and arranged my transfer to McGill University law school. In early September, less than four months later, we were back as residents of Montreal, something we have continued to be for all but one of the last nine years.

Our first lesson in Montreal came the day we arrived. Coming in late in the afternoon, we found a restaurant for dinner, then went for a walk along St. Catherine Street, the city's main street. Just west of Guy Street (which, knowing the French pronunciation, I was careful to call "Ghee," until baffled French-speaking Montrealers realized I meant "Guy," which they pronounced the English way), we saw "Toe Blake's Tavern," owned by the former great player and coach of the Canadiens. It was one of the few landmarks we had heard of (the others being the Forum, Expo, the Queen Elizabeth Hotel, McGill, Delorimier Stadium, and Maurice Richard's "544 Tavern"—the latter two we later learned no longer existed). So we crossed the street and went in. At first, we heard what sounded like cheering, so we looked around until we were sure it was directed at us, then realized it wasn't cheering, but shouting. A waiter approached us and quietly explained that this was a tavern, and that in Quebec, women were not allowed in taverns. More embarrassed than angry, we left.

A little more than a month later, British Trade Commissioner James Cross was kidnapped, followed six days later by Quebec Labour Minister Pierre Laporte. On October 16, citing an apprehended insurrection, Prime Minister Pierre Trudeau invoked the War Measures Act, and troops were moved into Montreal. For more than a month, as I walked along McGregor Avenue from the law school to the Forum, I passed army trucks, jeeps, and armed soldiers, but, preoccupied with other things and new to the province, I had little sense of the momentous events going on around me. Like everyone else I went home each night and learned the exciting details of the day from TV, and everything looked the same as it had in every other drama I had seen, except this time I recognized the setting.

In those early years, Montreal seemed like a wonderful, exciting foreign city with all the comforts of home. It had a different look, a different sound, a different *feel*, and, like New York or London, was just challenging enough to give immense satisfaction to those who could cope with it, and succeed. But it was a foreign city with a difference. Whenever it got too difficult, whenever it was more than I could handle, I could flip a channel, turn a page, drive west of St. Laurent Boulevard, or switch from French to English, and it was easy again. It turned language into a game—I watched French movies subtitled in English, and English movies subtitled in French; I took French courses at McGill, planned vacations in French-speaking places, did a French play-by-play of highway signs, stores, buildings, cars, people, *anything*, between our house and the Forum; and I said *merci* so often that I said it to startled cabbies in New York and Buffalo. As a game, it was something I could dabble in, all the time thinking I had really committed myself. But language is not a game.

In Montreal, language is the single dominant fact of life. Two languages, French and English, side by side, on signs, newsstands, and grocery shelves, on TV and radio dials; they are what make the city distinctive, capable of delighting the visitor with its charm, its *ambiance*; they are what give Montreal its romance. But language is also the source of Montreal's division. While the city is no longer quite the "two solitudes" of novelist Hugh MacLennan's wonderfully evocative phrase, for the French and the English who once divided demographically east and west, culturally, and in the workplace, and who now more often confront each other directly, language is the principal source of tension and rivalry. It has to do with status—majority status and minority status—and the correlation between numbers, influence, and language that has never been quite direct. And while the image of English-speaking Montrealers ghettoed into executive suites and high-income areas is now hyperbole, historically there has been enough truth in it for the image to remain.

As a hockey player, I live a special existence in Montreal. I feel little in common with the English community here. I have never enjoyed special opportunity, nor have I earned more money because of the language I speak. The special status I have, the income I earn, come only because of hockey, and that isn't being threatened. Nor is the language of my workplace changing. If it has a language, it is English, but it could be French and it would make no difference, as most of my work is alingual. And because language is not a factor, I feel no pressure to leave. My future here is what it always has been; neither the legislation passed to protect the French language at the expense of the English nor the consequent disquiet in the English community have changed it.

Nor has very much changed for my French-speaking team-mates. If they grew up suffering the slights of the English community, they suffer few now. They earn no less money, they earn no fewer promotions because of the language they speak. They feel no inferiority complex, they hold no second-class status within their province or country. Rather, they are *stars*, celebrities, special wherever they go, travelling easily and for much of the year, not language-locked in one area of the continent. And if language is not an issue of their work, just as it is not of mine, the tension and rivalry, the division caused by language, are not features of their workplace.

At first appearance, that would seem to be so. For the Canadiens look an immensely compatible team: compatible personally and professionally, sharing special skills and common goals, at once capable of great joy *and* great satisfaction, a team that, by and large, seem genuinely to like each other. A second look, and it might not seem the same—unconnected pockets of English conversation, or French, in dressing rooms, airports, at team meals; best friends—Larocque-Lambert, Risebrough-Jarvis, Savard-Lapointe—that divide by language; the highly publicized "incidents" that seem to embroil the team so frequently—Al MacNeil–Henri Richard, Pete Mahovlich–Mario Tremblay.

But take a third and closer look, and it will look different again. These are not divisions, because they don't feel like divisions; they are unconscious and unintended, and almost always unnoticed. We are not a linguistic version of *All in the Family* or *The Jeffersons*. We are not football teams or baseball teams in the second generation of their race relations, so anxious to show how well they get along, so conscious of division, so preoccupied with division, that they laugh too loud at the "honky" and "nigger" jokes they can't stop telling. We are a team that has gone one step further—we know there are differences, we just don't think they are that important. Only one player, defenseman Gilles Lupien, tells roundhead (French) and squarehead (English) jokes. Perhaps he felt he needed them, carving an identity for himself in the years he spent in Halifax with the Voyageurs before he got to Montreal. But while we often find what he says funny, his jokes begin and end with him.

Indeed, if best friends seem to share one language, they also share other things just as conclusive—common backgrounds, common junior or minor pro teams, common status on a team as rookies or veterans, a friendship between wives whose isolation in one language, in most cases, is far more complete than their own. And if the "incidents" seem often to involve English and French players or coaches, there is something else involved as well. To anyone who has grown up in this province, at one time especially to a French-speaking Quebecker but now equally to both, if *un Français* and *un Anglais* have a problem, it is a French-English problem.

In 1971, after the fifth game of the Stanley Cup final with Chicago, Henri Richard told reporters that Canadiens' coach Al MacNeil was "incompétent." The next day, everyone in Quebec understood. It had nothing to do with the frustration of an immensely proud but aging star who was benched in a game that had to be won, but was lost, a frustration which later caused him to insist that he would have said the same thing about Claude Ruel or Toe Blake. Rather, it was as if his phrase "MacNeil est incompétent" was really in code, a special French-English code which everyone in the province understood the same way—"MacNeil, a unilingual English-speaking Canadian, cannot relate to French-speaking players." Two games later, after the Canadiens had won the Stanley Cup and Richard had scored the winning goal, MacNeil became coach and general manager of the Nova Scotia Voyageurs.

Several years later, Mario Tremblay and Pete Mahovlich got into a fight in a hotel room in Cleveland, as a result of which Mahovlich, a notoriously poor fighter, ended up in the hospital with stitches. The fight had nothing to do with being roommates and being drunk. Mahovlich, the code said, and everyone understood, did not like French Canadians.

And so, while language may not divide us, others—the public, the press—whose experience is different, who themselves are divided by language and who find tension and rivalry by language in their workplace, understand us and explain us in *their* way, and in doing so, sometimes cause division. That will not change. For if the team is no longer truly of the society of which it is part, it remains its most visible symbol. It has been, and will continue to be, used by both sides as they play out their tensions.

My wife and I have lived in Montreal since our marriage. We bought our first house here, our two children were born here. It has been a time of extraordinary excitement and change, for the city, for the province, for us. When we first came to Montreal, we left in the summers and travelled, just as we would have done if we had lived somewhere else. Now, with children, except for the trips to visit family we cannot visit the rest of the year, we stay here in summer, as we would if we lived somewhere else. I grew up in Toronto, but it has been many years since Toronto has been home. At times, Montreal has felt like home, but it has never really been home. For beyond the team, beyond the celebrity culture we inhabit, we have few roots here. With a house, with a family and friends, roots can develop, but in Montreal, real roots come only with language. There is no more interesting place to be than Montreal only if you can be a part of what makes Montreal interesting and special, only if you can live in one culture and partake fully of the other. If you cannot—and now even fluently bilingual English Quebeckers are finding it difficult, since language is irrelevant if the issue is cultural separation—then Montreal is a relatively small English city, spectator to a much larger and more exciting one. Montreal/Montréal, where the Canadian dream of French and English living and working side by side has had its best chance; Montreal, a city just close enough to be a frustrating reminder of what I am not.

Living in Montreal now, I feel like I do when I lose my glasses. I know that there is much going on around me, but I can't see what it is. And when I can't see something, I get afraid of what I can't see, so I go off by myself until I can. But then, feeling more and more isolated, I begin to feel different; and the more different I feel, the more I begin to feel that it is *they* who are different. And I don't like that feeling.

Early in 1972, I was invited to appear on a late-night talk show called *Appelez-moi Lise*. It was hosted by a bright, dynamic woman named Lise Payette, at the time the most popular TV personality in Quebec, a few years later a cabinet minister in the PQ government. That show frequently featured Canadiens players as guests, and Payette invited me because I spoke French better than most of my English-speaking teammates. I was reluctant to go on at first, explaining to her that I didn't speak or understand French well enough for the kind of interview I was sure she had in mind, but after she promised to switch into English if I ran into trouble, I accepted. (As it turned out, no matter how much trouble *I* thought I was in, she appeared not to notice, for we spoke only in French.)

I don't remember what we talked about, only that some of the questions she asked I could understand, and others I couldn't understand at all. Though my answers were often incomplete, when the show was over I felt relieved, satisfied that I had survived the experience. But those who had watched the show apparently thought differently. For years afterward, people would remind me of that interview, telling me how much they had enjoyed it, how much they had appreciated my speaking their language, how well they thought I had spoken.

The next year, I was one of ten finalists in "le Plus Bel Homme du Canada." Despite its name, this was a popularity contest in Quebec which in the aftermath of the 1971 playoffs and in Lafleur's pre-superstar days got me consideration. It was run in conjunction with Payette's show. With the exception of one politician (who did not appear), the others nominated were television or movie "personalities," each of whom arrived for the show in a tuxedo. I wore a burgundy-colored suit. The countdown began at 10. At 7 (6th runner-up?), they called my name. I walked down the spiral staircase to be greeted by Madame Payette. The previous three contestants had given her a kiss; the five that came after me also gave her a kiss. I shook her hand. When I did, apparently she said to me, "Aren't you going to give me a kiss?" Not understanding what she had said, I leaned in closer for her to ask again. When she saw me leaning down, she thought I was leaning down to give her a kiss. As she raised her head, as I lowered mine, we collided.

Later in the show, Quebec *chanteuse* Diane Dufresne sang a song to the nine of us as we stood in a line, stopping for a moment to sing to each of us in turn as she passed. When she stopped in front of me, I reached into my jacket pocket and pulled out a small English-French dictionary and leafed through it. The audience laughed. The next day in *La Presse*, there was a large picture of me, Diane Dufresne, and my dictionary.

I was on *Appelez-moi Lise* one more time. Again, I understood much of what Payette asked, answering sometimes in complete sentences, at other times in fragments she had to complete for me. When the show was over, her producer asked me to appear again a few weeks later. I said no. I told her that the first time was fun, and the second time was too, but that years were passing and still I couldn't express myself the way I wanted to. I told her I would come back when I spoke better French.

Yesterday was a reminder of spring; today, harsh confirmation that this is Montreal and still the winter, cold and gray and not much else. The radio warns of new snow tomorrow or the next day, and again I feel a quick desolate twinge, knowing that what I had counted on won't happen for at least a few more weeks. Every year I am surprised at how late in the fall the winter begins. Remembering the endlessness of winters before, I expect it with the start of the hockey season in mid-October, and when it doesn't come, I think that maybe it won't come as it has in other years. And each year about this time, I am reminded that it's at the other end that Montreal winter hits hardest. When the fury of January is spent, when the worst is past, it doesn't go away; it lingers like an unwelcome guest until you wonder if it ever will. But experienced in winter, Montrealers adapt and cope, triumphing over it. Streets and sidewalks get tractored and plowed, underground shops and walkways are built; snow tires go on, furs and boots appear, the heat goes up, and life goes on uninterrupted. Winter defines life in this city. It is fresh and bracing, an invigorating test; it is only its length I can never get used to.

I drive down side streets narrowed by drifts and snow-shrouded cars. Traffic is light today, and the few cars on the road move easily, unconcerned by the conditions. After the awkward caution of a winter's first snowfall, for Montreal drivers, like riding a bike, it all comes back, and slippery streets are driven as if bare and dry. I park several blocks away from the Forum and walk. The wind, gusting up Atwater Street, is bitter and cold, and hunching over, I try to cover up, but can't. I start to jog, then run, faster as the wind bites harder. At de Maisonneuve, the light turns red but I continue across.

Peter, a tiny round elf-faced boy of about fourteen, a Canadiens sweater visible beneath his parka, runs from in front of the players' entrance and meets me at the corner. Six or seven others, boys and girls, bigger than Peter but about his age, follow behind. Many of them are also wearing Canadiens sweaters under their parkas. I recognize most of them; a few ask for autographs. They walk thirty quick feet with me as they do with each player, we ask them how they are, they answer with "Great game" or "Too bad about last night," then, out of time and at the door, we say "Thanks." They leave their classes at nearby schools an hour before practice, stay most of that hour, returning two hours later as we leave. For games, they wish us luck as we go in; five hours later, after 11 p.m., they're there again, some having gotten in to watch the game, most having not. Peter has been coming for nearly two years; a year or two from now he will have new interests and commitments—girl friends, school, a job—and gradually he will stop; and there will be others. During that time, the boys never change; the girls, once thirteen, suddenly seventeen, do. In a life where games and seasons blend together, it is one of the few ways to know that time has passed.

I'm late again. I come in another door, hang up my coat before anyone sees me, and walk in the room as if I've only been unnoticed, not absent, all these minutes. My laces are cut again. Risebrough says, "I tried to stop him." Lapointe says, "Hey, get the right guy," and everyone laughs. Larocque arrives after me and gets the same reaction, then Savard. Pierre Meilleur, the pudgy assistant trainer, who likes to introduce himself as "Pierre 'Boom

Boom' Meilleur, personal trainer Serge Savard, team trainer Montreal Canadiens," sits down next to Savard and begins to replace his shredded laces. We shout at Meilleur, gibing him for his self-inflicted status, but he just laughs and continues. There is something he doesn't hear though, something he should hear; it is anger. For while Bowman lets us get away with his "thirty minutes in the room before practice" rule, except when we're losing, the team, in its own way, does not. We all like to test his rules, getting away with as much as we can, but by cutting laces, we remind each other that there is *some* price for being late, that it *has* been noticed. By fixing Savard's skates, Meilleur has gotten in the way of a team as it disciplines itself, and the anger is real.

The room is alive and bursting with energy. It is what happens when a team gets together—in a bar, on a plane, anywhere, every time. Everything louder and faster. Half-naked players move hurriedly about, laughing, shouting for tape (black or white, thick or thin), cotton, skate laces, gum, ammonia "sniffers," Q-Tips, toilet paper, and for trainers to get them faster than they can. It is the kind of unremitting noise that no one hears and everyone feels. But there is another level of dialogue we all can hear. It is loud, invigorating, paced to the mood of the room, the product of wound-up bodies with wound-up minds. It's one line, a laugh, and get out of the way of the next guy—"jock humor." It is like a "roast," the kind of intimate, indiscriminate carving that friends do to keep egos under control. Set in motion, it rebounds by word association, thought association, by "off the wall" anything association, just verbal reflex, whatever comes off your tongue, the more outrageous the better. Elections, murders, girl friends, body shapes, body parts—in the great *Tonight Show/Saturday Night Live* tradition, verbal slapstick dressed as worldly comment, mother-in-law jokes for the media-conscious, it is anything for a laugh.

Amid the business of getting ready for practice, there is talk of beer.

"*Câlisse*, you see the paper?" Houle moans. "Beer's goin' up sixty-five cents a case. Sixty-five cents!"

His words bring a grumble of memory.

"Shit, yeah," says a mocking voice, "the only thing should go up is what they pay fifteen-goal scorers, eh Reggie?"

There is laughter this time. Across the room, Guy Lapointe stares at the ceiling, lost in thought. Suddenly he blurts, "That's it, that's it. No more drinkin'."

There is loud laughter.

"Hey, Pointu," Steve Shutt says, "ya just gotta learn to beat the system—drink on the road." His quick, chilled, high-pitched laugh follows.

Steve Shutt is a curious-looking hockey player. Short, with a wide round face, a permanently quizzical grin, and a body shape he feels is deceptive—"Hey, that's not fat," he insists, referring to a small puddle of fat around his middle; "I'm swaybacked"—he is often disparaged as a "garbage man." But he is not. Rather, he is what laughingly he says he is—a "specialist." He lurks about "in the weeds," as he would put it, away from the play, unnoticed in a game that centers around his linemate Lafleur. Then, as the puck enters an opponent's zone, he accelerates to the net like a dragster, with quick, chopping strides, to sweep in a goalmouth pass, to deflect a shot in some improbable way, to snap a rebound to a top corner. It is a style he learned as a boy on a small backyard rink his father built. Crowded with neighborhood kids, there was little room to skate and only time for short, quick shots that gave no second chance.

Off the ice, he is the same. Lurking about in a corner of the room, he takes in everything, his head bobbing about like a bird, ninety degrees at a time, ready, waiting for an opening. Then, at the moment we're most vulnerable, he springs into action, throwing out a stream of "quips," as he calls them, in quick staccato bursts, always with the same shivery giggle—hee hee hee—like Ernie on *Sesame Street*. He is our foil, a perfect Shakespearian fool; his greatest delight comes in interrupting life's careful, ordered rhythms to catch people with their pants down. Some of his quips are good, some are not so good, some are genuinely bad. But it doesn't matter. Irrepressible, irresistible, funnier than anything he says, after a while he just opens his mouth and we laugh.

The talk rebounds from Margaret Trudeau to the price of gas to "Sheik Khomeini" to harems to "real service stations" ("no self-serve"). Houle, who as a boy was poor enough that now he worries about losing what he has, puts on his sweater, grateful that the subject he started has now been forgotten. Savard adjusts his shoulder pads and looks across the room at him.

"Hey, Reggie, relax," he yells, and Houle, no longer relaxed, jerks up his head. "What're you worryin' about," Savard continues. "All those annuities you got. Hell, they'll pay ya six per cent the rest of your life. In ten years they'll be worth five, ten thousand bucks a year," he says soothingly, then pauses for his own punch line, "just because they're worth fifty [thousand] now."

There is loud laughter. Suddenly, we're back to the price of beer.

"It's that fuckin' government," someone says. "Why the hell

don't they do something about that instead of the goddamn referendum?"

There are loud murmurs of agreement.

"Shit, they don't care," another voice says, "they got all the wine drinkers on their side. The beer drinkers gonna vote 'no' anyway."

"The government," someone else growls, "who gives a shit about the government. We win [Stanley] Cups with the Liberals, we win 'em with the PQ. What the fuck's the difference?"

Stunned, we go silent for a moment, then Lapointe looks over at Mondou. "What d'you think, Mousse?"

Pierre Mondou, a funny, likeable second-year player, with a mind too fast for his tongue and a tongue too fast for any ear to comprehend, in English *and* French, looks up like he hasn't done the reading.

"Huh, oh, um, *câlisse* goddamn, heh heh heh."

We all stop what we're doing and look at each other.

"What the hell was that?" more than one of us asks.

"*Câlisse*, I thought it was English," says Lapointe, looking puzzled. "Hey Mousse, easy for you to say," and there is more loud laughter.

Today, we practice at Verdun Auditorium, a short bus ride from the Forum. With the work involved in packing the equipment needed for practice and taking it to another rink, all but Larocque and I dress into full equipment at the Forum. Because of the awkward bulk of our leg pads, we put our pads, skates, gloves, and masks into an equipment bag to change at Verdun. It will be one of the few times this season we have not practiced at the Forum.

As soon as the NHL schedule is released in late summer, Bowman and Grundman meet with a Forum executive and Bowman tells him the days he wants the building reserved for practice. The day after a long road trip, the day before an important game— if any of the dates then or later conflict with a possible Forum event, there may be negotiation, but final discretion always remains with Bowman. It is a power almost anachronistic in a time when a building's high operating costs demand as close to nightly use as possible. But though busy more than two hundred nights a year with rock shows, ice shows, circuses, and other events, the Forum remains first and foremost a hockey arena. Tonight, the Harlem Globetrotters are in town and the ice has been covered with a gray bounceless floor.

Carrying sticks and helmets, with skate guards protecting their skate blades, players walk from the building to a chartered city bus waiting at a bus stop on Atwater Street. Across the road, shoppers at Alexis Nihon Plaza go about their business. A few stop suddenly, do a quick double-take, but distrusting their instincts, certain it must be someone else, they continue on. We spread around the bus, sitting singly or in twos, reading the newspapers that are passed around, some of us with legs crossed, others stretched into aisles—looking much like any bus passengers. The door of the bus remains open while we wait for the trainers. A plump middle-aged woman, laden down with parcels and bags, runs across the street against the light, dodging traffic, looking anxiously toward the bus. Lapointe yells something to the driver. The woman reaches the bus badly out of breath, but at least a little triumphant. The driver says nothing. She climbs the steps, reaches into her purse for the fare, glances quickly down the bus at the smiling helmeted heads, screams, and runs off.

It's a sense of fun more than a sense of humor. It's pie in the face, seltzer in the pants, duck and get the other guy—slapstick, up front, but rarely the way it seems. So free of malice—the mangled pies and ruined ties exist only in fun. So well done that the fiftieth pie is as funny as the first. And Lapointe is a natural. With the team as his audience and his more than happy victim, he lets us share hundreds of pranks in the making—on the other guy. When it's on you, you never see it happen.

It was at lunch before my first game with the Canadiens, an exhibition game in Halifax against Chicago:

"Ah, I'm full," Lapointe announces, wiping his face with his napkin. "Anybody want my ice cream?"

Shaking their heads, murmuring, everyone says no. Finally, after looking around, certain that no one else wants it, "Um, yeah sure," I say tentatively, "ya sure ya don't want it?"

Lapointe shakes his head, and hands it to me. I take a bite. Before I can taste what I have eaten, the room explodes in laughter—sour cream with chocolate sauce.

"Pointu!"

In Colorado, Lapointe in a garbled French accent addresses a young stick-boy anxious to please:

"Oh garçon, uh, uh bud-dy, les boys uh, zey ont bes—uh zey, zey need un, un bucketa steam."

"Excuse me?" the boy says.

"Les boys zey, zey un bucketa steam. Vas-y, vas-y, go, go, go."

The stick-boy, still anxious to please but a little puzzled, leaves to find a bucket of steam.

A serious Lapointe:

"*Câlisse*, now I done it," he groans. "Kenny, who's a good lawyer? I need some help."

He looks genuinely worried this time. "Call a guy named Ackerman," I tell him earnestly.

"What?" he says.

"*Ackerman*," I repeat louder, and suddenly I know what's coming next.

"I'm not deaf," he says indignantly, and walks away laughing. "Pointu!"

Sugar in salt shakers, ketchup on shoes, shaving cream on sleeping heads, petroleum jelly on the ear-piece of a phone, and never once do we wonder—why does a 31-year-old man do these things? To others, it might seem just adolescent humor, adults playing a little boys' game playing at being little boys. But up close, we don't worry about that. To us, it is simply fun. Seven days on the road, walking through an early-morning airport, tired, laden with carry-on bags, starting up a long escalator, and suddenly it stops—without looking up, with no one else in sight, six or seven voices chorus into the wind, "Pointu!"

We learn to count ketchup bottles, check ear-pieces, salt shakers, and ice cream, but it doesn't matter; and we don't care.

In the early and mid 1970s, except for Bobby Orr, Guy Lapointe was the best defenseman in the NHL. He was strong and powerful, an explosive skater with a hard, low shot, but what made him unique was the emotion he could bring to a game. During flat, lifeless stretches, uncalculated, he would suddenly erupt with enormous impatient fury, racing around the ice, daring and inspired on offense and defense, giving the game a new mood; turning it our way. It is a rare ability, and even as Potvin and Robinson matured in mid-decade to push him onto second all-star teams and beyond, it was a skill that even they couldn't match. Only recently, with accumulating age and injury, has some of that fire gone out.

When I think of Lapointe, I think of three games. The first, in 1976, was the fifth game of the Stanley Cup semi-finals against the Islanders. We were ahead three games to one, having won the decisive fourth game in New York, and were back in Montreal to finish the series. The game began slowly, both teams playing as if it were only a formality. The Islanders, then a young, emerging team, seemed intimidated by the task before them, and waited for the game to take shape—as we did, apparently believing that our accumulated reputation, home ice advantage, and series lead would give us the win. Early in the second period, drifting in a tie, the game was there equally for either team to take. The Islanders continued to wait; it was Lapointe, not Potvin, angry and impatient, who finally took hold of the puck and with it the game. We scored two quick goals, and by the end of the second period, the game and the series were suddenly over.

A year later, we played against the Islanders again. We had lost the fifth game in Montreal in overtime, and we played the sixth game in New York, ahead 3-2 in the series. Lapointe had missed nearly half the season with injuries and illness, and had struggled in the playoffs, playing poorly in the overtime game. In the sixth game, however, he was brilliant. While it is usual, indeed expected, that a defenseman will block shots at least occasionally, Lapointe prefers not to. He did it at times earlier in his career, but less often in recent years and with more injuries that year, less often still. And whenever he *did* block a shot, whether from accident or mindless desperation, he would always follow it with the same routine— slowly getting to his skates, wincing painfully, limping in a way that said he was finished for the game, moving imperceptibly towards the bench, looking at Bowman, wanting to go off; seeing Bowman turn and look away. But Bowman knew that when the puck was dropped, Lapointe would play as if nothing had happened. That night he blocked several crucial shots—intentionally— and we won 2-1.

Then last year, in a game against Detroit in the Forum, it finally happened. After practice the day before, Lapointe had gone to a dentist to get some new teeth. These teeth were bigger than his old ones, longer, in fact too long, especially the front two. They might have gone entirely unnoticed except for another change. His hair. Tired of it falling on his forehead like a bowl, he had had it permed into a round, black aura. The next night he wandered into the dressing room before the game and sat down as if nothing had happened. One by one our sightless glances turned to double and triple takes, open mouths, and finally fits of laughter:

"Je-sus Christ, will ya look at that head!" someone said at last.

"Hey Pointu, the beaver put up much of a fight?"

Laughing at first, then embarrassed, then making it worse by trying to explain—"Yeah, the dentist said he might have to file 'em down a bit"—Lapointe removed his teeth and slipped out to the bathroom for water and petroleum jelly to stick down his hair. When he came back, he looked almost like Pointu, but the memory wouldn't go away. Every few minutes there was a snigger or a snort, then we'd laugh until we were all aching and teary-eyed again.

When the game began, it got worse. The water evaporated, and the petroleum jelly washed away with his perspiration. I didn't notice anything for a while; even after the first period nothing seemed unusual. But suddenly, early in the second, when he skated back for the puck, he looked different. He had grown. His aura was much bigger than before. With the heat and the bright lights, his hair had straightened, stiffened, and shot up like an umbrella in a wind storm. At the end of the period, we were beside ourselves.

"For crissake, Pointu, put a helmet on. I got a game to play."

"Hey Pointu, I got the electrician. Which socket was it?"

Finally, the right guy.

If the bus were to continue past our destination a few blocks, we would come to an area called "the Avenues," the six numbered avenues that run north-south between Verdun Avenue and Bannantyne. It was on "the Avenues" that Scotty Bowman grew up.

In 1930, John Bowman, a blacksmith, left the small market town of Forfar on the east coast of Scotland and arrived in Canada. He was twenty-eight. A year later, his wife Jean joined him. They were Depression immigrants, and like many of their ancestors who began settling in Canada in large numbers more than a century before, they came first to Point St. Charles, a low-income working-class area east of Verdun, less than a mile south of the Forum. There, surrounded by countrymen, they learned to adapt quickly to life in their new country. In time, as the men found jobs, and as families settled in, most left "the Point," many moving west a few blocks into slightly newer and larger accommodations in Verdun.

In 1935, with two young children, the Bowmans moved to 2nd Avenue in Verdun. Two years later, they moved again, west onto 5th Avenue, where they remained for the next twelve years.

More than 150 families lived on 5th Avenue in the city block between Bannantyne and Verdun. It was a street of sixplexes, one beside the other, thirteen on each side of the street, each with two doors on the ground floor, a flight of outside stairs to a balcony and four more doors, two of which led to second-floor flats, the other two to inside stairs that connected to flats on the third floor. Inside, the flats were identical—a narrow hallway running from the front door to the back, and extending off it, a small sitting room, two small bedrooms, a kitchen and bathroom on the other side near the back. For $22 a month, the Bowmans lived in one of the bottom flats; the landlord, as was the custom, lived in the other. Years later, Bowman and his friends would joke about living in

Harlem, but the flats, while small, were well-built and well-main-
tained. Size, in fact, was little problem, for the children of Verdun
spent most of their time outdoors.

They spent it on the streets—in the 1930s and 1940s, streets
largely empty of cars—or at Willibrord Park, where each winter the
city of Verdun put up five outdoor rinks. On these rinks or in back
alleys, from late November to late March, at noon, from school-
end until dinner time, Saturdays, Sundays, and holidays from
morning to night, Bowman and his friends played hockey. In
summer, they played baseball. It was a simple, invigorating life, the
cliché childhood of Canadians of their generation. Years later,
asked to remember his childhood, Bowman said simply that
"everything was sports."

After playing his minor hockey in Verdun, at sixteen Bowman
joined the Montreal Junior Canadiens. A left-winger, he was a
good skater with a fine instinctive sense of the game, though
surprisingly weak defensively, and in his first season scored the
promising total of twenty goals. That year in the playoffs, the
Juniors played Trois-Rivières. It was March 1951 and Bowman
was seventeen. Ahead 5-1 in a game that would eliminate Trois-
Rivières, with thirty seconds remaining Bowman got a
breakaway. Chasing him a few strides behind was Jean-Guy Talbot,
a talented defenseman who would later play sixteen seasons in the
NHL, three in St. Louis with Bowman as his coach. Talbot had
played poorly, taking several costly penalties, and with his season
about to end, he was frustrated and angry. He reached out and
came down hard with his stick on Bowman's shoulder. Bowman
kept going. Talbot brought his stick down again, harder, this time
on Bowman's head. Bowman went down, his skull fractured, his
career over.

Talbot was suspended for a year, though his suspension was
lifted the following November. Bowman, after a few anxious days
in the hospital, slowly recovered. He tried playing again the
following year, this time with a helmet, but found that he couldn't
play as he had before. Late in the fall, Frank Selke, then general
manager of the Canadiens, sponsors of the Juniors, called him to
his office and told him it wasn't worth the risk to him or to the
team for him to continue. Having just turned eighteen, Bowman
decided to quit, accepting Selke's offer to coach a midget-age team
in Verdun. Years later, he held no bitterness. Uncertain of a
professional career in the tightly competitive six-team NHL, he
saw his injury as an opportunity to get a head start in a new life.

For sixteen years, almost a coaching lifetime, he apprenticed—
coaching and supervising minor hockey teams in Verdun and

recruiting players for Jr. A teams, coaching a Jr. B team, for two years assisting Sam Pollock with the Hull-Ottawa Juniors, moving to Peterborough to coach for three seasons, scouting eastern Canada for the Canadiens for two, coaching Omaha, his first professional team, for a few unhappy weeks, then returning to Montreal for two more years with the Juniors. At first, it was a rapid rise. Then, too young to advance beyond junior hockey, Bowman began a long and at times frustrating wait, moving sideways several times until much of his early promise seemed to have deserted him. But during this time, working with Selke and Pollock, he got immensely varied and valuable experience. So, early in 1966, a year before the NHL expanded from six teams to twelve, when Lynn Patrick, coach and general manager of the expansion St. Louis Blues, called and asked him to be his assistant, at thirty-three, Bowman was ready.

Before twenty games had been played in the Blues' first season, Patrick had stepped down as coach and Bowman had replaced him. In his first three years, the Blues finished first twice and third once in the expansion Western Division of the NHL, going to the Stanley Cup finals each time. In his fourth season, the team slipped to second and lost to expansion rival Minnesota in the quarter-finals of the playoffs. After an uncomfortable plane ride home from Minnesota, the next day Bowman met with Sid Salomon III, son of the principal owner of the team. In a stormy meeting, Salomon made it clear that he didn't want Al Arbour as his coach the following year, Cliff Fletcher as Bowman's assistant, or Tommy Woodcock as the team's trainer. Bowman decided to resign. Little more than a year later, only Woodcock was still with the Blues, his job saved by a players' protest.

A few days after Bowman resigned, Henri Richard called Al MacNeil "incompétent," the province of Quebec heard him say something quite different, and the Canadiens needed a new coach. At thirty-seven, Scotty Bowman returned to Montreal to take the job he had trained for during most of his life.

If you ask the players who have played for Bowman if they like him, most will stand shocked, as if the thought never occurred to them, as if the question is somehow inappropriate, as if the answer is entirely self-evident. No, they will say, Scotty Bowman may be a lot of things, but he is not someone you like. A few, usually those who played for him the longest but who now no longer do so, might brighten and answer quickly, as if they *had* thought about it, maybe a lot about it, in the years since.

"Yeah sure, I, I really *respect* the guy. I really *admire* him. He sure did a lot for me."

Scotty Bowman is not someone who is easy to like. He has no coach's con about him. He does not slap backs, punch arms, or grab elbows. He doesn't search eyes, spew out ingratiating blarney, or disarm with faint, enervating praise. He is shy and not very friendly. If he speaks to reporters or to a team, he talks business, and his eyes sweep several inches above their heads. If he speaks to you alone, as a few times each year you force him to, explaining something that is annoyingly unclear, you share three or four intimate, surprising minutes that bring you closer to him than you ever thought possible. Then, as if he suddenly remembers where he is and what he is doing, he cuts it off—"Yeah, yeah, is that it? Good, good"—and before you can answer, it's over. And if, by chance, your path crosses his away from the rink, at first there will be several awkward "caught in the act" moments. Recovering, he may ask how you are, but if he does, he'll blurt something about Tremblay's rash or Lemaire's injury before you can answer. And all the time you talk, one foot on the brake, the other on the accelerator, he lurches away, inch by inch. In the intimacy of a team, Bowman calls Bunny "Michel," Sharty "Rick," and Pointu "Guy." Bo and Bird and Co and Shutty are Bob and Larry and Jacques and Steve. He doesn't call anyone by his nickname.

Abrupt, straightforward, without flair or charm, he seems cold and abrasive, sometimes obnoxious, controversial, but never colorful. He is not Vince Lombardi, tough and gruff with a heart of gold. His players don't sit around telling hateful-affectionate stories about him. Someone might say of him, as former Packers great Henry Jordan once said of Lombardi, "He treats us all the same—like dogs," but he doesn't. He plays favorites. His favorites, while rarely feeling favored, are those who work and produce for him. He is complex, confusing, misunderstood, unclear in every way but one. He is a brilliant coach, the best of his time.

He starts each season with a goal—the Stanley Cup—and he has no other. It is part of the Canadiens' heritage passed from Selke to Pollock, through Dick Irvin, Blake, and Bowman, to the Richards, Béliveau, Lafleur, and the rest. A good season is a Stanley Cup; anything else is not. So in September, in November, in December, and in March, he never loses sight of May. With schizophrenic desperation/perspective, he treats each game as an indicator, as a signpost, en route to May; yet he makes no compromise for any game. He sees an inextricable link between the months and games of a season—"You can't turn it off and on," he says, as other coaches say. But Bowman believes what he says, and practices it. Like his mentor, Sam Pollock, he lives with a conviction, what others, less strong, might call paranoia, that no matter how good the team is, it might never win another game. He can see in every game the beginning of a chain of events he cannot stop a careless loss at home, a tougher game on the road, an injury, three games in four nights, Chartraw missing a plane, a sweep of winter sickness, an opponent on a hot streak, building pressure at home, a media scandal, a team that shows you less respect, then another, and another, and quickly several more.

For someone of his obvious ability, Bowman seems a remarkable contradiction of strength and weakness, realism and insecurity; but he is not. As others have discovered, at the top, where Bowman is, strength, weakness, realism, and insecurity are really just symptoms of each other. So while he surely knows that we are better than any other team, if he has ever thought about it, he has done so only fleetingly and not without wincing at his own dangerous thought. For he knows that May is always ahead, and when May is over, September is never far away. With each Stanley Cup, we look for, and sometimes find, signs he is loosening up. But he has never really changed. We know that when two or three days of uncharacteristic pleasantness leave us talking to ourselves, as winger Jimmy Roberts once said, "It's nothing that a loss won't cure."

Not long ago, I asked him his most important job as coach. He sat quiet for a moment, his face unfurrowed and blank, thinking, then said simply, "To get the right players on the ice." In an age of "systems" and "concepts" and fervid self-promotion, his answer may seem a little unsatisfying; but though misleadingly simple, it is how he coaches. No one has ever heard of a "Bowman system" as they have a "Shero system." Fred Shero's Flyers, a good but limited team, needed a system. To be effective, they needed to play just one way, and to play that way so well they could overcome any team. Bowman's team is different. Immensely talented, immensely varied, it is a team literally good enough to play, and win, any style of game. For it, a system would be too confining, robbing the team of its unique feature—its flexibility. Further, Bowman understands, as Shero did, that the flip side of winning with a system is losing *by* that system. So Bowman, a pragmatist with the tools any pragmatist would envy, coaches with what he calls a "plan."

It starts with speed. It is the essence of the Canadiens' game— "firewagon hockey" someone once called it—and Bowman understands speed. He knows that speed is disorienting, that, like an old man in a thirty-year-old's world, it robs an opponent of coordination and control, stripping away skills, breaking down systems, making even the simplest tasks seem difficult. He knows that with

Lafleur, Lemaire, Shutt, Lapointe, Gainey, and others, speed is an edge we have on everyone else; so Bowman hones that edge and uses it. His practices are in constant motion, shooting, passing, everything done *on the go*, *with speed*, every drill rooted in high-pace skating (in the Canada Cup and the Challenge Cup, when Bowman coached players from other teams, they tired quickly in early practices, unused to his pace). In games, he tells us in his earnest way to "throw speed at them." Other teams forecheck, then fall back quickly to pick up their men, but Bowman frees his skaters to chase the puck in all but the defensive zone. In the 1976 Stanley Cup finals with the Flyers, in a high-pitched, impassioned voice, he reminded us repeatedly, "Don't respect their speed." He wanted to pressure the Flyers with all five men in their zone, unworried by 2-on-1 breaks that would sometimes result. He knew that against the Flyers, a methodical, even slow, team, our speed would let us recover easily.

But speed is not enough. Quick players are often small, and in smaller rinks against bigger teams, are frequently subject to intimidating attack. Bowman knows that Lafleur, Lemaire, and Lapointe, players whose skills turn the Canadiens from a good team to a special one, must be made "comfortable," as he puts it; they must be allowed to play without fear. So never farther than the players' bench away, to balance and neutralize that fear, Bowman has Lupien and Chartraw, sometimes Cam Connor, in other years Pierre Bouchard, and of course, Larry Robinson. With a game-to-game core of fourteen or fifteen players, Bowman fine-tunes his line-up, choosing two or three from among the six or more available to find the "right mix," as he calls it, for every game we play. He believes that a championship team needs all kinds of players, and that too many players of the same type, no matter how good, make any team vulnerable. So for games against the Flyers and the Bruins, and for many road games, he goes with a "big line-up"; for other games, different combinations which an opponent and the circumstances of a season make appropriate.

It gives him the kind of flexibility that no other coach has. He knows that only a special set of circumstances can beat us, so he coaches as if preoccupied with minimizing those circumstances. He can do nothing to prevent slumps and injuries, but he can make sure that well-prepared replacements are ready when needed. We carry five or six extra players, more than any other team. It can be a problem at times, since players who play little complain often and disturb a team. But when a team is winning, these players say little, for few in the press or public will listen to them. And while Bowman maintains even stricter isolation from them—his attitude seems to be "If you don't play the way I want you to, why should I speak to you?"—he keeps them around and uses them. He plays them occasionally, and gives them ice time with Ruel before and after practice, reminding the regulars that good players not out of sight, never out of mind, are only the barest margin away from playing more often. It is with these marginal players that Bowman feels he has the greatest impact.

Once he remarked to me that Guy Lafleur seemed obsessed always to do better; that while he was a good team player, being the foremost player in the league carried with it a larger responsibility, and that for him anything less than a scoring title was not enough. Bowman feels much the same way about the team's other exceptional players—about Gainey, Robinson, Savard, Lapointe, Shutt, Cournoyer, Lemaire. He believes that while he can set a constructive tone for the team, and can prepare these players physically and tactically, reminding them from time to time to their annoyance that they are not playing as they can, ultimately what drives them is *them.*

Not so the marginal player. Young players whose styles are not yet set, older players on the other side of their careers, their egos battered until they're willing to listen: these players are vulnerable and can be manipulated. So Bowman manipulates them—Tremblay, Chartraw, Larouche, Larocque, and others—sometimes cruelly. Benching them, ignoring them for long periods of time, he makes them worry, and makes them wonder why. Then the team hits injuries or a slump and he uncovers them again. He works them hard in practice, watching them, telling the press how hard and well they are working, making them feel they are earning their place in the team. Given a chance, usually at home, they give back an inspired game. A few games later, the inspiration fades, and it all starts again. He holds them by their emotional strings, often for many years, manipulating them until he gets out of them what he thinks is there; then, when he gets it, when he feels it is grooved into place, he stops.

"He's not honest," they often complain, though translating "honnête" too literally they mean, in part, that he isn't "fair." Several times each has asked to be traded, but it won't happen. Bowman knows that a championship team needs two goalies capable of winning a Stanley Cup; that it needs Chartraw's versatility and toughness, Tremblay's infectious enthusiasm, the prodigal goal-scoring of Larouche. In important games, when each team fixes on the other team's best, holding them in check, it is often the quality and readiness of the rest that make the crushing difference. In the third game of the 1976 finals against the Flyers, Chartraw made that difference; two years later, Tremblay scored two goals and Larouche one in a 4-1 Stanley Cup winning game against the Bruins. It is all part of getting "the right players on the ice." Bowman knows the enormous strength he has, and squanders none of it.

On a team of talented, tough-minded, egotistical players, Bowman is the boss. His captains—earlier Henri Richard, now Cournoyer—have no special role. A few years ago, he formed a committee of the senior players on the team—Lemaire, Savard, Lapointe, Cournoyer, Roberts, Pete Mahovlich, and me ("the Magnificent 7" the others called us) to meet with him periodically to discuss the team. We held one meeting. (That we had only one meeting didn't surprise us; that he formed the committee did.)

Unmistakably, and to an extent that may surprise even him, Bowman is in charge. Not Grundman, not Pollock before him—in distant upstairs offices, with *technical* authority, we feel little contact with them. It is Bowman who sets the tone and mood for the team. He may say less than he seems to say (when asked, most players admit to their own surprise they "never really had any problem with him"), but his presence, belligerent, nagging, and demanding, like a conscience that never shuts up, is constant. And every so often, when some internal threshold is passed, he will blurt out something in his acerbic, biting way, to others usually, but really to all of us. Just words we've all heard before from others, but coming as they do *without* malice, with nothing in them that can be for his benefit, we hear them as words that might be right, and probably are. It is what he says and what he might say that make us fear him. It is his hair-trigger sense of outrage at those who don't measure up; and the feeling, the fear we all share, that at any moment that outrage will be directed at us.

He knows each of us too well; he leaves us no place to hide. He knows that we are strong, and are weak; that we can be selfish and lazy, that we can eat too much and drink too much, that we will always look for the easy way out, and when we find it, that we will use it. He knows that each of us comes with a stable of excuses, "crutches" he calls them, ready to use whenever we need them. The team with the fewest crutches will win, Bowman believes. So he inserts himself into our minds, and anticipates these crutches— practice times, travel schedule, hotel, the menu for our team meal—then systematically kicks them away, leaving us with no way out if we lose. And when we don't lose, we get our revenge, we pretend that we did it ourselves. We want him to have no part of it; and he lets us. He never challenges the integrity of the team. Just as he will allow no player to stand above the team, he will not stand above it either. The team must believe in itself.

More than any coach I have had, Bowman has a complete and undistractible team focus. He has one loyalty—to the team; not to individual players on the team, though most coaches prefer to ignore the distinction (as most players do until they are traded or become free agents); not to fans or to anyone else. Most of us like to pretend the primacy of personal relationships in our work (then are unforgiving of those who let us down); Bowman doesn't pretend. To him, loyalty is doing what you can and doing it well. If you don't, and play less often or are traded away, it is not he who is being disloyal.

He is uncompromising, unmellowing, unable to be finessed; he is beyond our control. Being a nice guy doesn't count; going to optional practices, coming early, staying late, doesn't count. As Pete Mahovlich, Cournoyer, and Henri Richard have discovered, what you have done before counts only until you can't do it again. No politics, no favors, it is how you measure up to what you can do, how you help the team, how you *perform*—they are what count. It is thin comfort.

Many times, I have sensed in Bowman a personal loyalty beyond the team, but I have been mistaken. I always believed that he played me the way he did because he understood me. He played me often because I needed to play often to feel part of the team; he put me into a game after a bad game because he knew that the humiliation I felt wouldn't go away until I played better; he played me on the road, when I was sick or injured, against the Islanders, Bruins, and Flyers because he knew I needed the exciting challenge that each offered. And when he talked to the press of my outside interests, he always spoke positively of them, as if he understood my need for distractions from the game, my need to scheme with myself to justify continuing in hockey, my need to pursue other things for their own sake. Two years ago, I allowed four goals in a first period against Vancouver, then was jeered by Forum fans the rest of the game. When I didn't play at home for more than a month until we met the Bruins, I thought he had been protecting me, keeping me away from the Forum until we played a team against which I always played well. In fact it was none of those things; it was *nothing personal* at all. I played often, I played after bad games, and against the league's best teams when I was sick or injured, because I play well then, and because when I play well, the team is better off. It is because he understands me *as a goalie* that he plays me when he does; he does it for the team, not for me.

A few weeks ago, the NHL all-stars played the Soviet National Team in the Challenge Cup in New York. While I had played against the Soviets only a few times in my career, I had done poorly enough in many games that there seemed a clear and disturbing pattern to my play. Simply, I began to wonder, as others did, if I was too big to cope with the quickness and dexterity of the Soviet game.

I had always been able to adapt before. I had moved from Jr. B. hockey to college hockey, from college to the National Team to the American League to the NHL. As a seven-year-old, I played against teenagers in backyard games. I had played against teams that had seemed too good—RAC, the Weston Dodgers, North Dakota, the Bruins in 1971. Many times, I was certain I would fail. Many times, I did not want to play, afraid of being humiliated if I did. But I always managed to cope, and found a way. This was different. This was not the first time I had played the Soviets. I knew exactly what I would face. And because I did, as if finally reaching the point where a coach would send me home, I was afraid I was up against something I could not handle.

I arrived in New York with my teammates three days before the first game. I went directly to my room and set myself a schedule, determined not to repeat the mistake I had made three years earlier. The night before a New Year's Eve game with the Soviet Central Army Team in 1975, I got away from the bustle of visitors who were arriving at our house and went to a downtown hotel. There, alone with myself for twenty-four hours, I built slowly for the game, and kept on building until the game and I became a fixation. I thought and worried and filled up with doubts, I could never get mentally free enough just to play, and while the great Soviet goaltender Tretiak stopped thirty-five shots, I stopped ten in a 3-3 tie.

This time, I would do it differently. I would keep busy, always moving, never allowing a moment alone with myself, never a chance to dwell on other games, to think/worry about those ahead. I got up early, and walked around Manhattan, shopping, looking, always moving; I went to Madison Square Garden for practice, ate a quick lunch, and walked again; I went to a movie, to another movie, ate dinner, walked, went to another movie—then did the same the next day.

We won the first game 4-2.

Friday was a day off. I repeated Tuesday and Wednesday, blanking my mind, building up energy, comfortable, confident, getting ready for Saturday. After a good start, we were outplayed in the last two periods and lost 5-4. I spent Saturday night with teammates talking about the Sunday game. We talked about what we hadn't done, and what we needed to do to win. I felt confident, comfortable, almost relaxed. Sunday morning, Bowman told me he was making a change. Bruins' goalie Gerry Cheevers would play the deciding game.

If the New Year's Eve game was my most disappointing moment, this was the most crushing. (After moping in a catatonic sulk for several days, back in Montreal I sat in the dressing room slouched against the wall, jotting something on a piece of paper. Looking over at me, Risebrough asked Shutt beside him, "What's he writing?" Shutt: "A suicide note.")

Friends and others found relief and vindication for me in the 6-0 loss and were surprised when I didn't feel the same way. They didn't understand. The third game was a game we *had* to win. Against a tough opponent, after a loss, it was *my* game, the kind Bowman always put me in, the one he knew I would deliver. A few days later, unable to keep to myself any longer, I went to Bowman and asked him why.

He said that he and Ruel and the team's general managers, Harry Sinden (Bruins), Bill Torrey (Islanders), and Cliff Fletcher (Flames), had talked at length about it and had made the decision jointly, hoping to give the team a spark that the second game had showed we needed. But Bowman, not hiding in that, said further that as coach, if he had insisted, he could probably have had his way. He didn't insist, he said, because looking at all the circumstances, he didn't feel certain enough. It was then that I understood for the first time.

Each year when the season ends, Bowman invites me to spend a day or a weekend at his farm south of Montreal. And each year, I intend to go, but I never have. It is because other things come up and gradually I forget about it until the summer runs out, but in part, perhaps in larger part than I'm willing to admit, I don't go because I'm afraid that knowing him better, and having him know me better, things might change. And I don't want them to change. We are a good combination. Together we have shared four Stanley Cups and many other satisfying moments. I know that nothing would change, yet I don't want to take that risk.

As a goalie, I am in Bowman's hands. I play when he says I play; I don't play when he says I don't. Much of my happiness, much of the mood I carry with me away from the rink, come from when and how often and against whom I play, and that depends on Bowman. It can be a helpless feeling for a player but with Bowman I am comfortable. We are in someone else's hands in everything we do, but how often are any of us in hands that know us so well? Hands that insist we be as good as we can be, that tolerate nothing else, hands we trust.

There are many successful ways to coach. There are autocrats and technocrats, mean SOBs and just plain folks. What makes Bowman's style work is an understanding, *the* understanding that must exist between a coach and his team: *he* knows the most important thing to a team is to win; *we* know he does what he does to make us win.

I like him.

The forwards and defensemen take off their skate guards and go directly onto the ice. Larocque and I remain behind in a small dressing room to put on our skates and pads. By the time we get to the ice, the others are warmed up and anxious for practice to begin. The rink is cold, and I move stiffly through the skating drills, unable to get loose. Then, as I skate around one net and start up ice, out of nowhere, with only his usual warning, Chartraw wipes me out.

It is not the first time. Rick Chartraw, a big slab-thick forward/defenseman, man-about-town, and designated team eccentric—"a classic," in the language of the team—has the annoying habit of spinning out of control at almost any time, in almost any place. The only warning he gives is a sudden, though not surprised, "oops," followed by the sound of furiously chopping skates as he tries to regain his balance. It is no use. Falling onto his back, out of control, he slides like a turtle on its shell until someone or something stops him. Several times it has been me, usually in pregame warm-up; twice he has injured Pierre Larouche in practice, both times when Larouche was his linemate. No one is quite sure why it happens. Some think it is inner-ear trouble, others that one leg is shorter than the other. Knowing Sharty, most believe that, faced with a sudden rush of options, his mind blows.

He gets up, apologizes as he always does—"Oops, sorry"— and skates off. More surprised than I should be, I pick myself up and get back in the drill. Before I get warm and loose, I am whistled into a net for shots.

In more than an hour, I never catch up. The forwards and defensemen skate through drills to get warm and stay warm. I started out cold, and now, unable to move enough to get warm, I get colder. I wanted a good practice today. I wanted to sweep Sunday's feeling uninterrupted into tomorrow's game, to reconfirm that Sunday's skills were still there. But too many pucks go in. When I'm playing well—today, tomorrow, practices, games, Leafs, Rangers, Flyers, it doesn't matter—I put on my equipment and play. But when I'm not, when I stutter between bad games and good, desperate to make a connection between yesterday and today and tomorrow, each puck I don't stop becomes important.

In an endless panorama of games, practice is the routine, unseen link in a season. One practice a day every day with few exceptions from season-opening to season-end: an hour the day before the game, and hour and fifteen minutes or more on other days, twenty minutes the day of the game. It brings a team together, binds it, gives it practice at being a team; gives it a "team feeling." Sometimes it is drudgery, sometimes pure remembered fun, usually it is just fast-paced emotionless routine. But filling up time that easily can go astray (a few years ago, Bowman changed our practice time from 10 a.m. to noon to interrupt afternoons and discourage outside activities), it joins one day to the next to keep up the tempo of the season.

What practice is not is a time to teach. In Europe, and in U.S. colleges and high schools, teams play fewer games and practice more often. With more days between games, they can vary the tempo of a season to create the right environment for practice. They can use practice for preparation and instruction, to develop team and individual skills. The Canadian tradition is different. We have never learned how to practice. We are told at an early age, and we believe, that only with game competition can we improve. So we play games, three games a week for much of our lives, and, preoccupied with the last game until preoccupied with the next, we have little energy and less attention span for anything else. Only when things go wrong do we interrupt ourselves and focus on specific parts of our game—on power plays, faceoffs, forechecking, breakout patterns. The rest of the time, our conditioning and skills building gradually from seasonal causes, we move through practice less to improve than to sustain what we already have.

Bowman blows his whistle; our bodies burst into motion, already in the rhythm of the next game. He lets us go, orchestrating with a loose, unfelt hand. "Between the lines," "Two-on-ones," "Line rushes out of both ends," he shouts. Power plays, shots, in sixty minutes we never look at the clock. It's the kind of high-energy pre-game practice Bowman wants. For me, lost at the start, trying to catch up, I survive unhurt, my usual goal at Verdun.

Finally, Bowman blows his whistle again and we skate to one end of the ice for some skating drills. Larocque stands beside the boards, I stand near the middle of the ice beside Risebrough.

Bowman yells "Blues!" and Lemaire, Shutt, and Lafleur, in light-blue sweaters, sprint down the ice to the other goal-line and back again. As they cross the blueline, straightening up to coast the final few feet, Bowman yells the name of another color and three more players sweatered in that color break forward as the blues had done. Larocque and I false start with each new group that is called. I skate faster than Larocque, but only marginally, and to compensate he stands near the boards, using their curvature to line up ahead of me without being detected. I move up so I am even with him. The first round through, I wait for Bowman to yell "Goalies!"; for every other round, the order set, from the corner of my eye I watch Larocque. When he starts, I go. I know that our respective speeds and wills are invariable. I know if I watch him and leave just a reflex behind, I will win. Bowman yells "Goalies!" and Larocque takes off. By the center line, I am even, but he stops before I expect him to, and at the turn he is ahead. By center, I am even again; at the blueline, straightening up, I coast to the end a few feet ahead.

Larocque and I compete with each other constantly. We compete in scrimmages and skating drills, by win-loss records and goals against; by going to optional practices and by how often and how long we stay when practice ends. Our competition is undeclared, its results are known only to us; we say nothing to each other about it. But we know. We compete though we are teammates and share the same goals for the team. We are friendly, if a little guarded with each other, and personally compatible. We know that the team needs two capable goalies, we know that we need each other to avoid the sloppy complacence a season can bring. But only one goalie can play at a time, and if he plays well, the other may never play. It means I am happy when we win and happier if I have played; unhappy when we lose, less unhappy if I haven't played. And if the game is close and I am not playing, I will forget myself and hope for Bunny without reservation. But if it is not, I want Bunny to play well, but not too well.

At one time, I thought I could "beat him out" fully and completely, just as I'm sure at times he has thought the same thing. I thought I could play sufficiently better than he to monopolize more than 60 of our 80 games and force him somewhere else or into a permanently subservient role. I could not do either. After we had played together a year or two, I realized that I could stay ahead, but I could not win. And while each year on the second day of training camp the Montreal papers report what I tell them the day before—that I hope to play 60 games—and what Bunny tells them—that he hopes to play 40—we know we have reached a kind of competitive equilibrium at about 50-30. Yet still we compete. In the last few years, I have been the one on the defensive. As it has long been assumed, and is now confirmed, that I will soon retire, and as Larocque has shown himself a strong and competent goalie, clearly the Canadiens' goalie of the future, that future is now uncomfortably close. I am a lame duck, and as more of the discretionary games go to Larocque to make him happy, my game total this year will be less than 50 for the first time.

Bowman blows his whistle again, this time harder and longer, and practice is over.

It is 1:13 p.m. The sun peeks through, the sweat that today did not come easily now feels good; our work day is over. We get on the bus and go to the seats we sat in on our way here. Chartraw skips to the back and lies down curled across the top of the seat like a back-window ornament.

"Hey Sharty," Shutt chirps, "your eyes light up when the brakes go on?"

Chartraw ignores him, waving to the driver of the car behind us.

"*Câlisse*, they always look that way," Tremblay growls.

"Hey Sharty, that's it!" Robinson yells excitedly, remembering Chartraw's most recent problems. "You've been skatin' with your brakes on."

We read the newspapers we read before and talk about fishing trips and golf games still months away. The bus passes a stylish coat and hat worn by a tall, slender body. The talk continues but heads turn like those at a tennis match, then snap back, disappointed. The stop light turns amber, then red, and the bus lurches to a halt. Lapointe looks out his window at the car below. Its driver, a well-dressed man of about fifty, stares diagonally past the front of the bus, waiting for the light to change. With his left hand, he distractedly rubs at his face, then his nose, finally picking at it more and more earnestly.

"*Ta-berr-nac*," Lapointe yells, "lookit this."

Instantly we rush to Lapointe's side of the bus.

"Ooh, oooh, that feels good," someone moans.

"*Ta-berr-nac*," Lapointe exclaims again, "ya think his contact's stuck?"

The man continues. Finally he stops, looks down at his finger, ahead at the light, and gets ready to go. Just to be sure he doesn't think he has gone unnoticed, several players bang at their windows. The man looks up. Looking down at him he sees a busful of laughing faces.

Back at the Forum, we have only started to undress when the press come in. They spread around the room, looking for an angle for their stories on tomorrow's game against the Leafs. Two reporters go to Napier, another to Hughes, both from Toronto, and both so young that returning home to play means something to them. In a few minutes, the reporter talking to Hughes walks over to Napier, and the two with Napier move across to Hughes. A fourth reporter is in the stick room with Lemaire, asking about his injured shoulder. As they talk, each reporter glances often at

Larouche. Pierre Larouche, sitting quietly in one corner, stares blankly across the room. After a stretch of games in which he scored well and again seemed ready to become the regular he was supposed to be when he was traded here from Pittsburgh a year ago, last week he played poorly in consecutive road games in St. Louis and Chicago. He played well last Saturday at home against Minnesota, but Bowman didn't dress him for the game in Buffalo. Today, while the regular lines wore their usual blue, yellow, orange, and green sweaters, Larouche wore black; the only other player in a black sweater was Chartraw. Now a reporter walks by and says something to him, but Larouche, staring straight ahead, says nothing. They are waiting for him to say what he has often said in similar circumstances, that he wants to be traded, that he is fed up with the way Bowman treats him. But today Larouche only looks sad and a little bewildered.

The dressing room has lost the leisurely pace it had yesterday. Players assembly-line in and out of the showers, equipment bags get packed, checked, zipped, locked, and carted away, clothes get hurried on. We have just a few hours to do what can't be done tomorrow; this show is packing up and moving on the road.

Houle ices down a shoulder, Risebrough a knee that gives him more trouble than he wants to admit. Napier, Hughes, Jarvis, Shutt canvass the room for extra tickets for relatives and friends in Toronto. Tremblay picks up Shutt's Coke, then Lafleur's, and drinks them both, and with a wink, a laugh, and a devil-may-care leap, darts to the shower.

Larocque and I pack our spare catching gloves, skates, and masks into our equipment bags. Lafleur, Shutt, and Larouche have gone; our corner of the room is vacated. Without looking up, I turn slightly towards him. "We had our meeting yesterday," I tell him, my voice barely above a whisper. He stops a moment, and without looking up, he nods; and we go back to what we were doing.

The Canadiens have two rules that are almost inviolable: the team must travel together, and the team must stay in the same hotel. It took me a long time before I would even ask about the flexibility of those rules. We play in Toronto only twice a year. My parents live in Toronto, and the few hours we have there each time we play are never enough to do all that should be done. A few years ago, I asked Bowman if I could leave Montreal early and stay at my parents' house. He thought about it for a moment, then, after satisfying himself that he would give the same perk to anyone who asked, he agreed.

I get dressed and walk to Bowman's office, a small concrete-block cubicle he shares with Ruel, across a corridor from the dressing room. He sits at his metal desk strewn with papers and equipment; Ruel, a few feet away, unlaces his skates. Bowman hands me my plane ticket, and tells me to be at Maple Leaf Gardens for an 11:30 skate tomorrow. I turn and start to leave, then stop. I am certain that I will be playing tomorrow—because of the way I played in Buffalo, because of the patterns of today's practice, because I always play in Toronto. But Bowman hasn't said, and won't say unless I ask him. I ask him because I want to know. He says I am playing.

Wednesday

*"...[I]t is part of the painful process of history that
people are always made by the world they reject and that the
rage at it they express is in large measure rage at themselves."*

—Fouad Ajami (reviewing
V. S. Naipaul's *Among the Believers*:
An Islamic Journey)

TORONTO

I WAKE UP IN MY OLD ROOM. THE CURTAINS ARE DRAWN tight, and though it must be mid-morning by now, the room is a deep gray. I feel for my glasses on a table beside the bed, then reach over my head and tug at one of the curtains, opening it a few inches. Light streams in over me. On the other side of the room, in the corner that is now lighted, I see a crib.

To those not from Toronto, I have always said I grew up in Toronto, but I didn't. I grew up in Islington, at the time a western suburb, now a mid-western suburb, of Toronto. When Toronto boomed after the Second World War, it was in places like Islington that it boomed. Uncramped by the city, houses, churches, schools, and parks suddenly spread out. Match-box bungalows became side-splits and ranch-style homes; schools one story high spread over large grassy playgrounds in a maze. Even the churches discarded city stone and an old-world style for blocks and bricks and a distinctive suburban look. This was the 1950s. TV was still a wonder, new chrome-covered cars drove on new clover-leafed expressways, and first-generation postwar parents moved from cities to suburbs to build a clean, healthy, church-going, family-oriented, college-educated world for their children. We felt immensely privileged growing up when we did, where we did. We felt that in the 1950s, in Islington, a middle-class suburb when being middle-class and suburban was considered a virtue, there was no better place to be.

My father, Murray Dryden, was seventeen years old, almost eighteen, when he left his family's farm near the tiny village of Domain, Manitoba. It was October 1929, after the harvest, and he moved to Winnipeg, twenty-five miles north, to live with his aunt. There he hoped to earn enough money, the few hundred dollars he needed, to buy mushroom spawn for a one-acre plot he had prepared on the farm. But with little education, and economic times worsening to depression, he could find work only as a commission salesman, selling ladies' silk stockings. He went door-to-door in Winnipeg that winter, earning only enough money to feed himself. When spring came, embarrassed by what he regarded as his own personal failure, he decided not to return to the farm, instead moving west to Saskatchewan. It was no better. Hitchhiking, busing from town to town, he found few buyers, and by fall he moved again. This time he went east, travelling by train across Northern Ontario, stopping in each town as he came to it, staying until he had earned enough money to pay his fare to the next one. In the spring of 1931, he arrived in Toronto. A few months later, he moved forty miles west and south to Hamilton.

For the next eighteen years (except for four years during the war) he travelled Ontario, going door-to-door or store-to-store selling can openers, fertilizer, soda pop, washing machines, window boxes, men's cosmetics ("Let Masculine Mask change your pimples to dimples"), ecclesiastical clothing—carrying one or two products at a time, a few months later dropping one or both for something that seemed certain to be better. In 1949 a new job took him to Toronto, and my father, my mother Margaret, my grandmother, my brother Dave, then eight years old, and I moved to Islington. Within weeks, my father quit his job and was out of work. He told no one, not even my mother. Each morning he would leave the house as if going to work, and instead spend the day searching through want-ads, pounding on doors, looking for a new job. He found one nearly a month later, selling concrete blocks. Later, he sold bricks and other building materials as well, selling on commission as he always insisted on (he dismissed salary salesmen as "nine-to-fivers"). After more than fifteen years selling the wrong products at the wrong time, he finally found the right ones. He hit the postwar construction boom just as it began, and rode it successfully for more than twenty years, retiring in 1972.

Dave's bed was where the crib is now. Mine was along the same wall, on the other side of an attic door. Above and behind our heads as we slept, we each had our own gallery of sports pictures.

They were full-page color photos taken mostly from *Sport* magazine, pasted tightly together in horizontal rows, covering the wall from the top of our headboards to the ceiling. Most were of baseball or college football players, but there were some of boxers, golfers, tennis players, Olympic athletes, even a few hockey players. They stayed on that wall for many years, untorn, unreplaced, in time almost unnoticed. Then, in his mid-teens, Dave moved to a room of his own in the basement, and my light-green/dark-green room got painted blue, and no new pictures went up in their place.

Now the room is lime-green, with whole sections of walls covered in orange, brown, and yellow floral wallpaper. After I left for Cornell more than thirteen years ago, and after a respectful wait, my sister Judy, four years younger, made this room hers. The curtains changed, the book cases and dressers changed, the beds changed, and new ones were put across the room beneath the windows at the back. Then she grew up and went away, and the crib came in, used and outgrown by one grandchild, ready for the few days a year that a second, Michael, comes to visit. There is one more thing—the light in the middle of the room that hung from the ceiling until it was forehead-high, the one I tied up and out of the way so I wouldn't walk into it, has been untied and let down again.

I get out of bed and pull back the curtains. It has snowed overnight and traces are still gently falling. For several minutes I stand there, my forehead pressed to the window, watching the snow, looking out at the backyards of the houses behind, where the Pritchards, the McLarens, and the Carpenters lived, and down below at the winter's depth of snow, and at the backyard where I spent my childhood.

"Dryden's Backyard." That's what it was called in our neighborhood. It was more than 70 feet long, paved curiously in red asphalt, 45 feet wide at "the big end," gradually narrowing to 35 feet at the flower bed, to 25 feet at the porch—our center line—to 15 feet at "the small end." While Steve Shutt and Guy Lafleur were in Willowdale and Thurso on backyard rinks their fathers built, while Larry Robinson was on a frozen stream in Marvelville and Réjean Houle on a road in Rouyn under the only street light that his street had, I was here.

It was an extraordinary place, like the first swimming pool on the block, except there were no others like it anywhere. Kids would come from many blocks away to play, mostly "the big guys," friends of my brother, a year or two older than him, seven or eight years older than me. But that was never a problem. It was the first rule of the backyard that they had to let me play. To a friend who complained one day, Dave said simply, "If Ken doesn't play, you don't play."

We played "ball hockey" mostly, with a tennis ball, its bounce deadened by the cold. A few times, we got out a garden hose and flooded the backyard to use skates and pucks, but the big end was slightly lower than the small end, and the water pooled and froze unevenly. More important, we found that the more literal we tried to make our games, the less lifelike they became. We could move across the asphalt quickly and with great agility in rubber "billy" boots; we could shoot a tennis ball high and hard. But with skates on, with a puck, we were just kids. So after the first few weeks of the first year, we played only ball hockey.

Depending on the day, the time, the weather, there might be any number of kids wanting to play, so we made up games any number could play. With four and less than nine, we played regular games, the first team scoring ten goals the winner. The two best players, who seemed always to know who they were, picked the teams and decided on ends. First choice of players got second choice of ends, and because the size of the big end made it more fun to play in, the small end was the choice to defend. Each team had a goalie—one with goalie pads, a catching glove, and a goalie stick; the other with only a baseball glove and a forward's stick. When we had more than eight players, we divided into three or more teams for a round-robin tournament, each game to five. With fewer than four, it was more difficult. Sometimes we attempted a regular game, often we just played "shots," each player being both shooter and goalie, standing in front of one net, shooting in turn at the other. Most often, however, we played "penalty shots."

In the late 1950s, the CBS network televised NHL games on Saturday afternoon. Before each game, there was a preview show in which a player from each of the teams involved that day would compete in two contests, one of which was a penalty-shot contest. The goalie they used each week was an assistant trainer for the Detroit Red Wings named Julian Klymquiw. Short and left-handed, Klymquiw wore a clear plexiglass mask that arched in front of his face like a shield. None of us had ever heard of him, and his unlikely name made us a little doubtful at first. But it turned out that he was quite good, and most weeks he stopped the great majority of shots taken at him. So, during backyard games of "penalty shots," we pretended to be Julian Klymquiw, not Terry Sawchuk or Glenn Hall. And before each of our contests began, we would perform the ritual that Klymquiw and announcer Bud Palmer performed each week:

"Are you ready, Julian?"

"Yes, Bud."

But the backyard also meant time alone. It was usually after dinner when the "big guys" had homework to do and I would turn on the floodlights at either end of the house and on the porch, and play. It was a private game. I would stand alone in the middle of the yard, a stick in my hands, a tennis ball in front of me, silent, still, then suddenly dash ahead, stickhandling furiously, dodging invisible obstacles for a shot on net. It was Maple Leaf Gardens filled to wildly cheering capacity, a tie game, seconds remaining. I was Frank Mahovlich, or Gordie Howe, I was anyone I wanted to be, and the voice in my head was that of Leafs broadcaster Foster Hewitt: ". . . there's ten seconds left, Mahovlich, winding up at his own line, at center, eight seconds, seven, over the blueline, six—he winds up, he shoots, *he scores*!" The mesh that had been tied to the bottoms of our red metal goalposts until frozen in the ice had been ripped away to hang loose from the crossbars, whipped back like a flag in a stiff breeze. My arms and stick flew into the air, I screamed a scream inside my head, and collected my ball to do it again—many times, for many minutes, the hero of all my own games.

It was a glorious fantasy, and I always heard that voice. It was what made my fantasy seem almost real. For to us, who attended hockey games mostly on TV or radio, an NHL game, a Leafs game, was played with a voice. If I wanted to be Mahovlich or Howe, if I moved my body the way I had seen them move theirs and did nothing else, it would never quite work. But if I heard the voice that said their names while I was playing out that fantasy, I could believe it. Foster Hewitt could make me them.

My friends and I played every day after school, sometimes during lunch and after dinner, but Saturday was always the big day. I would go to bed Friday night thinking of Saturday, waking up early, with none of the fuzziness I had other days. If it had snowed overnight, Dave and I, with shovels and scrapers, and soon joined by others, would pile the snow into flower beds or high against the back of the garage. Then at 9 a.m. the games would begin.

There was one team in the big end, another in the small; third and fourth teams sat like birds on a telephone wire, waiting their turn on the wall that separated the big end from Carpenter's backyard. Each team wore uniforms identical to the other. It was the Canadian midwinter uniform of the time—long, heavy duffel coats in browns, grays, or blues; tuques in NHL team colors, pulled snug over ears under the watchful eye of mothers, here rolled up in some distinctive personal style; leather gloves, last year's church gloves, now curling at the wrist and separating between fingers; black rubber "billy" boots over layers of heavy woolen socks for fit, the tops rolled down like "low cuts" for speed and style.

Each game would begin with a faceoff, then wouldn't stop again. Action moved quickly end to end, the ball bouncing and rolling, chased by a hacking, slashing scrum of sticks. We had sticks without tops on their blades—"toothpicks"; sticks with no blades at all—"stubs." They broke piece by heart-breaking piece, often quickly, but still we used them. Only at the start of a season, at Christmas (Dave and I routinely exchanged sticks until one year he gave me a stick and I gave him a pair of socks) and once or twice more, would we get new ones. All except John Stedelbauer. His father owned a car dealership and during the hockey season gave away hockey sticks to his customers as a promotion. Stedelbauer got all the new sticks he needed, fortunately, as they weren't very good. One year he broke nineteen of them.

A goal would be scored, then another, and slowly the game would leapfrog to five. Bodies grew warm from exertion, fingers and toes went numb; noses ran, wiped by unconscious sleeves; coats loosened, tuques fell off; steam puffed from mouths and streamed from tuqueless heads. Sticks hacked and slashed; tennis balls stung. But in the euphoria of the game, the pain disappeared. Sitting on the wall that overlooked his backyard, Rick "Foster" Carpenter, younger and not very athletic, gave the play-by-play, but no one listened. Each of us had his own private game playing in his head. A fourth goal, then a fifth, a cheer, and the first game was over. Quickly, four duffel coats, four tuques, four pairs of weathered gloves and rubber "billy" boots would jump from the wall to replace the losers; and the second game would begin. We paused at noon while some went home and others ate the lunch that they had brought with them. At 6 p.m., the two or three who remained would leave. Eighteen hours later, after church, the next game would begin.

When I think of the backyard, I think of my childhood; and when I think of my childhood, I think of the backyard. It is the central image I have of that time, linking as it does all of its parts: father, mother, sister, friends; hockey, baseball, and Dave—big brother, idol, mentor, defender, and best friend. Yet it lasted only a few years. Dave was already twelve when the backyard was built; I was six. He and his friends played for three or four years, then stopped; I played longer but, without them, less often. Yet until moments ago, I had never remembered that.

The backyard was not a training ground. In all the time I spent there, I don't remember ever thinking I would be an NHL goalie, or even hoping I could be one. In backyard games, I dreamed I *was* Sawchuk or Hall, Mahovlich or Howe; I never dreamed I would be like them. There seemed no connection between the backyard and Maple Leaf Gardens; there seemed no way to get to there from here. If we ever thought about that, it never concerned us; we just played. It was here in the backyard that we *learned* hockey. It was here we got close to it, we got *inside* it, and it got inside us. It was here that our inextricable bond with the game was made. Many years have now passed, the game has grown up and been complicated by things outside it, yet still the backyard remains—untouched, unchanged, my unseverable link to that time, and that game.

Seventeen years after we played in the backyard for the first time, my father took a train to Montreal, hoping that something special might happen. He went to see a game between the Canadiens and the Buffalo Sabres, and in the middle of the second period, Canadiens' goalie Rogie Vachon was injured and had to leave the ice. I had been called up from the Voyageurs less than two weeks before, and was sent in to replace him. As I skated to the net, Sabres coach Punch Imlach motioned his goalie, Joe Daley, to the bench, and Dave skated out in his place. It was like it had been all those times before.

I didn't enjoy that game very much. I had played only two previous NHL games, and seeing Dave in the other end was a distraction I didn't want or need. And while I became more comfortable as the game went on, I was surprised and disappointed that I didn't feel more. All those hours we had spent in the backyard, all our childhood fantasies, the different routes we had taken, the different careers we had seemed destined for; then, years later, Montreal, the Forum, our father in the stands—the unexpected climax. Yet try as I did, I couldn't feel that way. I could sense the curious excitement of the crowd, I could feel its huge vicarious pleasure, but my own excitement was vague, it had no edge to it, as if somehow it wasn't new; as if in fact we *had* done it before.

When the game was over, proud and relieved we shook hands at center ice. A few hours later, I began to feel differently. What had surprised and disappointed me earlier, I found exciting and reassuring. It *really* had been no different. Those backyard games, the times we stood at opposite ends of the yard, the times we dreamed we were Sawchuk and Hall, we *were* Sawchuk and Hall, there *had been* a connection, we just never knew it.

Now, when the snow melts in the spring, the backyard looks like an old abandoned runway. The red of the asphalt has been worn away to gray, roots from nearby poplar trees have heaved and cracked its surface and clusters of tall grass have pushed their way through. Along the base of the bank that rose to McLaren's backyard, the concrete block wall that was our "boards," the target of balls and pucks in winter and baseballs in summer, has slowly pitched forward from the pressure of the bank, and soon will fall. Over much of the big end, where games opened up and skills were freed and given their chance, a huge compost heap lies like an ancient earthwork under the snow, growing faster each year than my father can use it. And a few feet from it, up against the back of the garage and under its eaves where I can't quite see it, a net, red with rust, its mesh completely gone; the other one loaned away years ago and not yet returned. It has been twenty years since Dave played here for the last time; fifteen years since I did. With no children or grandchildren to use it, fixing it up, restoring it as a monument to ourselves, doesn't seem right. Still, it's the most vivid memory I have of my childhood, and now when I come home, when I stand at this window and look out at the backyard as I sometimes do, I don't like to see it without its snow.

I go downstairs. My father is out on an errand; my mother is in the kitchen ironing, waiting for me before beginning her breakfast. Outside, the snow has stopped and sun streams in, filling the room. I get the cereal, my mother makes the toast, and with no place to go and nothing to do until my father picks me up an hour from now, it is a rare relaxed time for the two of us. It is how it is with my mother. While my brother, my sister, my father, and I rush around always in search of something, my mother, at home, seems to have found it. I can read it in the letters that she writes to us each week. In her small, clear, legible handwriting, unhurried, she tells us about her days—about my father's projects; the dinners and functions they attend; her church groups and bridge club ("I had punk cards," she always says); the news from Judy in Vancouver and Dave in Edmonton—always in the same even, tranquil tone.

I think my mother has always known the life she wanted to live. Like most women of her generation, it was to get married and have a family, and to raise that family and make a home for it. She was a kindergarten teacher when she was young; later she ran the office for my father's business out of our house, always making sure we were fed, dressed, and ready, no matter the hour, for whatever it was we had to do. Soft-spoken and gentle, she has always stayed in the background, but she has a strength and a will about her that seem surprising, though they show themselves manifestly in her family. While at times it has not been easy for her, to a remarkable extent the life that she set out for herself is the life she has lived. Now, as we talk, hearing her as she sounds in her letters, with three children raised, educated, and married; with grandchildren, and more time for herself, she seems deeply content.

She asks me about Sarah and Michael and talks of her trip to

Montreal to visit us when my father goes away. I tell her of my meeting with Courtois and Grundman, matter-of-factly at first, then rambling on into things I never intended to say, building up a case I no longer need to build, pausing, breaking my own silences until, with nothing more to say but no place to stop, I shrug and leave it at that. She tells me that she thinks it is a "wise" decision. Sounding more sure than I am, I go on about my plans for the fall—taking my bar exams, writing a book, or doing unspecified "other things." With a nod and a murmur, my mother fills in the blanks.

My father arrives home, I pack up my bag, and we get ready to go. I shouldn't have come home this time. In the right frame of mind to wander through my past, I'm in the wrong frame of mind to dwell on it, and as I leave, I feel a strange melancholy, as if something that was always there is gone. My life had always moved ahead in easy, comfortable sequence, from grade to grade and age group to age group, from elementary school to high school to university to law school, from Islington to Ithaca to Winnipeg to Montreal, hockey always at my side to smooth away the changes. But now I am at the end of something, and for the first time I find myself looking back. I'm thinking about things I was too busy to think about before, finding confusion where once I felt none. I had always sprinted through the present, the future an exciting day away, the backyard, my parents and family just glib anecdotes from the past. Then the present slowed down and the future changed direction.

I now have a past that will get longer and more pervasive. It is the life of an athlete, the life of any prodigy who makes it young and has to move along. Just a quick climax in the first act, and a long denouement to the end. Always *ex-*, always *former*, pushed and talked into the past, the future a place where others get their chance; where we find "something to fall back on," if we're lucky. But forty years is a long time to pay out the string.

Yesterday, I felt excited by the challenge a week away; today, I'm back in my past, bouncing from the past to the future, not liking it anywhere. Everything I see, everything I do at home is a reminder. I've got to get out of here.

My father drives me to the subway.

The summer before I left for Cornell, I worked for a demolition company tearing down houses to create a narrow above-ground strip for the latest extension to the Toronto subway. It is now more than ten years since this station was completed, yet only the gloss of newness has gone from it. Even closer to downtown, as I pass in and out of stations older and busier, the only hint of age comes from color juxtapositions more popular in another time. The subway cars show the effects of hard winter use, but, like the stations, nothing looks so dirty that it cannot, or will not, be cleaned. More remarkable in a modern city is the almost total absence of gratuitous abuse. There are no graffiti; no seats have been slashed, no initials carved. For the visitor from New York or Boston, the Toronto subway is a jarring, disorienting experience, an object of wonder, and, as if somehow authoritarian and un-modern, one of lingering suspicion. It has none of the monumental quality of the Moscow subway, or the aestheticism of the newer Métro in Montreal, but, clean, civilized, efficient, not quite exciting, the Toronto subway is an apt metaphor for the city.

I sit back in my seat, reading a newspaper. Two teenage boys, sitting in front of me, are talking.

"You think Laflooor's any good?" one asks.

"Naw, he's overrated. Sittler's better than he is," the other says, and they both nod. I look up to see who is talking, then look back at my paper.

"Yeah, him and Salming are the best," the first one says again.

"Yeah, Palmateer too. That guy's great. Shit, if he ever played for the Canadiens, nobody'd ever score on him."

I change at Yonge Street and get off at College, and follow the sign that reads "Maple Leaf Gardens," emerging onto the street less than a block away from it. A giant theater-like marquee hangs over the sidewalk:

WED 8 PM

MONTREAL

When I was growing up, in an insular world before Guinness and *The Book of Lists*, there were certain things we were told so often that we knew them to be true: "Toronto is the fastest-growing city in North America"; "Toronto has the world's largest annual fair, the Canadian National Exhibition"; and "Maple Leaf Gardens is the finest indoor arena in North America." The Gardens was built in 1931 by a Toronto entrepreneur named Conn Smythe, and by the time I first saw it more than twenty years later, it was still a wondrous place. It is now more than twenty years later again, and thinking back on it, it seems quite incredible to me that the Gardens could ever have existed. There was a large portrait of the Queen, framed in royal maroon drapes, above the mezzanine in the south end, and beneath it, a bandshell, extending out in a balcony where 31-man regimental bands played during intermissions, and before and after games. Hidden away above was Horace Lapp's giant Wurlitzer organ, its pipes cut into the south wall and covered over with gold-colored slats that opened and closed like vertical venetian blinds. Suspended by a torrent of cables, the huge "Sportimer," a four-sided scoreboard-clock with the faces and venerability of Big Ben, hung over the center of the ice; across from it, exactly fifty-four feet above the ice, was Foster Hewitt's famous "gondola," so named because it reminded a Gardens director of the cabin of an airship; and below were 14,850 unobstructed red, blue, green, and gray seats, and the aisles between them which always looked clean. It was a period piece—elegant, colonial Toronto—perfectly, shamelessly preserved from a time before glitter and spectacle came to the city; and came to sports.

I used to go to junior games Sunday afternoons at the Gardens, and between periods I would look at the pictures that hung from its walls. There were team pictures in the front lobby—"World Champions and Stanley Cup Winners" some of them said, and at the time, it was an indisputable claim. There were action pictures and ceremonial pictures; pictures of players from the thirties—Charlie Conacher, Joe Primeau, King Clancy, Lorne Chabot, Busher Jackson—players whose names were already legendary to us, but with whom, because of their curious haircuts and equipment, we felt no connection; players from the late forties, their equipment distinctly modern, their faces, like pictures we had seen of our fathers, broadly smiling, with the postwar look of robust good health. I liked to follow the faces from year to year, guessing at where they went and why. Taking what little I knew of them, finding clues in the pictures, imagining their stories. Looking to see if the faces had stayed the same from picture to picture (maturing together? getting old as a team?); if they had won or lost the year before; if faces had disappeared, then reappeared in consecutive years (sent to the minors), or after a lapse of several years (gone to war); if they had disappeared entirely (traded or retired). And each time I was in the Gardens, as if to reconfirm what I thought I had seen each time before, I would run through the names under the pictures until I found "Happy" Day, the Leafs' long-time coach; then quickly again the faces, looking for Garth Boesch's mustache, the only mustache I had ever seen on a hockey player.

But while I looked at each picture, there were two I always lingered at a little longer. One was of Rocket Richard, his body bent, his right leg frozen in the air moments after his skate had shattered the Gardens' herculite glass. The other showed Canadiens' goalie Gerry McNeil, on the ice and fallen in his net, a puck hanging against the mesh above him, and in the foreground, his back to the camera, a Leaf player almost horizontal to the ice. The caption read: "Bill Barilko scores Stanley Cup winning goal 1950-51 season." We knew that a few months later, before the next season began, Barilko had been killed in a plane crash.

With the kids at the back waiting for the team bus, the sidewalk in front of the Gardens is clear. I open a door to the lobby and drop my eyes to the floor, moving quickly for an entrance gate so as not to be recognized. I needn't have bothered. The lobby has the near-empty look of a bus station at midday. There are a few untidy lines at ticket windows marked for future Gardens events; several unhurried clusters of mostly middle-aged men, tourists perhaps, talk idly, glancing here and there at the pictures on the walls. On the day of a game, a Canadiens game, I expected more. I wanted clamor and excitement, but except for a few general-admission tickets that disappeared like phantoms many weeks ago (always to someone else), the rest of the tickets have been gone since season-ticket subscriptions were renewed last summer.

I am a few minutes early, happy/unhappy to go unnoticed, and decide to look around. Many of the same pictures are still here—the team pictures in the lobby, the pictures of Boesch and Day, of Barilko's goal—but as I look at them, at the haircuts and the equipment, at the maskless goalies and bareheaded skaters, it is those pictures that now look old and dated to me. I look for the Richard picture, but it is gone; several action pictures from the Stanley Cup-winning teams of the sixties—of Frank Mahovlich, Tim Horton, Johnny Bower, Red Kelly, Bob Pulford—have gone up, but as I get to the end, I notice that I have seen few from the present. One or two action shots, a few ceremonial ones, of Leafs captain Darryl Sittler and owner Harold Ballard, of Sittler and Ballard and Sabres captain Danny Gare, of Ballard and Bobby Orr—

"Two Hockey Hall of Famers
Bobby Orr 1979   Harold E. Ballard 1977"

the caption reads—but little else, as if the legacy of the Leafs died with those teams more than ten years ago.

Now in his late seventies, Harold Ballard is the new star of the Leafs. He has become a Toronto, even a national, celebrity. Known locally as jovial and outrageous, nationally above all as outrageous, as owner of the Toronto Maple Leafs he is *ipso facto* a celebrity, and there is nothing he can say or do, nothing *anyone* can say or do, to change that. He can be unfair and erratic; he can be unequivocally wrong. It doesn't matter. He is Ballard, owner of the Leafs. What he says, what he does, we pretend is news. In turn, used to the attention, he pretends that it isn't his money that has bought him his celebrity. It is the disease of the sports entrepreneur.

Ballard, George Steinbrenner, Ted Turner, Nelson Skalbania, Peter Pocklington, Jerry Buss—money buys celebrity, and celebrity means being able to say anything about anything and someone will report it as if it were true; money and celebrity together mean thinking that no one, *nothing*, can stop you. The cost is small—just a few millions among the scores you have—except sometimes to the fan. It is easy to say that a fan can stay at home, or at home he can change a channel and watch something else. But it isn't as simple as that. A sports fan loves his sport. A fan in Toronto loves hockey, and if the Leafs are bad, he loses something he loves and has no way to replace the loss.

Not long ago, I was speaking with a friend. I knew he was not a Leafs fan, and I was laughing at the team's snowballing demise. My friend was laughing too, until suddenly, looking pained, he stopped. He explained that when he had lived in Montreal, he was happy to see the Leafs lose. But now, living in Toronto, he felt differently. "You don't understand," he said. "I'm still not a Leafs fan, but I want to see good hockey and who else have I got to watch?"

Yet as his team sinks lower, Ballard continues to parade himself before us, apparently invulnerable—his Maple Leaf Gardens filled by more and more events, his television revenues increasing, his team selling out as they have since 1946; his celebrity status intact. The press and the public vie with each other in attacking him, then pause to praise his charitable generosity or his devotion to his late wife (maybe we've got him all wrong?); then, like the wrestling villain who touches his audience to make his next villainy seem worse, he does something or says something to start up the cycle again. But, check and checkmate—the currency of the celebrity is attention, and each angry attack only means more attention for him.

As a member of the Gardens board, as vice-president, he was perfect. Likeable, convivial, able to be disregarded at the proper time, without the title that brings the platform that brings the rest; but as president, as principal owner, he is very imperfect. And the Leafs fans suffer. Yet I can't help feeling sorry for him. Though he confronts the public, almost challenging fans to stay home if they dare, laughing at them when they don't, taking their money, telling them that he cares for nothing else, in part it must be a pose.

For as someone who has spent most of his life in hockey and with the Leafs, it is impossible to imagine that he doesn't feel some of the immense sadness and anger a Leafs fan feels at seeing a once great team, a once great *institution*, now shabby.

The team arrived from Montreal by charter this morning. Lafleur and Robinson, in their longjohns, stand outside the dressing-room door, talking to Toronto reporters; Risebrough, a few feet away, planes and files some sticks for the game. When I walk into the room, Tremblay looks at me sharply.

"*Câlisse*, Dryden," he snarls, "one set of rules for the team, another for you," then, as I begin to feel uncomfortable, he smiles and slaps me hard on the back. Napier and Hughes shout around for unused tickets for more family and friends than they had yesterday, but too late, they are mocked and find none. Reading a Toronto newspaper, Lapointe suddenly crumples it in disgust.

"Lookit this," he roars, pointing to the paper. "'The great Leafs-Canadiens rivalry.' Who the hell they think they're kidding? Shit, they must think we're the goddamn Pittsburgh Penguins."

Startled, we look up, waiting for a smile, waiting for a punch line, but none comes.

The conversation returns to Houle and his breakaway against the Sabres. Quickly it moves to Houle's other breakaways, and as each is remembered, several others come to mind. I yell out my favorite—one last season in Chicago against Tony Esposito. Houle's smile disappears. "*Câlisse*, you can't stop me," he growls. I stop laughing—he's right, I can't—but he presses on. "Some of the goals you let in. *Câlisse*, Reggie Leach, Schmautz," brightening with each name he says.

He is beginning to sound like a catalogue, so I interrupt him. "Hey, what're ya starting in on me for?" I ask, trying to sound wounded; but it's no use. The bandwagon has stopped, turned, and is coming my way. Ten voices, busy with their skates, come alive,

"...McDonald..." someone shouts.

"...Ramsay..." says another.

"René Robert..."

"Barber..."

The names stream out—Dionne, Gare, Tommy Williams—stored away waiting for this moment, each name bringing a quick laugh, then a longer one as the memory of the goal returns. Finally, it is Shutt who remembers; it would be Shutt. "Hey, what about Plager's goal?" he chirps, and there is a scream of laughter.

I had had a promising start, then everything came unravelled.

In the next ten minutes, St. Louis scored three goals, at least two of which I should have stopped. I survived goalless the next few minutes, and began to feel better, wondering if I had finally settled down enough, if Bowman thought I had settled down enough, to play the rest of the game. With eight seconds left in the period, there was a faceoff in our zone. The puck went to the boards; Bob Plager, a big, ponderously slow defenseman for the Blues, came in from his left point position and flipped it towards the net. I reached out to catch it, and felt it hit off the heel of my glove, then watched mesmerized as it rolled up my wrist, through my legs, onto the ice, and over the goal-line, just as the siren sounded to end the period. When the second period began, I was on the bench.

"*Câlisse*, Bob Plager," Lapointe mutters to himself, still disbelieving, "it was so slow, there were three minutes left when he shot it . . ."

Hah hah hah.

" . . . the ref almost called it back—delay of game . . ."

Hah hah hah.

The next year, when we were back to play the Blues, a local announcer asked me for an interview. He apologized for not knowing much about hockey, but I reassured him, going into my "you don't really need to know anything about hockey; it's just like everything else" routine. Suddenly, his eyes brightened.

"Hey, you're the guy Plager scored on from the parking lot last year. That was his last goal, ya know. Hell, it was almost his first. Hah hah hah, well I'll be. . . ."

The names continue on without a break. A little desperate, I try again.

"Hey wait a minute. Wait a minute!" I shout. "Getting back to your breakaway, Reggie . . ." But no one is listening.

" . . . hey, remember Larry Romanchych?" someone shouts, and there is more laughter.

" . . . and Simon Nolet?"

" . . . and what about Tom Reid's goal?"

Tom Reid's goal! That was seven years ago! How did we get on to this?

It is not easy to say what Réjean Houle does for a team. On the one hand he is a good skater and forechecker, capable of playing any of the forward positions, a better-than-average playmaker and penalty-killer; on the other, he is not big, not strong, not tough, often injured, a worse-than-average shooter, and has surprisingly little goal-scoring touch. On a winning team, where goodwill and kind words abound, it is often easy to pretend that someone is better than he is (on the Orr-Esposito Bruins, Derek Sanderson was a "great" player), but by his own admission Houle is "very, very average." He says it without bravado, without the survivor's ubiquitous pride, not intending to appear modest as others insist on doing (preferring to praise themselves by implication for having the character to overcome their defects), but because, as he says evenly, "It's the plain truth."

If he was a slightly better player, but mostly if he allowed it to be so, his story would have an almost monumental quality to it. Instead, typically underplayed, it is a quiet story, a *nice* story, a story sure to have a happy ending, though it is far from over.

Up close, he has a little boy's face, lumped and scarred by a decade of pucks and high-sticks. But stand back, a few feet more each year, let the lumps and scars go out of focus and disappear, and you will see the real Réjean Houle, still untouched: the eyes and smile that tighten and twinkle; the shock of thick brown hair, his too-long sideburns, his persistent wisps of cowlick, the fan of hair that falls on his forehead. And listen to his voice—its high-pitched, exuberant bursts, never far from a laugh, his guileless candor and simple eloquence that sound naive. It is the look and sound of a fourteen-year-old boy, and it is both real and deceptive.

He was born in Rouyn, a small mining town in northwestern Quebec, neighbor to Noranda and to the small mining towns of northeastern Ontario a few miles away. In the heart of the Canadian Shield, a vast sweep of lakes and forest and mostly rock, it was an area largely unsettled until early this century when rich ore bodies were discovered—nickel and silver mainly to the south and west, gold to the west, iron, lead, zinc, and copper in and around Rouyn—and towns went up as if overnight. Houle remembers Rouyn as a town of *travailleurs*, workers—Québécois, Italians, Poles—miners like his father, who worked for the giant multinational Noranda Mines. Noranda, on the other side of the tracks, north and west, was where "the big bosses" of the mines lived. They were English ("as usual," Houle laughs) from Montreal and Toronto, and lived in big white houses, with big gardens and beautiful lawns. Houle was rarely in Noranda, except for hockey games, and remembers being uncomfortable there, as if he didn't belong. Yet asked if he ever felt any bitterness or resentment, he said without apology, "No, I respect people for what they are."

His father was a driller, working in stopes, big hollowed-out caves deep underground, drilling holes for dynamite charges in the face of the ore body. The base wages at the mine were low, and he worked hard for bonuses, sometimes working faster than he should. One time a heavy wrecking-bar bounced back, hitting his face and knocking out several teeth; another time, he badly injured a hand. It was dangerous work, Houle recalls; then, suddenly remembering a jaw he had broken twice, a leg, finger, toe, and collarbone once each, a shoulder separated, the other dislocated, and the more than two hundred stitches that line his face, "like a hockey player," he says, and laughs with great delight.

But his father's injuries were mostly inside him, and, like his fellow miners, he tried to keep them there, avoiding doctors as best he could. Finally, at forty-two, his health deteriorating, and spitting up black saliva, he was retired from the mine, later to work in a halfway house for delinquents in Rouyn. I asked him if his father had ever made his experience in the mine a lesson to him. Houle said that his father often talked about his work, and like every other father wanted something better for his children, but that no, it was never a lesson. His father liked being a miner, he said.

Houle remembers his childhood mostly in a series of hockey images: the games under a solitary street light, the only one that his street had; a friend's backyard rink, with lights for the early northern nights; Saturday morning, every second week, his father working from 7 p.m. to 4 a.m., sleeping for two hours, then taking him to play; Saturday afternoons and Sundays at a local *collège* (high school), where on a single rink there were four pucks, scores of kids, and four games played simultaneously—three across its width, one down its length; and Saturday nights, on a couch in the living room with his family, listening to announcers René Lecavalier and Jean-Maurice Bailly, and watching the Canadiens on TV. They were his team, and "Boom-Boom" Geoffrion was his favorite player—"I thought he was spectacular," he would say later. "A kind of showman, and when he scored goals, he showed lots of expression, smiling, jumping up and down. I liked that." Yet while those around him dreamed of playing in the NHL, Houle did not. Not until latert when he was fourteen or fifteen years old. I asked him why. He paused a moment, choosing his words carefully as if unsure I would understand. "You see, working-class people have no confidence," he said in his quiet, straightforward way. "It just takes a while to get some." Later, he explained it to me another way, and in doing so told much about himself. "I never dream of something I cannot be," he said.

He was a star in Rouyn, later in Thetford Mines, he had scouts at many of his games, but it wasn't until he reached Montreal and starred for the Junior Canadiens that he thought he might be good enough to be an NHL player. Asked how it finally happened, he answered quickly, "I was lucky," then stopped himself, and quietly started again. "No, not lucky," he said. "Lucky's a funny word, eh?" and pausing while I nodded, he continued again, "I was given the chance to prove I was good enough."

When we were rookies together in the 1971 Stanley Cup playoffs, as teammates talked of money and pride, Houle, wide-eyed at the magic, kept repeating, "I wanna kiss the Stanley Cup." (It became a dressing-room rallying cry of sorts—"C'mon guys, Reggie wants to kiss Stanley's cup.") Two years later, he signed a lucrative contract with the Quebec Nordiques of the WHA. He had been torn between his enthusiasm for the Canadiens and his even more instinctive quest for financial security. Three years later, he was back with the Canadiens, this time with the contract he wanted.

He has always been careful with his money, investing much of it in annuities to guarantee his future, but in recent years he has seen inflation rise and his annuities-secured future shrink agonizingly away. For the first time, he has seen the end of his hockey career—three years, four, perhaps five years away, but sometime; and soon. It was his one gift, his one chance, the source of security he never had, the source of confidence he always needed, the rallying point for the people he has learned to crave, the underpinning of his way of life—he could feel it slipping away, with nothing to put in its place.

He was clearly bothered by it all, though his friendly, open, self-mocking manner never changed. He read "doom and gloom" financial newsletters, and magazines; he announced out loud each jump in interest rates, each fall in the dollar, until teammates, noticing his torment, gleefully announced them to him first. There had seemed such an urgency about him; he seemed always to be running after "deals," promotions, endorsements, openings—anxious to conspire on the latest and hottest tips, wheeling for nickels and dimes like a French-Canadian Sammy Glick. He began even to look the part, wearing three-piece pinstripe suits (closer to Frank Nitti than to Brooks Brothers), smoking big cigars. Yet always there was that laugh. At our hotel in Newport Beach a few weeks ago, he looked out over the pool, his hands in his vest pockets, puffing on a big cigar, and said, "You know, I oughta be a millionaire. I got all the moves," then, laughing at himself, "I just don't have the money."

But this season, I have begun to notice in him an ease that wasn't there before. He still talks constantly of inflation and interest rates, but the edge in his voice has gone, as if he does so now only because the team expects it of him, as part of his team persona. I see him reading biographies of Moshe Dayan, Martin Luther King, and Trudeau, talking politics with Savard or with one of the reporters, sitting quietly in a lobby with piles of newspapers he has brought from home. He seems involved in more and different things with new people who like being around him, and, doing well, he seems happy with himself. All his life he has searched for confidence and security, and now it seems he has found them. Their original source may have been hockey, but when hockey leaves, they will remain. The nicest part of his story is that he is now beginning to realize it himself.

What does Houle do for a hockey team? Any team, even a great team, has many more Réjean Houles than it has Lafleurs and Robinsons. Grinders, muckers, *travailleurs*, they form the base of any team; they do the kinds of diligent, disciplined, unspectacular things that every team must do before it can do the rest. But more than that, players like Houle make it fun to be on a team; it is a rare skill.

A few days ago, over breakfast, I asked him how he felt. With characteristic eloquence, he said simply, "I feel just the way I want to feel. I feel great in my skin."

The door swings open and Pierre Meilleur strides in, looking like someone whose brother is the toughest kid on the block.

"The Leafs are off [the ice]," he sneers. " 'Piton' [Claude Ruel] says if ya aren't on right away, don't bother goin' on."

Only Lapointe looks up. "Hey Boomer, see this," he says, holding his stick upright, pointing to its butt-end, "sit on it."

Until recently, teams had only a "morning skate," often in civvies or sweatsuits, simply for players to test that their skates were properly sharpened. But for a player, putting on skates means picking up sticks, and sticks mean pucks, and sticks and pucks mean easy shooting and informal games. That means the risk of an injury and the need for full equipment. And with full equipment, coaches began to ask themselves, why not have a practice? So for fifteen or twenty optional but demanding minutes, we practice.

I don't like practicing the day of a game. I am afraid of getting hurt, not seriously, but perhaps a bruise on my catching hand, or on my arm or my shoulder, just enough to nag at me through the day and make me wonder how well I can play. What a morning practice does, and does well, is kill time, something not unimportant on the day of a game. On a day when nothing matters until the day is nearly complete, it is something to get out of bed for, to get dressed for, to get to, to get undressed and dressed for, to do, to get undressed and dressed again, to get back from—to get us through more than two hours of a purposely uneventful day.

We file out singly to the ice, along a narrow rubber path that comes out behind the net at the north end. The ice is still being resurfaced after the Leafs' practice, and, cursing Ruel and Meilleur, we pool up near the boards and wait. *Hurry up and wait.* The bright TV lights have been left off and the Gardens lies in a kind of amber twilight. Half the ice surface away, two or three Leafs players stand behind their bench, being interviewed for the 6 p.m. sports. We sit in the seats, bored, impatient, our legs propped over the seat backs in front of us, or pace on the spot beside others who do the same. Tremblay yells something not quite in the direction of the Zamboni driver, then quickly looks away, but the driver doesn't hear him. It is the day of a game, repeated eighty times and more a season. With too much energy, too much time, and not enough to do—hurry up and wait.

I look around, then again more slowly, gradually aware of what I see. The enormous Sportimer is gone; an even larger, more versatile scoreboard-clock, the kind you might find in any large arena, is in its place. Foster Hewitt's gondola was taken down last year; the portrait of the Queen, the bandshell, and Horace Lapp's giant Wurlitzer were removed nearly twelve years ago when more than 1,500 unobstructed seats were added. The "reds" are now "golds," though they appear more a mustard-color; the "blues" are "reds," except in the mezzanines; the "greens" and the "grays" and the aisles that always looked clean remain.

I don't much like the Gardens now. Competing against a child's memory, that is perhaps inevitable, but it is more than that. The building's elegant touches are gone, but anachronistic perhaps even in that other time, most deserved to go. It has been expanded and modernized for contemporary needs—more seats, more private boxes, a bigger press box—but I dislike the haphazard, graceless way it was done. There is a veneer of newness about it now that doesn't quite fit. It has been stranded in awkward transition; no longer what it was, it cannot be what it wants to be. Now, after nearly fifty years, there is nothing special about it. It is just another rink; just another place to play.

The Zamboni drives off the ice and we burst on. For twenty minutes we skate easily, then harder, whistled into drills by Bowman—one-on-ones with the goalies, three-on-two line rushes, two-on-ones—like every other practice except each drill is shorter and quicker. When it is almost over, as we are changing from one drill to another, I look up in the seats and see Johnny Bower.

Now a scout and goaltender coach for the Leafs, Bower, in 1958, at the age of at least thirty-three (because he had enlisted in the Canadian army in 1941, it was often thought he was even older), joined the Leafs for only his second NHL season. It was a time when the Leafs were assembling and maturing into a team that would win four Stanley Cups during the next decade, and

Bower, a relentless worker and competitor, with an awkward, almost comic, style, became an important member of those teams. A few miles away, I was nearly a teenager and playing in my last few backyard seasons. I felt too old to pretend in quite the way I had done before, but when I did, I was Johnny Bower.

Last year, I met Bower for the first time. It was at an NHL awards luncheon in Montreal, and, leaving the hotel together, we shared a taxi to the airport. We were both uneasy at first, but gradually we just began to talk. As we were nearing the airport, he was telling me about his goaltending partners Sawchuk and Don Simmons when suddenly it struck me—he was speaking to me as a fellow goalie, as a colleague. It was not NHL star to star-struck kid, it was as if we were equals. For the length of the cab ride, it was just Johnny and Ken.

I know that I am doing now what he did then, but still I cannot make the connection. I have this strange sense of unreality that never diminishes, no matter how long I play, a feeling that I'm not really playing for the Montreal Canadiens, that this isn't really the NHL; that I am the victim of a wonderful, cruel hoax, and that some day, today, *now*, it will end. Pierre Bouchard and I used to have a routine that we would go through several times a year. Prompted by nothing in particular, one of us would say, "We've fooled them this long," and the other, shaking his head, would reply, "Yeah, but how much longer can we do it?" Then we would laugh. But then I started to wonder—who is fooling whom?

I remember my first training camp, and wondering what *I* was doing there. *Me.* Then stopping Béliveau and Cournoyer and *knowing* what I was doing there, but wondering where I was. Feeling excited/disappointed/confused—was this the real Béliveau I had stopped? The real Cournoyer? Was this really the training camp of the Montreal Canadiens? Was this the NHL, the league I had never dreamed of playing in—even when I was young and knew no better; even when I was older and had been scouted and drafted and offered a contract—because I knew I wouldn't be good enough? Instinctively I knew what the answer must be—that if this was the real Béliveau, if this was the real Cournoyer, I couldn't stop them.

It was the same wonder I felt in 1973. I had played two seasons with the Canadiens, two successful seasons, and had returned to Toronto to work with a law firm. I began watching NHL games on TV just as I had always done until two years before. As I watched, wondering at saves that a year earlier I would have thought routine, I found that no matter how I tried I couldn't put myself in the game I was watching. I couldn't see myself on the ice, in one of those uniforms; I couldn't feel what the game felt like.

Instead, I had an overwhelming disorienting sense of *jamais vu*, as if those two years had never really happened.

Bower-NHL; NHL-me; Bower-me—it is a connection I know to be real, but it's a connection I cannot feel. There is only one moment when I can almost make it. It happens when I see a kid in a driveway or on a street, playing hockey as I once did, wearing a Canadiens sweater, and on his back a number 29.

Hall, Sawchuk, Jacques Plante, and Bower—they were the heroes of my childhood. Performing before my adolescent eyes, they did unimaginable things in magical places. Everything they did was braver and better than I had ever seen before. Then later, when I got old enough to get close to them, they had gone. And so it was that as a boy, my impression of them was fixed and forever frozen. They were the best. It meant that later, when I would get better, they would get better too.

For any goalie who came before—Georges Vézina, George Hainsworth, Frank Brimsek, Bill Durnan, Turk Broda—I have only record books and someone else's opinion, invariably exaggerated by time. For those who have come later—Bernie Parent, Tony Esposito, Gump Worsley, Vachon, Ed Giacomin—I have seen each of them up close, too close. I have seen their flaws and remember more than their highlights, and I have fixed on them a thirty-year-old's cold, jealous judgement. I know that pucks are now shot faster by more fast shooters. I know that players train harder and longer, and receive better coaching. I know that in any way an athlete can be measured—in strength, in speed, in height or distance jumped—he is immensely superior to one who performed twenty years ago. But measured against a memory, he has no chance. I know what I feel.

Nothing is as good as it used to be, and it never was. The "golden age of sports," the golden age of anything, is the age of everyone's childhood. For me and for the writers and commentators of my time, it was the 1950s. For those who lived in the 1950s as adults, it was the 1920s or the 1930s. Only major disruptions like wars or expansions can later persuade a child of those times that what he feels cannot be right. For me, the greatest goalies must always be Hall, Sawchuk, Plante, and Bower.

As I skate off at the end of practice, I wonder what Johnny Bower is thinking.

I walk back to the hotel with Risebrough and Houle, and go directly to the banquet room reserved for our team meal. The meal has been arranged for 1 p.m. and it is now only 12:30, but more than half the team is already there. Across the room, I see Shutt with an empty seat beside him.

I have played with Shutt for more than five years, sharing the same corner of the dressing room, hearing and (mostly) enjoying thousands of his good and bad one-liners, and I've decided I want to know more about him. A few weeks ago, a friend, a professor at McGill, asked me about the players on the team. He wanted to know where they had grown up, where their families had come from, what work their fathers had done, what vivid childhood memories each carried with him. I couldn't answer him; I didn't know. I had never asked, and no one had ever said. Yet it never occurred to me that there was something more that I didn't know. I had seen each of them almost every day, often for many years, through wins and losses, slumps and scoring rolls, in unguarded and indiscreet moments. I *knew* them, everything about them, far more than they could ever tell me. Still, except for the slow news/no news mid-week bios that newspapers run, offering each of us an athlete's formula childhood (backyard rinks, supportive parents, glorious minor hockey triumphs—athletes and politicians have none of the torment in their childhoods that writers insist on in theirs), I knew none of the details. Last week, over breakfast, I had a chance to talk to Houle. Now I want to know more about Shutt.

I walk over and sit down beside him. He is looking the other way. I pour myself a glass of Coke and ask him for the salad dressing. Then, as if the question had suddenly occurred to me, I start with an easy one.

"Hey Shutty, you were born in Toronto, weren't ya?" I ask casually, reaching for some ice.

"Hmm, I'm not sure," he chirps, "I was so young at the time."

About 12:45, the rest of the meal arrives.

After lunch, I meet a writer friend in the lobby and we go for a walk just to talk. Two years ago I helped him with a play he was doing on the Canadiens, and now, recently back from Mozambique, he is finishing another play he began work on several months ago. It has been giving him trouble. I listen as he explains; offering back what I can, but quickly I realize that I am not helping. Too abruptly, I ask about his trip; he begins to answer, but soon I am lapsing in and out of what he is saying. I am not thinking about the Leafs; I am not thinking about hockey at all. I am spinning four or five things around in my head, each unrelated and unimportant, there, spinning, only because I can't focus on anything for more than a few seconds at a time. It is what happens to me on the day of a game. I do not think about the game, but I am preoccupied with it. As it gets closer, my mind and body discover its rhythm and build with it towards game-time. Yet I am never aware that it's happening. Suddenly, I lapse back and hear him say something about the land-reform policy of the Frelimo government. I find a disjointed parallel with the Leafs. We both laugh.

On the way back to the hotel, we pass a construction site. Stretching half a city block in all directions, it is surrounded by a high white plywood fence, with nothing yet far enough out of the ground to be visible above it. On the fence, every seventy-five or a hundred feet, "POST NO BILLS" has been painted in black stencilled letters. About midway along the fence, painted above a section framed with molding to make it look like a large bulletin board, it reads "POST BILLS HERE." Scores of notices in tidy rows have been pasted up, each tight against the one next to it until the space is completely filled. Along the half city-block of high white fence where several times it says "POST NO BILLS," no bills have been posted.

Only in Toronto.

I go to my room. Risebrough is in bed reading a book called *Wind Chill Factor*. Though he insists he really hasn't been reading it all season, it seems he has. Indeed, with a cowlick of a hundred pages or so that stands straight up when the book is at rest, he seems even to be at the same page. But every road trip he brings it out and reads it as a necessary part of his routine. Getting on the plane, he finds his seat, folds his overcoat carefully into the overhead rack, puts his bag on the floor in front of him, takes his book from his bag, sits down, buckles up, and starts to read. Moments later, the plane in the air, his seat angled back, he's asleep. An hour later, the plane on the ground, he wakes up, takes his book from his lap, stuffs it back in his bag, and walks off the plane, ready for the next trip. Recently, apparently anxious to finish, he has taken to reading it in the room. When I look over at him, I see him reach up his hand and stifle a yawn.

A few years ago, a sports columnist for the *Montreal Star* left Montreal for Boston, and for his final column he wrote about the ten most memorable athletes he had met in Montreal. It turned out to be a rather predictable list of the city's celebrated and notorious (if the reasons he gave were not always so predictable), except that one of the names he included was Doug Risebrough. Why Risebrough? A small, versatile, and useful twenty-goal scorer, he is handsome, but much too discreet, and certainly no swinging bachelor (after seeing him in another of his gray, blue-gray, brown-gray suits, someone once remarked, "Dougie, I didn't know drab came in so many colors"). Why would he be included? I don't remember the writer's precise reasons, but I think they were the same as my own. Risebrough is a *nice* guy. Not wimpy, ingratiating nice, not "try like hell" nice. *Nice.*

Athletes, entertainers, politicians, all public persons live at the center of their own world. Things revolve around us; things we do, and do with others, reflect back on us alone; others exist as they relate to us, they are there to ask us what *we* think, how *we* feel, how *we* are, as if it is somehow important to them. After a while, preoccupied with ourselves, we forget to ask—how are *you*? Risebrough asks. Not as a pattern of speech—"How're the wife and kids?"—not as practiced courtesy, not out of curiosity, but out of *interest*—he wants to know. In Toronto, he asks about my parents, though he has met them only a few times—is your father back from his trip? How was his Christmas-tree season? He asks about Lynda, Sarah, and Michael, and if I tell him only they are "fine," he will ask about Sarah's school or Michael's black eye. No big thing, nothing intended to reflect back on him—he cares; he just wants to know.

On a plane, in a bar or hotel lobby, when people talk to him, he talks to them, easily, comfortably, about anything, about *them*, and he listens and reacts to what *they* say. Like most hockey players his formal education ended when he turned professional after high school, but he has such a natural intelligence and passion for people and things that he can talk to anyone about anything. Five minutes, ten minutes, an hour later, when the conversation ends, you will both go away feeling better, and knowing you have learned something.

Periodically, prompted by nothing we are aware of, Bowman changes around the roommates. I have roomed at various times with almost everyone on the team, but most recently with Bill Nyrop, for two years with Lapointe, and now for more than a year with Risebrough. I am not someone easy to room with, but we get along well, mostly because of him. I go to bed later than he does and like to read in bed or watch TV. I am usually awake for many hours after a game, alternating between bathtub and bed; I get up early by our standards (about 8 a.m.); I get frequent phone calls; I like to make phone calls the afternoon of a game when others wish to sleep. For him, it means noise and disturbing lights, interrupting the fragile sleep we seem always in a hurry for. But through it all, Risebrough appears unbothered. Instinctively I like to be alone, and have often thought I would prefer a room by myself, but if I am alone too much, I cut myself off from the team and from the shared feeling I, and we, need. As well as being a friend, Risebrough, like Lapointe before him, is my point of contact with the team, and a steady reminder of the feeling I am missing if I stay away.

I settle back uncomfortably on the bed, leafing through a newspaper, unable to decide what I want to do. I ask Risebrough if he wants to go for a walk. He says nothing. Still glancing at the paper, I ask him again. Finally, I look up. His book open across his lap, he's asleep.

I call a friend, a lawyer north of Toronto, who grew up with me in Islington. His secretary answers the phone in a perfunctory way, but when she asks my name and I tell her, I can hear a trace of pandemonium in her voice as she relays the message to him.

Not surprised by the call, he comes on the phone as if in the middle of the conversation, laughing, pleased to remind me of something unkind that a New York writer wrote about me recently. We speak by phone only the twice a year we play in Toronto, and see each other only two or three days each summer at his home, but our friendly dressing-room banter, our occasional lapses into something more serious, easily come back to us. Yet as we talk, there are moments when everything sounds different. It is not because time has passed and we see each other less often, fumbling at the details of each other's current lives. It is a tone, a little too respectful, as if he is talking to someone that he doesn't know so well. More and more he knows me now only as others know me, and even though what he reads and hears is not what he remembers, he can no longer be sure.

A few summers ago, in Toronto, he took me to a health club he had recently joined. He talked at length about its facilities on our way over; then, not wanting to sound too positive, he interrupted himself, complaining in his raspy, passionate way about the high cost of its membership. When we arrived, he showed his membership card to the man at the desk and took some money from his wallet to pay the guest fee. The man never looked at the card, or at the money. He looked at me, quickly recognizing who I was, and after talking hockey for several moments, reached into his desk and gave me a free membership to his club.

The conversation winds down after several minutes, I remind him that I'm paying for the call, and he talks on—about the Leafs, about Ballard, expressing his angry disbelief at the season-ticket holders who return year after year. Though he means what he says, it is also his way of letting me know that he doesn't want to go to the game tonight. He is like friends in other cities, most of them former classmates at Cornell, who a few years ago were anxious for tickets they couldn't get otherwise, and would go to a game each time we came to town. But they are now married, with children, and often live far from the center of a city. The excitement of the game and the novelty of having a friend who plays it have worn off; there are now the complications of family, baby-sitters, and cost, and though they would never say so, they do not want to go any more. So when I talk to my friend on the phone, I no longer ask him if he wants tickets. I know that if he wants them, he will tell me.

I make one more call. It is to the secretary of an Ontario government advisory committee of which I am a member. I have not attended any of its meetings for several months and I want to find out what the minutes and other materials I am sent don't tell me. Excited at the coincidence, the secretary tells me the committee is meeting this afternoon about an hour from now, and asks if I would like to come. I fumble for a moment, uncertain what I will say. Finally, not too convincingly, I say no, I won't be able to make it.

In the first three years I played with the Canadiens, when I was given a form to complete for my American immigration visa, under "occupation" I put "law student." Later, after I had graduated from law school and returned to the Canadiens from a year of articling in Toronto, handed the same form I started to put "law student," then "articling student," then "lawyer"; then I realized I was none of them, and wrote "professional hockey player."

Because my hockey identity is secure and well known, as often as not I am referred to as "Ken Dryden" comma "lawyer," or "Ken Dryden" comma "former Nader's Raider." As much as stopping pucks, like Joe Namath and his life-style, like Bill Lee and his off-the-wall "spaceman" routine, it is what makes me publicly distinctive, it is what makes me celebrated as a hockey player. And while hockey has been my number one consuming priority when I'm playing it, something else is when I'm not. It takes much of my time and more of my energy, but hockey never took away other interests. It never forced on me a choice.

That had always been so. Until I graduated from law school five years ago, I had been a full-time student and a full-time hockey player at the same time. When I returned from Toronto in the fall of 1974, law school finished, my articling over, I felt immensely free. I was back as a full-time player, and now had all my law-student time to pursue new things. Quickly I became disoriented, picking up things, dropping them, moving on to something else, but gradually new interests developed, and therein lies the problem. I could be a full-time law student and play hockey because I could do law-school work on my own time. Missing most of my lectures (scheduled on someone else's time), I could still find time after games, on planes or buses, for the more important course reading. But with other things, things that involve other people, where it isn't just *my* time, it doesn't work. Slowly, so slowly I didn't notice it happen, I have become a full-time hockey player and a part-time everything else.

It is a life that can fool you. Eight months a year in good years, fewer in others, three games a week, an hour a day at practice, there should be time for other things, plenty of time; but there isn't. There are no weekends for families and friends, no nighttimes; then there is a summer of weekends and nighttimes, catching up to fall behind the rest of the year. Hurry up and wait. Hockey had always been a game, something I had done with something else alongside it that would go on after it had ended. Even with more games, more practices, more travel, being paid like a full-time job, with all those other hours in a day that seem vacant, those other months in a year, it can't be a full-time job. But it is.

And now I am beginning to learn the choice I have made. When I was twenty-four or twenty-five, I did more interesting and challenging things, more exciting and remunerative things, than every other twenty-four- or twenty-five-year-old I knew. Three or four years out of college, my friends started in the middle, working slowly up the corporate ladder. Playing hockey, I was happy doing what I wanted to do, and happy not doing what I didn't want to do. Now, things have changed. I am thirty-one years old. Other thirty-one-year-olds are doing interesting, challenging, exciting, and remunerative things, and they will continue to do so. I am beginning to feel I am missing out.

When asked why I continue to play, I have always said it is because I enjoy playing, and because I enjoy it more than anything else I might be doing. It is for the same reason I will now retire. The irony is, that when I retire at the end of this season, I will do so as more of a hockey player than I have ever been before.

I am not going to the meeting today because I would only sit and listen as a bystander, and I don't want to be a bystander any more.

The Leafs are not yet a mediocre team, though they are surely moving that way. After their wonderfully successful years of the 1960s, their great old veterans got old, first during the long seasons, then finally in the playoffs, and they haven't been close to a Stanley Cup since. For a time, they imagined they were in a slump, one that would end when those veterans who had done it so often before would do it again. But the veterans couldn't do it

again, and the slump didn't end. It was a decade in which good
young prospects had been exchanged for better veterans; four
Stanley Cups were won, but left was an unpromising mix of
deteriorating age and mediocre youth to carry on. Several disastrous seasons followed; then unexpectedly things changed again.
In the early 1970s, a combination of good fortune (the signing of
free-agent Swedish defenseman Borje Salming), good draft picks
(Lanny McDonald and Ian Turnbull in 1973; goalie Mike Palmateer and Dave "Tiger" Williams in 1974), and the gradual
maturity of Darryl Sittler into the team's new leader, transformed
the Leafs into an immensely promising team. Indeed, by mid-
decade, led by this talented core of players (by performance and
promise, arguably as good as any six players on any team in the
league, including the Canadiens), the Leafs became a genuine
Stanley Cup contender, not quite ready to win, but good enough
that in each year they seemed set for a final breakthrough. Their
star players in place, all they would need was a stronger supporting
cast, something they could reasonably expect to build through the
draft by one or two players a year.

But it hasn't happened. A series of ill-conceived drafts and
poor trades has left the supporting cast no stronger now than it was
four years ago; and the Leafs are slowly dying. I can see it in Sittler,
Salming, and McDonald. At their playing peaks, having given as
much to their team as they can give, they now look tired and
frustrated, as if suddenly they understand that nothing they can
give any longer will be enough.

I can see it in Tiger Williams. For four years, he ran around the
ice, high-sticking, charging, fighting on hair-trigger impulse,
always excitingly involved. He distracted fans and teammates into
greater passion, distracted opponents away from their style of play
to his, then scored timely, infuriating goals, always celebrating
them in his outrageous, mocking way. But now his joyful fire
seems calculated and forced. As if sensing the fall around him, he
tries harder, running around the ice in a desperate binge of effort,
but with much less effect. He is now out of step with the game; his
penalties and fights come annoyingly at the wrong time; he looks
only a parody of himself. It is just Tiger Williams and his "routine."

Most of all, I can see it in Turnbull and Palmateer. They are
two immensely gifted but undisciplined players who need the
temper of competition to distract them out of their wallowing self-
preoccupation. Both have been pampered too long for their superstar skills; both have seen how good they can be, mistaking it for
how good they are; both can play brilliantly, as each did last year in

the Leafs' playoff upset of the Islanders. But now, as the team settles easily onto a competitive plateau that will lead nowhere until it leads down, they find time for the kind of petty self-indulgence that makes them frustratingly ordinary.

On paper, the Leafs would seem a superior team to their predecessors a few years ago, but they are not. The energy and excitement they felt at being good and promising, so important to their success, have worn away and nothing has been put in their place. They are a beaten team. They have already lost Turnbull and Palmateer; they are quickly losing Sittler, Salming, McDonald, and Williams. As players, they have been in the hands of their owner, and in the hands of the owner's general manager, his scouts and coaches. Depending on them to draft the right players, to make the right trades, to give them a chance to do what they were good enough to do, they have been badly let down. The tragedy is that what they had has been squandered and is now gone, with so little to show for it.

There is a different crowd in the Gardens for a Canadiens game, a season-ticket-holder crowd. While for games against other teams tickets get spread among family, friends, and business clients, for the Canadiens they are kept and used by the subscribers themselves. It means seeing more adults and fewer children, more sports jackets, suits, and ties in the crowd. While it seems almost incredible now, until Conn Smythe left the Gardens in 1964, a jacket and tie was considered compulsory attire for season-ticket holders of red (now gold) seats. In letters to subscribers, Smythe would sometimes remind them of this rule, warning that repeated violations of it could lead to non-renewal of their season-tickets. Tonight, and each time we play here, it's as if that rule was back in force.

The Leafs start quickly, moving the puck into our zone and keeping it there for most of the first few minutes. But it's only the knee-jerk commitment of a home team, without much depth or resolve, and as we stiffen and push back, the game turns and moves to the center zone. Play is sloppy, possession changing with every pass, but scoring chances given away are quickly given back on offsides and more bad passes, and the game remains scoreless. Near the middle of the period, Napier swings wide of Turnbull, who hooks him down for a penalty. With the extra man, we find the composure and coordination we were missing, but Palmateer is spectacular, stopping Lafleur and Robinson in succession, then Shutt on a rebound, and we don't score. Moments later, with

Turnbull caught deep in our zone, Salming swoops back and steals the puck from Lambert as he moves to the net with Tremblay. Then, lying in the corner, the puck safely at center, with a petty gamesmanship unworthy of his great skill, Salming reaches up with his stick and trips Lambert, getting a penalty. A few seconds later, Lapointe scores and we go ahead, 1-0.

The Leafs tie the game quickly, Boutette scoring after a penalty to Houle, but when the game resumes, the sloppy play continues. Already the fans, even some of the players, can sense that the real game is being played the one minute in every three that Jarvis, Gainey, and Chartraw play against Sittler, McDonald, and Williams. Because the Leafs depend on Sittler's line for a high percentage of their scoring, our approach is simple—stop Sittler, McDonald, and Williams and we will win. To do that, Bowman wants the Jarvis line, our best defensive line, to play them head-to-head. At home, with the advantage of the last change of players, Leafs coach Roger Neilson works to keep Sittler away from Jarvis, but finding he can do it only by moving him on and off the ice too quickly to be effective, he soon abandons the effort. Thereafter, whenever Sittler's line goes onto the ice, Jarvis's line follows. Within that match-up there is another, which for me has always been the best part of a Leafs-Canadiens game. It is when Lanny McDonald and Bob Gainey play against each other. They are two strong, proud, willful players, Gainey on left wing, McDonald on right, face to face, as if theirs is a personal test—skating, hammering at each other with shoulders and hips, hard and often in painful exhilaration, like two well-matched fighters taking their best shots, grim, respectful, and inside, grinning with enormous pleasure. As I watch them on the ice, uncomplaining, never acknowledging the other, friends competing as good friends often do, it is as if they understand what we can only sense—that whoever wins their private contest will win the game.

It is a great temptation to say too much about Bob Gainey. It comes in part from a fear, guilt-edged in all of us, that Gainey, a fifteen-goal scorer in a league full of do-nothing thirty-goal scorers, goes too often unrewarded. But mostly it is admiration. If there is such a thing as a "player's player," it would be Gainey. A phrase often heard and rarely explained, it is seldom applied to the best player of a sport, as Gainey is not, for performance is only a part of it. Instead, the phrase is for someone who has the personal and playing qualities that others wish they had, basic, unalterable qualities—dependability, discipline, hard work, courage—the roots of every team. To them, Gainey adds a timely, insistent passion, an enormous will to win, and a powerful, punishing playing style, secure and manly, without the strut of machismo. If I could be a forward, I would want to be Bob Gainey.

I first saw him play on TV. It was the fall of 1973, a few months after I had left the Canadiens to article in Toronto, and I was in Fredericton, New Brunswick, for a sports banquet. When the banquet ended, still early in the evening, the guests and many of those who attended reconvened in a large room where there was a TV turned on to a Canadiens game. The noise from scores of conversations was loud enough that no one could hear the game, but watching whenever I could, I kept seeing an image I didn't recognize. All I could tell was that whoever it was, he could *really* skate. Later that year, after I decided that Gainey would become a big star for the Canadiens, I found out he couldn't score.

It took more than two years for Montreal's press, fans, coaches, and management to agree that Gainey had an indefinite future with the team doing simply what he had been doing. I remember a brief talk I had with Bowman on the way to an airport after a game in Gainey's second year. Gainey had just played what I thought was an outstanding game, characteristically without a goal or an assist, and I was talking extravagantly to Bowman about him. Bowman was agreeing, but once or twice, wincing, fighting his own feelings, he said that Gainey really needed to score more often, that a regular forward on the Canadiens team had to score at least 20 goals. The next year, after he had scored several times early in the season, when others were predicting 40 goals or more for him, Gainey talked of 25, not with any longing, but simply as a total that would remove the pressure from him, that would release him to play the game he knew he played best. Soon after, when the team was in the midst of a slump, he began to think differently. He said he had come to realize that if he was to do his job well, he couldn't score even 25 goals a season. He felt that if he did, the negative trade-off in goals against would make it a poor bargain for the team. He scored 15 goals that year.

The same year, Doug Jarvis joined the team, and with Gainey and a 35-year-old defenseman-right winger named Jim Roberts, they formed the "Jarvis line." Playing one minute in every three, on a team that scored more than 380 goals, they scored 33. But playing the first shift of every game, often the last shift of a period and the last minute of every game when the score was close, playing the Clarke, Sittler, Perreault, Dionne, Esposito, and Trottier lines, the league's best lines, head-to-head, they allowed even fewer. It seemed inconceivable to us. After losing just twelve games (eleven regular-season games, and one playoff game) and winning the Stanley Cup, there was a clear and unequivocal consensus by the end of the 1976 season—there was room for a low-scoring but peerless defensive forward, for a low-scoring but superb defensive line.

That is an important moment for a defensive player, particularly a forward—to know that his play will be judged against a standard suited to his natural game; to know that a general manager will ignore statistics, or emphasize different ones, and reward him for what he does for the team, not for what he doesn't do. If he scores only rarely, as he always has, it is important to know that the press and the fans won't wonder out loud why he is playing. To feel the pressure taken off, to feel accepted and appreciated for what he does, no longer feeling himself at a halfway house, safe for now, but getting older, and knowing he must soon be something else— that is decisive. For without that consensus, the incentives—more applause, more kind words, more money—are too much, tempting him away from what he can do to what he cannot, at great cost to the team, and to him.

It doesn't mean, it will never mean, that as a defensive forward he stops craving the glory and excitement of scoring goals. It is only in the last few years that Gainey has not gone home in the summer intent on returning to Montreal a more complete player, practicing several times a week, working on his shooting and puck-handling, using the summer as a breathing space, as time to de-program himself from his defensive rut, to redirect his mind to new and broader roles to play. In the 1976 Canada Cup, with linemates who played a quicker, less defensive style, Gainey discovered he could successfully play a more offensive role. When the tournament ended, he returned to our training camp and recalls now that he scored nine goals in nine exhibition games (it was actually four—to a defensive player it only *seemed* like nine). When the season began, however, old habits, old instincts, returned, and gradually he scored less and less, ending the year with fourteen goals.

In part, it is because he lacks a goal scorer's skills. He is a power player, a strong, tireless skater with great straight-ahead speed, coming as he does from behind the play into the open at center for a pass, then around a back-pedalling defenseman for a low, hard, sharp-angled shot. But he is without the quickness and deft maneuverability in his skates and hands that puts the offensive player into scoring position, and without the delicate goal scorer's touch that does the rest. But as well as his lack of offensive skills, it is the role he plays on the team that holds him back, a role best suited to his skills and to the needs of the team; a role where scoring has little priority; a role he will not compromise. So, while he always feels he can score more often, by now he also knows that he won't. Like the 30-handicap golfer who shoots 40 on the front nine, somehow he knows that his final score will still be 100.

He is the consummate team player. An often misunderstood phrase, it does not mean that Gainey is without the selfish interests the rest of us have. It means instead that without the team's tangible rewards, without the wins and the Stanley Cups, there are few tangible rewards for him. For Gainey's skills are a team's skills, ones that work best and show best when a team does well; ones that seem less important when it doesn't. While other players, in their roles, constantly battle the tension between team and self (it is surely good for Larry Robinson to score a goal; if the team is ahead and the score is close, it may not be good for the team that he try), simply put, what's good for Bob Gainey is good for the team; and vice versa. In many ways he is like former basketball star Bill Bradley. Without virtuoso individual skills, team play becomes both virtue and necessity, and what others understand as unselfishness is really cold-eyed realism—he simply knows what works best, for the team and for him.

When Gainey was eighteen, he joined the Peterborough Petes. A leading scorer in his Junior B league the year before, as a rookie with the Petes he scored less often, with the offensive game monopolized by older players. It was a difficult year for the Petes, normally one of the strong teams in their league. Having to replace several over-age players from the year before, they were not very good, something their coach, Roger Neilson, and the players realized early in the season. But slowly, and only out of the necessity of their own circumstances, the players learned how a team not good enough to win can win. Late in the season, Neilson brought his team together and told them what they already knew. He said that if they were to succeed in the playoffs, they would have to play as a team, working for each other, *depending* on each other. Then, unexpectedly, the shy, unemotional Neilson looked around at his players and one by one asked them if they agreed with him. Uncomfortably at first, yet with more than ritual solemnity, one by one the answers came back—yes, yes, yes. Later, Gainey would remember it as a moment of bonding, a time when a team declared a commitment to itself. That year, Peterborough won the Ontario league and went to the national final, losing the Memorial Cup to Cornwall.

Now, Gainey thinks of that moment only with the slight blush of someone who is older. But the blush is for those who wouldn't understand, for those who don't remember being young, and who have never been emotionally entwined in a team. When the season ended, Gainey had been left with a feeling, and from that feeling slowly came an understanding. He had learned the lesson of team sport. He had found joy in scoring goals and would continue to, but now he felt a greater joy, a greater satisfaction, a greater sense of personal achievement, than he had ever felt before. At that moment, he realized he could accomplish more, and feel more, *within* a team. It would change the direction of his game.

Like a coach, like a goalie, Gainey plays with a constant perspective on a game. But unlike a coach or a goalie, he plays a game in its passionate midst, where perspective is rare, perhaps unique to him. He is sensitive to a game's tempos, to its moods, if it moves too fast or too slow, if we are in control, or they are, or no one is. And each time he goes on the ice, his role becomes the same. More than to score and to stop his man from scoring, it is one almost of stewardship. When he leaves the ice sixty seconds later, he wants the puck in his opponent's zone, the tempo of the game to be right for the score and for the time of the game; he wants the game under control. Then, as the next line comes on to do what it does best, Gainey stays with the game, watching for the link between what he has done and what comes next, and if a goal is scored a minute or two minutes later, he will find satisfaction or despair that is more than just vicarious.

Once I asked him what gave him his greatest pleasure in a game. Personally, he said, it was a big play, a hard body-check that stripped an opponent of the puck and caused a goal, or perhaps a goal itself, but something where the cause and effect, the emotional link, was close and direct. He gave as his most satisfying game the sixth game of the 1977 semi-finals, when he scored both goals in a 2-1 win that eliminated the Islanders. For the team, he said, it was the feeling he got when a game was under control. He mentioned a game the following year, 1978, the sixth game of the finals against the Bruins. After beating the Bruins in four straight games the year before, we started the same way, easily winning the first two games in Montreal. Then, shocking both ourselves and the Bruins, we went to Boston and lost twice. We won again in Montreal, and returned to Boston Garden for the sixth game. In the early minutes, Brad Park scored for the Bruins on a long screened shot. Quickly we tied the score, then at 9:20 of the first period, Mario Tremblay scored to put us ahead 2-1. It was the winning goal.

Late in the second period, the score 3-1, I was waiting for a faceoff in the Bruins' zone when it happened. It was as if the game suddenly stopped, and I stepped outside it for a moment and saw everything as I had felt it all along. I could sense the same feeling in the crowd, and in the Bruins players. Our control was so complete, so unshakably complete, that while there were more than twenty minutes to play, and the score was close, Tremblay's goal would be the winner, and we all knew it.

Because of his style, because of the role he plays on a team, the moment a game is under control is the moment of Gainey's triumph. For us, that moment usually comes when we score so often that the gap of goals is so wide and the time so short that a comeback is no longer possible. On this night, we scored only four goals, the Bruins were never far behind, and there was always time for something to happen. But nothing could happen. The tempo of the game was set; the mood was set; our control was absolute. For more than half the game, Gainey could savor that moment in triumph.

One time, reading something which mentioned repeatedly that Gainey scored very few goals, Lynda turned to me a little surprised and said that while she had watched him play for almost five years, she had never realized that. Then she shrugged, and went on to something else, as if in Gainey's case it somehow wasn't relevant. While a team needs all kinds of players with all kinds of skills to win, it needs prototypes, strong, dependable prototypes, as examples of what you want your team to be. If you want it to be quick and opportunistic, you need a Lafleur and a Shutt, so that those who can be quick are encouraged to try, and those who cannot will move faster than they otherwise might. If you want a team to be cool and unflappable, you need at least one Savard, to reassure you, to let you know that the time and the team needed to do what you want are still there. If you want a team to be able to lift a game, to find an emotional level higher than any opponent can find, you need players like Lapointe and Tremblay, mercurial players who can take it there. And if you want a team game, where the goal is the team and the goal is to win, you need a player with an emotional and practical stake in a team game, a player to remind you of that game, to bring you back to it whenever you forget it, to be the playing conscience of the team. Like Bob Gainey.

Early in the second period, Lambert deflects Savard's long shot and we move ahead 2-1. The pace of the game accelerates, moving from end to end for a time, then gradually settling into our zone. Lapointe loses his stick, and, under harassing pressure, grabs at a loose puck and is penalized. For more than a minute, Jarvis and Gainey disrupt the Leafs' power play, but when Robinson falls going after McDonald in the corner, we start chasing the puck, always an open man behind. Finally, with no one in front of him, Salming moves in from the point. As three players rush for him, he passes to Sittler at the goal crease and the game is tied again.

While Sittler's line has been shut down by Jarvis, except on the power play, the Leafs' checking line has done the same to Lemaire, Lafleur, and Shutt, giving the Leafs enormous confidence. For it was here that they worried they would be badly outmatched. But now, with each shift that passes that shows they aren't, an excited feeling builds and spreads among their players—they now think they can play with us. The quality of the game improves, and the Leafs begin to take over. Suddenly, Napier intercepts a clearing pass and scores. Thirty seconds later, his linemate Hughes does the same. The effect is crushing.

Juggled in and out of the line-up by Bowman, Napier and Hughes trade places with Larouche, Chartraw, or Connor, depending on the game. Tonight, with the game in Toronto, they are playing because they are from Toronto. The Leafs began this game hoping to win, but afraid that Lemaire, Lafleur, and Shutt could not be stopped; afraid that Robinson, Lapointe, and Savard were too good to allow them enough chances to score. They have stopped the Lemaire line, they have made our defense look ordinary. But within thirty seconds, two players they didn't know would play have put them out of the game. At this moment, the Leafs players, those on the bench and those on the ice, are saying to themselves, "There is no way we can ever beat this team."

The Leafs begin the third period with a spasm of pressure, but Williams high-sticks Jarvis and the spasm ends. The crowd chants "Bull-shit! Bull-shit!" to the penalty call, sounding more titillated by its own chant than angry. Palmateer makes two more spectacular saves, both from rebounds he could have prevented, then Napier scores again. The rest of the game is a surly shambles. Without the feeling they had briefly in the second period, the Leafs look inept. It all looks very sad. Late in the game Mondou scores, then McDonald and Maloney for the Leafs.

After the game, I see my father, and the fathers of Risebrough and Jarvis, Napier and Hughes. They have watched their sons play many games for many years, and tonight, though they are careful not to show it, they look proud, as if it was all worth it. I walk over to where my father is standing and he introduces me to a friend he invited to the game. A few years ago, many years after she had wanted to say it, my mother asked Dave and me if we would mind if she did not attend any more games. She said that she had enjoyed going, but that the games made her worry, and she hoped we would understand. Later, my father told us that whenever she went to a game, she would watch until the puck came into our zone, then look at her feet until it had left again. Finally, she found that even that was not enough.

My father and I talk for a few minutes; the other man listens.

My father says something about the game, I say something back, quickly and flippantly, trying to tell him that I don't want to talk about it. After a few awkward pauses, we realize we said all that we wanted to say last night and this morning. We shake hands and say good-bye.

I walk out to the bus. The sidewalk is filled with a scrum of autograph-seekers, yelling, jostling, pushing out paper scraps and pencil scraps, sometimes getting the same ones back. As I near the bus, a dark, tired-looking woman, in her late thirties, asks me to autograph her hand. She holds it out and I cradle it in mine. Her pen bumps across her veins and tendons, tugging, skipping over loose skin almost illegibly. When I'm done, she thanks me, smiles, and gives my hand a gentle squeeze.

The lights are turned off, the bus is dark. I lie back in my seat. Outside, through the bus's tinted windows, scores of people stare, bobbing their bodies, straining for a familiar face, and when they see one, pointing at it, yelling for friends to see what they are seeing. Inside, someone makes a sound like a chimp.

"That's it, you bastards," another voice shouts. "Look at the animals. Take a good fuckin' look," and here and there I hear laughter.

I'm angry—at the last two goals, at the game, at the Leafs, at the Gardens, at me; at people who all day have promised me a Leafs-Canadiens rivalry. There is no Leafs-Canadiens rivalry. It's dead: the Leafs killed it.

I feel duped.

Thursday

"Our friends, the enemy."

—Pierre-Jean de Béranger,
L'Opinion de ces demoiselles

BOSTON

IT IS EARLY MORNING. THE BEER HAS BEEN DRUNK, THE MEALS have been eaten, the exuberant sounds that winners make when they win have been made, and now, drained out, are gone. It is quiet. Typewriters that hammered out word of our victory for an audience still hours away, backgammon boards, playing cards, have all been packed up and put away. The aisles of the plane are empty; the cabin, its overhead lights turned off, lies at dusk. For the thirty-five players, coaches, trainers, and journalists who make up this travelling band, yesterday is finally over. We sink back in our seats, suddenly weary.

I close my eyes, then open them again and stare out at the night. From under the wing, a red aura of light flickers on and off hypnotically. Down below, small unconnected islands of white and yellow light, the towns and villages of western Massachusetts, inch by several seconds apart. I lean forward and rest my head against the window, feeling its coolness, fogging it with my breath, blinking at the filigree landscape as it drifts beneath me.

Ahead, the patches of light broaden and run up against each other and I know that Boston is not far away.

The plane banks sharply to the right, south over the northern coastal towns of Swampscott, Lynn, and Nahant; then, levelling off, it leaves the coast and moves out to sea. Out from behind the plane, I see the moon for the first time, brilliant and full, its crystal-white light reflecting on the water, turning it the shimmering black of slate. The right wing of the plane dips gently, then steeply, driving me deeper into my seat, and the plane spirals back towards land. Over Hull, Cohasset, Quincy, and South Boston, over Boston Harbor, easing lower and lower until every light disappears for long suspended seconds, and we hit the runway. It is 2 a.m.

I stir, then I hear it again. Sharp and penetrating, again and again, until, gradually awake enough, I know what it is. "Yes?" I yell, my voice still muffled with sleep.

"Just checking for occupancy, sir," a voice sounds, and everything goes quiet again. It is the universal hotel maid, a pass-key in her hand, standing in front of my door inches from a sign that hangs from its handle and reads "DO NOT DISTURB."

A few seconds later, I hear the same sound, then again, less sharp and penetrating each time as she moves from room to room along the hall. It is 8 a.m.

ON THE ROAD AGAIN

For two days in the East, for four sunny, warm days in the West, I like the road. I like the feeling of moving, of being in a hurry, of doing something even when sometimes I'm not. Of being in one place, and a few hours later being some place else. I like the energy I get from airports and planes, from hotels and tall buildings, from downtown sounds and traffic jams of people. I like travelling a continent to walk on its streets, to see its people, to know its names and places, to observe, to get a sense of it before I leave; then weeks, months, years later, to go back to see if it or I have changed. I like finding the places I'm supposed to find, and then finding others, no undiscovered gems, just public places I can make private and important to me, that I return to each time—to Stanley Park, lush and green on rare and rainless days in Vancouver; to the mountains in Colorado, and deserts in California; to bookshops in Greenwich Village, to Washington Square at New York University for the menagerie of life's performers that gathers there; to Harvard and MIT, and along the Charles River which joins them, moving with Boston's joggers, cyclists, and crews as they push back the winter and reawaken with the spring. And by the time I leave a place, to feel some vague reassuring comfort, as if coping with freeways and frenetic life-styles, with the Rangers, Bruins, and Kings, means somehow I have made it there.

More than that, I like the spirit and freedom of the road, the chance to be alone in a life overcrowded with people. I enjoy walking downtown and going unrecognized; watching others, as in Montreal they watch me. With wife and children miles away and no family life to lead, I like to get up, to eat, to sleep, to walk, to talk, to shop, to read, to rent a car when *I* want to. With only a game to prepare for, with many hours to fill, I enjoy having unbusied, unbothered time *for me*. And for the team. With no appointments to keep, no agents, no lawyers or accountants to interrupt us, it is our chance to rediscover the team. It happens over a meal, at a table of empty beer bottles, on planes or buses, in card games or golf games, wearing clothes that seem right, but laughingly are not, in the awful, outrageous stories we tell that we've told too often before; it is our time, as Pete Mahovlich once put it, to "act stupid together."

But life on the road comes at a price. The energy it gives, the freedom you feel, it takes away, and more—twenty-six weeks a season, eighty games, from bus to plane to bus to hotel to bus to arena to bus to plane, to a leagueful of cities three times a week. A rhythm like any other rhythm, it is one you get used to; except this one is always changing and you never do. Like a skillful runner in a distance race, it sets the pace and plays with you; going slower than you want it to, speeding up before you are ready, gradually wearing you down, until after four games in five nights in four different cities, you are weak and vulnerable, and it sprints away from you.

Several times a year it happens to me—a game at night, chartering into the early morning, waking up in you-don't-know-where and you really don't care, hung over from fatigue, arms and legs aching for sleep, last night's snack five hours stale in your mouth. A shower, a shave, and they all go away; twenty minutes later, they're back. You take an afternoon nap to get you through a game; a game, a flight, a new hotel, and you can't sleep because you slept in the afternoon. It means going from nap to nap and from game to game, just one never-ending day with no big sleep to send you on to the next one. Then the phone goes off like electrodes in your brain, and you're up again. Morning, afternoon, a plane, a game, you don't know which and you really don't care. There are newspapers on the bed, shirt, jacket, and pants are slung in a chair, a tie, tied and untied until it's seersuckered, lies sprawled on the floor, still tied. You reach for your suitcase; inside you find fresh clothes, freshly wrinkled, and what the hell, you grab the old ones and put them on again. In. Out. Two points and a season to go. You're on the run and you'll never catch up until it's over.

It's life in a revolving door—home, away, home again—spinning around and around until Montreal is one more stop on the road, and you're never really anywhere but on the way. Just picking up, packing up, and moving on, you are never around to see how things turn out. A bump on the head, a trip to the hospital, and 2000 miles later you say, "How're ya feeling, Sarah?" You have an argument, time's up—"We'll talk about it when I get back." It's a road mentality, popping in, performing for the troops, popping out again. There are no commitments, no responsibilities; we let absence become the tie that binds. Then one day, "Daddy's coming home"—and lives get rearranged; new dresses are put on, rooms get cleaned up, and special meals are prepared. We arrive with gifts, are treated like special company, and everything is wonderfully the same. Except this time, where once you left loneliness, where you left a family to live off the goodness of neighborhood fathers, you come home to a family that has learned to cope; a family that has built a life without you.

I turn over and try to sleep, but quickly give up. Fumbling for my glasses on the bedside table, I roll upright to the edge of the bed, my elbows on my knees, eyes still closed. Slowly, they open. A few feet away, Risebrough stirs and is asleep again. I look around. The color of the wallpaper, the arrangement of the room—I have been here before. I try to remember yesterday, and piece it together—the game, the flight, the bus ride from the airport—and it comes to me. This is Boston. Slowly in my stomach and legs I get a feeling, a gnawing uneasiness, then in my chest and throat a fear. *I don't want to play tonight.* I don't want the hours of anxious waiting that must come first. The spasms of memory—the Bruins, my last game in Boston—that will interrupt me through the day; I don't want the two and a half hours that will come at the end, hours I can't control, that will make me work and sweat, that might embarrass me, that will give me a mood to carry around until the next game. I don't want it, any of it. In Boston, ready or not, I feel trapped, with no way out but to play.

Twenty minutes later, I am showered, shaved, and dressed, and the feeling is almost forgotten.

The elevators stop and go with the early-morning rush, opening and closing at every floor but too full for anyone else to get on. In the lobby, men, or men with women, in suits and ties, and carrying briefcases, stand in check-out lines, watching their watches, moving ahead one step at a time. Others crisscross hurriedly to the newsstand, to the front desk or the bell captain's stand, emptying up escalators to restaurants on the mezzanine, filing from restaurants and elevators, emptying to parking lots and taxi-stands outside. Near the front door, his back against a square lobby-high pillar, Larry Robinson is reading a newspaper.

Taller, broader, younger than those around him, he shuffles his body and straightens up as I get closer, and looks much bigger. Erect, angular like an Easter Island statue, a bush of curly brown-red hair covering his head, he is not football-big or basketball-big, but, pushing as he does the limits of *normal* big, to those who pass unable to keep themselves from taking a second look his size seems remarkable.

If you were to close your eyes and think of Larry Robinson, before you thought of his occasional punishing body-checks, or his amiable rawboned farmboy look, you would think of his size. It is his defining feature. As a boy, it was what held him back, and gave him his chance; what made coaches wonder and pro scouts drool; what gave him his potential, and made him slow to realize it. Maturing, slowly gaining control of his distant parts, it was what finally made him a star, and created the Bunyanesque expectations of him not always fulfilled. Like other big men, like a rich man's son or a beautiful girl, he has spent much of his life denying what he is, anxious to prove, ostensibly to others but really to himself, that he is more than just big, that he is what he is by his own merit, not by a quirk of genetics.

Although I must have seen him in two training camps before, I have no memory of him until his first NHL game in Minnesota. It was early January 1973, and with injuries to many of our defensemen, Robinson was called up from the Voyageurs. When I walked into the dressing room before the game, there he was, already half dressed, looking taller, more rawboned, more angular than he does now. With our defense depleted, seeing Robinson didn't make me feel any better. But he played a remarkable game—poised, in solid control defensively, moving surprisingly well, with only a hint of lanky awkwardness. And what I recall most vividly, a goalie's memory, was that he blocked shots. (It wouldn't last long. After the first burst of rookie's enthusiasm wore off, he became like the rest.)

When our injured defensemen returned, Robinson remained with the team, but for the rest of the year and for much of the next three, he was only occasionally as good. Alternating long moments where he did little with shorter frenzied bursts where he tried to do everything to make up for it, he seemed disoriented, as if searching for a game to play. A pet project of Al MacNeil with the Voyageurs, he became one with Ruel, spending long additional time with him on the ice before and after practice. Gradually his choppy, legs-akimbo stride lengthened and grew forceful; the dangerously erratic shots that had sent teammates from the front of the net to the relative safety of the corners now came in low enough often enough to bring them back for rebounds; his puck-handling and passing more confident and certain, he was becoming an immense ragbag of rapidly developing skills. But he needed something around which to organize these new skills: like Lafleur's quickness, Bobby Hull's shot, Maurice Richard's insistent passion, something to focus his game, the stereotype skill to which the others could attach and find meaning, something that was his own. The one original part of his game around which it might be done he seemed anxious to deny. He had been a "big stiff" all his hockey life, the promise of muscle and intimidation his major *raison d'être*. Now he wanted the satisfaction and self-respect he felt in another game. And so he continued to search and experiment. At times copying the all-ice consumption of Bobby Orr, at other times swooping around the defensive zone with the elastic grace of Salming, most often he played with the same non-violent elegance and disinterested cool as Savard. But nothing quite worked.

Then, in 1976, out of two separate events four months apart, Robinson became an original. The first was the Stanley Cup finals with Philadelphia. After they had won two consecutive Stanley Cups, this was the last go-round of the "Broad Street Bullies," but with Dave Schultz, Jack McIlhargey, Don Saleski, Bob Kelly, and others, they were still a hugely intimidating team. We knew that to beat them we would need to neutralize their intimidation (in order to free up the rest of our game, which we knew to be superior); so Bowman lined up Bouchard, Chartraw (in Philadelphia), Risebrough, Tremblay, and Robinson against them. We won the first game in Montreal, and were leading midway through the third period of the second, when Gary Dornhoefer, a tall, lean, irritating winger for the Flyers, moved across our blueline. From his left defense position, Robinson angled over to play him. In most arenas, when struck by colliding bodies, the boards whip obligingly out of shape, absorbing much of the force of the blow before whipping back into position again. Not so in the Forum. Forum boards are solid and punishingly unyielding, or always had been. Driving into Dornhoefer, Robinson hit him so hard that the Flyer's body dented a section of boards, leaving it an inch or so in back of where it had been just moments before.

The game was halted, amid an awestruck buzz from the crowd, and for several minutes Forum workmen used hammers and crowbars trying to undo what Robinson had done. But when the boards were banged back in place, the impression remained. He had done it with such crushing ease: no cross-ice leaping, elbowing, high-sticking charge; just simple "aw shucks" destruction, the kind that leaves behind the shuddering hint of something more to come. He had delivered a message—to the Flyers, to the rest of the league, to himself. A series that had been moving our way found its irrevocable direction, and we won in four straight games. Robinson was named *Sport* magazine's MVP of the playoffs.

Late that summer, the first Canada Cup was played, and Robinson, on the strength of his performance in the playoffs, was chosen a member of Team Canada. It was a team of highly skilled offensive players, and competing against the quicker, more wide-open European teams, Robinson had felt a need to prove his right to be there. But, pressed to raise the pace of his game, forced to handle the puck more often, to move it quickly and join in the offensive build-up, by the time the series was over he had discovered he could. All the pieces had finally fallen into place. He had found a game, *his* game. Not Orr's, not Salming's or Savard's. A game of strength and agility, a commanding mix of offense and defense, his size a lingering reminder of violence. If you closed your eyes and imagined Robinson, that is what you saw: vivid, sharply defined and original, a Larry Robinson game. It had been there for some time; it needed only the Dornhoefer check and the Canada Cup to bring it together and make it work. The next season, more than doubling his offensive totals, he was voted the league's best defenseman.

In the next few years, more than just an outstanding player, Robinson became a presence. It had to do with being so big, so strong, so tough, so agile, that no one knew how good he was, and no one wanted to find out. A burst of speed, a quick pass, triumphantly in the clear, then looking up and seeing *him*, and feeling everything inside you slowly sucked out. It had to do with knowing that anything you can do, he can do better, so throw up your hands, shrug your shoulders, put on the brakes—what's the use? He had a numbing reputation, an imperial manner, and the goods to back them up, a game rooted in defense, opportunistic on offense, limited, economic, and dominant. It had to do with what he did and what he didn't have to do because of how he did it.

He was the rare player whose effect on a game was far greater than any statistical or concrete contribution he might make. When he came onto the ice, the attitude of the play seemed to change. Standing in back of him, I could feel it, I could *see* it, change, growing more restrained, more respectful, as if it was waiting for him, to see what he would do. Nowhere was this more clear, or more important, than against the Flyers or the Bruins. They held him in such awe, treating him with an embarrassing, almost fawning, respect, that they seemed even to abandon their style of play when he was around, and with it any hope of winning. Each time we played them, I knew that an outraged Fred Shero or Don Cherry would send out players to hunt him down, to hammer him into the boards with elbows and sticks, to fight with him if he would let them, until, bruised and sweating, his mystique could only come crashing down. But they never did.

For a time, Robinson had it both ways. With the Dornhoefer check, with an impressive portfolio of fights, he had shown the flag and shown it in such a way that he could bring it down and it would still be seen vividly and unforgettably. He could put away the "big man's" game he never wanted to play, and, moving up ice, excitingly involved in all parts of the game, he could play the one he did. All he would have to do is bring out the flag and shake it occasionally as a reminder.

But he never really has. Convinced he can't body-check regularly through the season without injury, bothered by fights he feels have no part in the game, Robinson cruises the ice as a belligerent peacemaker, going nose to nose and stare to stare with anyone who threatens a teammate, stabbing at the air with a menacing right index finger. It is enormously important to the team, preventing as it does the fights we have no use for, but over time, appearing less threatening and more comic, it hasn't been good for Robinson. Each time he does it, he puts too much at stake—an immense reputation, unchallenged, building with memory, his size a constant reminder; a fight he can only lose. Schultz, who fought several times a week, could sometimes lose and fight again, his effect undiminished. But to keep from fighting, to keep *us* from having to fight, to be an entirely effective *deterrent*, Robinson can't lose. He has to be unchallengeable; the consequences of fighting with him must be so sure that no one will take the chance. The only way it can happen is if he doesn't fight at all. If he doesn't fight at all, he gets out of practice.

Once Bowman said about Robinson, "I was always fearful that some guy would deflate him with a lucky punch. He has so much to live up to." In our final pre-season game in Toronto last fall, with only a few minutes to play, Dave Hutchison, a big goon-defenseman for the Leafs, began shoving with one of our players. Predictably, Robinson rushed over to confront him. As everyone watched, the two of them wrapped their hands in each other's sweaters and glared stiff-eyed, their faces inches apart;

stalemated. Then, as things were cooling, Robinson began shoving Hutchison. Watching from the other end, I could see that Hutchison wanted to go no further, yet inexplicably Robinson persisted. Having already thought out the consequences a year or two earlier, I began to panic, muttering to myself for him to stop, telling him it wasn't worth it. Finally the fight started. It was over in a few seconds; the result, while not clear-cut, seemed decisive. Robinson, looking awkward and entirely mortal, emerged with a black eye.

Yet nothing happened. I was certain that word would spread through a league desperate for new ways to beat us, and we would find ourselves under attack for much of the season. But I was wrong. As usual, the team has been involved in very few fights; Robinson still intrudes on those that threaten and breaks them up, and with fighting gradually diminishing as a tactic, nothing seems different. But in another, and related, way, something has changed.

Close your eyes and think of Robinson again: his size, his occasional body-checks and fights—these images still come quickly, but they are no longer features of his game. Try again. What do you see now? What is the instant image you get? What is the focus around which everything finds its order and purpose? What is the quintessential Robinson? I see an imposing, erect figure, the puck on his stick, moving slowly to center, others bent double at the waist skittering around him. Then, as if jerked into fast-forward, the image speeds up: defensive corners, offensive corners, their net, our net, faster and faster, no pattern, like a swarming, sprawling force; everything blurred and out of focus. It happens every time I try it. I can see Lapointe; I can see Brad Park and Savard; I can see Denis Potvin's crisp pass, his unseen move to the slot, his quick, hard wrist-shot. But I can't see Robinson.

When you are a presence, there are many things you need not do, for it is simply understood you can do them. So you don't do them. You don't risk what you need not risk, you let others' imaginations do them for you, for they do them better than you can. Like the man who opens his mouth to prove he's a fool, often the more you do, the more you look like everyone else.

Someone once said after hearing George McGovern speak, "I always get the feeling he thinks that if he speaks long enough, he will say something worthwhile." The comparison to Robinson's game is too harsh, indeed Robinson remains one of the league's best defensemen; but, born of the same uncertain self-image, as he tries to do more and more, that same thought occurs to me.

What set him apart from other players was his size and

strength, his implicit toughness and chilling manner; what set him apart from other big men was his agility and puck-handling skill; what made him unique was the mix. What made it all work was a game rooted in defense—strong, limited, and commanding. *A big man's game.* His offensive game was the exciting appendage, but it needed his defensive game to work, emerging out of it as it did timely and unseen from behind the play. In 1976, Robinson discovered that big man's game, but mistaking its visible, dramatic symbols—the fights and the body-checks—for its essence, and not liking the symbols, later finding them too confining and unrewarding and giving them up, he has denied and given up the rest. By rejecting a big man's game for one of which he's less certain, and one of which he knows others are less certain as well, he feels driven to do more and more to accomplish the same; and therein lies the problem.

More skillful with each year, doing more things, stretching himself wider, he has stretched himself thinner. Working hard, he is making more good plays; but, overextending himself, his stride now chopping, his invincibility in question, he is making more bad plays as well. The numbers are still hugely in his favor, but now it *is* a game of numbers, concrete and measurable, as for everyone else. By exchanging a game he dominated for a larger, more demanding one he cannot dominate, Robinson is no longer a presence.

Crossing the lobby, before I can say anything Robinson looks up from his paper and tells me that the Islanders won last night. We both shake our heads, and say nothing.

It is a beautiful late winter day: clear, the sun so crisp it etches everything in shadow; cold, but not so cold that you can feel it right away. Outside the front door of the hotel, taxis in a line, businessmen in a line, move up, meet, and speed away. Across the street, joggers in shorts and sweatshirts amble past, mothers with other mothers stroll with their children, talking as they go. I cross the street and fall into step behind. I look at what they look at, smile when I hear them laugh, walking to feel the air and the sun, to feel alone and not alone. A few hundred feet ahead, our street winds gently into shadow, then opens to a field of red-brown brick dominated from one corner by the Capitol-like dome of the Christian Science Church. On its enormous plaza, there are many more joggers, more mothers and strollers, families posing each other in front of a reflecting pool many football fields long and wide. But the plaza was built for fields of people, and soon we are far apart. I find a concrete bench and sit down. For more than an hour, I read the paper, gradually piling its sections under me against the cold, here and there glancing at what's around me, closing my eyes and looking up at the sun.

I have been coming to Boston for more than twelve years, the last eight years with the Canadiens, and in sports parlance, Boston is *my* town, the Boston Garden *my* rink, the Bruins (Boston University, Boston College, Harvard) *my* team. In the endless panorama of any season, it is my own personal landmark—a city, a team, a rink, a game I always look forward to; a base where, when things go badly, I find solid ground; a launch pad where, when things must go well, they always do. Twice it is where I got my start, twice it is where I made my breakthrough; twice each year it is where I get renewed. Each new game is a random event, except that something always happens, unimportant in other places, but because this is Boston I notice it, and the remarkable connection seems more remarkable. In twelve years, playing on two non-Boston teams, Cornell and the Canadiens, we have won three Eastern College championships, one Christmas tournament and shared another, one NHL quarter-final series, and two Stanley Cups, *all* in Boston, all but one in Boston Garden, never losing more than a few scattered games.

In 1971, I was in goal when we played the Bruins in a Stanley Cup quarter-final series. Though we would need to go on and beat Minnesota and Chicago to win the Cup, though I've played more than four hundred games in more than six seasons since, in those seven games, games 7 through 13 of my NHL career, I did the only thing I've ever done that will last more than twenty years of a sports fan's memory.

Those were the Orr and Esposito years, but first and foremost they were the Orr years. Bobby Orr had turned twenty-three just seventeen days before the playoffs began, a Bruin since he was eighteen. In his almost five full seasons, he had won all the awards a defenseman could win, in some cases several times, and in 1970 he added one that until then had been thought so unlikely as not to be taken seriously, the Art Ross Trophy as the league's leading scorer. In a career that matched peaks with Esposito and Clarke, that overlapped those of the aging Howe, Hull, and Mahovlich and the emerging Lafleur and Trottier, Orr was *the* outstanding player of his generation.

In 1966, Bobby Orr joined a Bruins team that had missed the playoffs for seven straight seasons, finishing sixth and last in five of those years. It was a team of journeymen, fourth-line forwards or spare defensemen on other teams, players who had bounced to the bottom, where they would stay a season or two before being turned over for other, younger journeymen. Most were old and unpromising, a few—goalie Gerry Cheevers, defensemen Dallas Smith and Don Awrey, forwards Ed Westfall and Derek Sanderson—were young, but quickly losing whatever promise they had in the mire of failure. Later, as several went on to various levels of stardom, it would seem a better team than it was. But in 1966, beaten into emotional and physical resignation, the Bruins were merely a directionless supporting cast, badly in need of someone to support.

Orr, of course, would be the man, but it didn't happen right away. In his rookie season, also coach Harry Sinden's first season, the Bruins earned four fewer points than they had the year before and went from fifth to last in the six-team NHL. But by the time the following season had begun, they would complete the core of players that brought them two Stanley Cups in the next five years.

On May 15, 1967, Boston traded Gilles Marotte, Pit Martin, and goalie Jack Norris to Chicago for Phil Esposito, Ken Hodge, and Fred Stanfield. With the Hawks, Norris would play briefly, then move on to Los Angeles, where, after a career total of fifty-eight games, he would leave the NHL and soon retire. Martin would do better. A smooth-skating, all-purpose center, in Chicago he fulfilled the abundant promise he had shown as a junior and gave the Hawks ten useful seasons. For Chicago, however, the key player was Marotte. Short, squat, a thunderous body-checker— "Captain Crunch" as he was later called in Los Angeles—unlike Potvin and Robinson, who came later and used the body-check sparingly and selectively, Marotte's defensive game was *based* on it. It was a style made gradually anachronistic since the forward pass speeded up the game more than fifty years ago. But Marotte would continue to deliver checks that others still recall with a shudder and a laugh; he missed too often, however, and less than two years later, he too was gone from the Hawks.

It would prove the most one-sided trade in NHL history. It was not so much a disastrous one for Chicago, since Esposito, Hodge, and Stanfield had been disappointing and minor figures there, as one of incredible good fortune for the Bruins. In Boston, Hodge and Stanfield became inportant players; Esposito was a revelation.

A late-developing junior, Esposito had blossomed as a scorer in two minor-league seasons, and was brought to the Hawks, where he settled in to a comfortable career as Bobby Hull's center, averaging nearly twenty-four goals a year over three seasons, not insignificant totals in pre-expansion times. But the Hawks were an established team, presided over by two great superstars, Hull and Stan Mikita. On and off the ice, its relationships were set, its roles carved out, and in time, little could change because Hull and

Mikita were too good, and too young. Hull was the goal scorer, Mikita the playmaker, and the rest, including Esposito, fit in around them as support. On the ice, it was Esposito's job to get Hull the puck; off the ice, an emotional and spirited man, he became that other part of his personality, the funnyman, the clown. So when Hawks general manager Tommy Ivan traded him to Boston, he traded a funny, playmaking 24-goal scorer who had no room to be anything else, and perhaps never would have. Years later, at all-star games, and as teammates in the 1976 Canada Cup, after Esposito had broken Hull's scoring records many times, they would come together as if time had frozen in 1967. There remained the same deference, a relationship that Hull never forced, but that Esposito insisted on. Bobby Hull was still the goal scorer.

In Boston, Esposito would move into Orr's shadow, but with each playing a different position, and in different roles well-suited to them, they were perfect complements for each other—Orr the great generator, Esposito the great finisher; Esposito, ebullient and mercurial, Orr the driven perfectionist to keep him in check. With the Bruins, a team just taking shape, Esposito could create his own role. So with Hodge and Wayne Cashman to work the corners, he moved to the front of the net, wrestling defensemen for position, using his extraordinary strength and reach to free the big-bladed stick he used to receive their passes. Then, seven or eight times a game and often more, without hesitation, he redirected those passes towards the net. Never a sniper like Mike Bossy or Rick Martin, he was a volume shooter. Entangled with defensemen as he was, few of his shots were hard enough or accurate enough to guarantee a goal, but over time many would go in. Taking tentative steps at first, he scored 35 goals his initial season in Boston, 49 his second. Then, as if the 50-goal standard belonged only to a scoring elite—Richard, Hull, Geoffrion—that didn't include him, he backed away, scoring only 43 the next season. A year later, in 1971, he scored 76 goals.

Had he scored 50, or even 55, goals, he would have forced inevitable comparisons with Richard and Hull. He wouldn't have fared well, predictably, because there is nothing spectacular, nothing legendary, about his game—no primeval fire in his eyes, no irresistible will that carries defensemen from the blueline to the net, no 50-foot slap shots hard enough to kill a man.

He was just a slot player, unseen in a crowd that surrounded the net, somehow connected to a red light that flashed behind the goalie. But he had scored *76* goals, forcing people to say he was *better* than Hull, *better* than Richard, and few were willing to do so. Instead, resentful, they disparaged him, blaming his success on expansion, attributing it to Orr. A year later, playing without an injured Orr and an ineligible Hull (who had signed with the rival WHA), Esposito led Team Canada through eight desperate games with the Soviets, and an eventual 4-3-1 series victory. While he was the leading scorer in the series, that is almost forgotten. *The* scorer was, and is, Paul Henderson, with three game-winning goals, including the series winner thirty-four seconds from the end of the eighth game. Instead, Esposito is remembered for his remarkable all-round play, for being the emotional heart of his team, the man who made a poignant impromptu speech to the nation on TV after the crushing fourth-game defeat in Vancouver. Ironically, as time passes, the enormous accomplishment of Henderson, the goal scorer, fades, dismissed as a quirk of sports, more fluke than achievement, while Esposito's accomplishment, this time less empirical, not built on statistics, continues to grow.

Then there was Orr.

It is not easy for a hockey player to dominate a game. A goalie, any goalie, can make a bad team win or a good team lose, he can dominate a *result*, but that is not the same thing. He cannot dominate a game, because, separate from the action of a game, he is not quite part of it.

In basketball, one man *can* dominate: usually a big man—Bill Russell, Wilt Chamberlain, Willis Reed, Bill Walton, Kareem Abdul-Jabbar—able to play most of the game's forty-eight minutes, and, as with any goalie, it might be *any* big man. It comes with the position. But in hockey, seventeen players are rotated more or less equally five at a time, and rarely does anyone play much more than half a game. A forward or defenseman, a *special* forward or defenseman, might with unusual frequency find the right moment in a game and make a play that will swing a result. But for too long periods of time, the game goes on without him, and his impact can rarely be sustained. In the 1970s, only two players could dominate a game. One was Orr, the other Bobby Clarke. Clarke, a fierce, driven man, did it by the unrelenting mood he gave to a game, a mood so strong it penetrated his team and stayed on the ice even when he did not. Orr did it another way.

Great players have skills that set them apart. Virtuoso skills—Hull's shot, Lafleur's quickness, Frank Mahovlich's power and grace—skills that separate them from their opponents and from the game, but also from teammates less able. It is a platitude of sports that a great player makes everyone around him better, but when it is true, the effect is often just spillover and coincidental. Indeed, more commonly it works the other way—the great player has everyone around him to make *him* better. When a superstar comes onto the ice or onto a playing field, a game changes and is drawn to him. It is he who is at the center of the action, commanding it, directing it, his teammates little more than courtiers or spectators, their initiative sapped, their skills seconded. It is no petulant power play of a selfish superstar, it is the force and magnetism of his skills that have this effect. It is why great players rarely work well together (there can only be *one* ball or *one* puck at a time), and are more effective with players of complementary and subservient skills—and so Cashman becomes Esposito's cornerman, Jim Braxton O. J. Simpson's blocker. Orr was the profound exception.

Perhaps it was because he lined up as a defenseman. Set back a few feet from the game with the time and perspective that offered, he could watch it, "taking pictures" as Bowman would say of him, finding its pattern, its rhythm, then at a moment he could choose, accelerate into its midst to turn two-man attacks into three, three into four. Orr was a brilliant skater, fast, quick, wonderfully maneuverable. While the speed of Hull, Mahovlich, and Lafleur, as forwards, often isolates them from teammates who cannot keep up, and robs them of the time necessary for effective combination play, as a defenseman, Orr gave his teammates a head start. With more ice in front of him, Orr could play full out, using all his special skills, and never lose contact. From behind, he could shape the game. He could see where it might go, then with no forward's lanes to hold him back, he could take it there: pushing teammates, chasing them, forcing a pace higher than many thought they could play, supporting them with passes, bursting ahead, leading them, forcing them to rise to his game, always working with them. From behind, with several defenders in front of him, he *needed* his teammates, who in turn needed his extraordinary passing and intuitive skills to bring out *their* skills to make *him* better, in turn to make *them* better. It was what made him unique. By making everyone a contributor, he made everyone feel part of his own success, of *their* success. From last place to a Stanley Cup in four years, it could only happen because, as catalyst and driving force, Orr brought the Bruins along with him.

He was the rare player who changed the perceptions of his sport. Until Orr, defensemen had been defenders, usually stocky and slow-footed, their offensive game complete when the puck had cleared the defensive zone. Even so-called "rushing defensemen" in pre-Orr times, Red Kelly, Tim Horton, and others, rarely went much beyond the center line, moving up only as a forward moved back, dropping out of the play as soon as they made their first pass. It was Orr who broke down the barriers separating offense and defense. Lining up as a defenseman, when the puck dropped, he became a "player," his game in instant and constant transition, until with no real transition at all, neither defenseman nor forward, *both* defender and attacker, he attacked to score and keep from being scored against; he defended to prevent goals and create chances to score. It was what soccer commentators would call a "total" game, what we knew as hockey of the future, and it became the model for all defensemen to follow.

Earlier this season, after six operations on his left knee, after nine seasons spanning thirteen years, Orr retired. He has left defence a much-changed position. He has given it new perceptions, a new attitude that makes further change easier; but he left no heirs. The best of his contemporaries—Robinson, Potvin, Lapointe, Park, Salming—have tried at times to emulate him, but without the prodigious skating and puck-handling skills necessary for his all-ice, all-out, all-the-time game, they have settled back, never completely, not quite comfortably, into something more measured, more restrained. It is what works best for them. The style that was the style of the future remains very much that.

Orr and Esposito were the two great superstars of the time, and around them were the "big, bad Bruins," winners of the Stanley Cup in 1970, source of the "Boston flu"—a groin-pull, hamstring-pull, anything-pull to keep the faint-hearted out of Boston and safely away from them. It was a team of great personal chemistry, free-spirited in the worst of times, now as champions rousing and carousing like a pier-six brawl ready to happen. Hard living, hard laughing, a team both on and off the ice, they seemed the image of what every team should be. And on and off the ice, the wind finally at their backs, in the glow of good feeling that had taken over the city and their fans, they built an enormous roll of momentum.

When a player speaks of momentum, when a journalist nods and his reader nods with him, what each understands is an almost tangible feeling, in that player and in his team, that a season moving in a clear and distinct direction will not easily change. But while momentum comes and goes with wins and losses, it follows a player and a team when a game ends, and returns with them stronger for the next game. For off the ice, surrounded by suddenly smiling faces, everything seen from the angle of victory, everything easier, happier, every next thing easier still, living itself seems easier and fuller, and brimming with energy and confidence; playing does too. It is what happens when all teams used to losing finally win, but the Bruins, carrying the spirit of the team with them wherever they went, seemed to do it better. Scoring a record 399 goals and finishing easily in first place, as much as talent and muscle it was this powerful, uninhibited force so much a part of their personality that made them seem unbeatable.

Yet today, looking at a roster of the 1971 Canadiens, at first it seems hard to understand why we were such prohibitive underdogs. With players like Jacques Laperrière, Terry Harper, Lapointe, and J. C. Tremblay on defense; Béliveau, Cournoyer, Marc Tardif, Houle, Henri Richard, Lemaire, John Ferguson, Pete and Frank Mahovlich up front, it seems a formidable team. And in the playoffs that year, it was. But it was a team of players we remember from a different time: Béliveau, Frank Mahovlich, and Richard from the late fifties and sixties; Lemaire, Lapointe, Tardif, and Pete Mahovlich from the mid and late seventies; a team a little too old and a little too young, both past its prime and before it. Indeed, of all its players, only Cournoyer was at his peak in 1971. But for six weeks in the spring of that year, older players whose best years were past found what had made them special one last time, and younger players, their reputations still years away, found it for the first time, and we met the Bruins on even ground.

It was an eleven-day, seven-game kaleidoscope of scrambles, hotels, plane rides, and feelings, but very few memories now remain:

•   A bus ride from Boston's Logan Airport, the quotes of Bruins goalie Eddie Johnston in the *Boston Globe*, saying that his friends in Montreal had told him I was good. Rereading his words later at the hotel, never thinking it might be pre-playoff puffery, I took him seriously and felt better.

•   Surviving the first game and feeling an immense satisfaction I couldn't subdue, though we had lost 3-1.

•   Game 2. In the dressing room after the second period, behind 5-2, believing what he was about to say but almost embarrassed to say it, coach Al MacNeil telling us that the Bruins were too loose, that our chances would come, that the game was still unwon—then going out and scoring five goals in the third period and winning 7-5.

•   Seeing Johnny McKenzie, the Bruins' feisty winger, both his eyes blackened, a cut across his nose, and wondering how it had happened; finding out I had done it with my stick in a goal-mouth scramble.

•   Early in the second period of the fourth game, ahead 1-0, after I had made several improbable saves, I remember moving out of my net to knock away a loose puck, and instead watched as it looped off my stick and into the air. I saw Orr angle quickly to the boards after it, then reach up with his stick, swinging at it backhand. Frozen to the ice, I could only stand and watch the rest—as the puck flipped through the air, hit in front of the crease, and rolled into the empty net. Moments later, staring at the ice, waiting for the center-ice faceoff, I knew with deadening certainty what thirty-seven players, eighteen thousand Forum fans, and several million TV viewers knew with the same certainty—that my bubble had burst. A 5-2 loss.

• The heat in Boston Garden for the fifth game, the ice that felt like sandpaper, losing 7-3, and feeling confused by the mood of reporters afterwards; a series only three hours before tied 2-2 and considered a toss-up was now finally and unwinnably over.

• A goal, then suddenly hearing my name announced for an undeserved assist. Trying to follow the puck as it went into the Bruins' zone, slowly I became aware that people in the Forum were getting to their feet and cheering. Still following the puck, not sure what else to do, I was too busy, too shocked, to enjoy the only standing ovation I ever got.

• In our hotel near Boston, the eve of the seventh game, turning on a TV to "Bruins' Highlights" to watch in a relaxed way what had not been relaxed the first time. Then watching 15 Bruins goals on 15 Bruins shots and shutting it off.

• An anguished night's sleep, then being awakened by an early-morning phone call for tickets from a Cornell friend whose name I didn't recognize.

• Walking in back of the hotel, finding a small stream, sitting down on a bench beside it, waiting for the game.

• Hodge's goal, Bucyk's goal; and in between, four exciting goals for us by players I don't remember.

• A burning/freezing feeling. In my back, in my arms and neck, slow at first, then surging through my body. Hearing a referee's whistle, and looking at the clock—"0:32"—then at Orr, his stick across his knees, bent double, squeezing out the breath he couldn't find; at Esposito, sweat cascading down his face, his eyes, his cheeks and mouth drooping in weary sadness; then at our bench, standing, jumping, hugging each other, and *knowing*, for the first time, knowing it was over. Then it happened—seven games of feelings, too busy, too afraid to feel before, were suddenly released and swept over me, and for thirty-two seconds I got a rare and precious gift: I felt victory *while* it was happening.

• Noise, interviews, pictures that the next day showed me smiling more than I ever smile, then walking onto an almost-full team bus and hearing teammates clap, as if they didn't know me.

That's all. I remember nothing more, except that now when someone mentions that series, I get the same burning/freezing feeling through my body.

By the time I get back to the hotel, it is almost noon and the lobby has begun to fill again. Seminar groups and conventioneers spill noisily out of meeting rooms, businessmen who left alone return with others, disappearing quickly to the mezzanine for lunch. With only a few upholstered benches scattered around its edges, we are comfortable on railings and stairs, against pillars and walls, unnoticed, but unmistakably a team. We are younger and broader, in vibrant checked jackets and open-neck shirts; there is a look of youthful decadence about us. Many of us are unshaven, some have facial cuts or bruises, most have had their noses thickened, flattened, or bent in some way by years of elbows and high-sticks. But though we are widely dispersed in the lobby, it is a group that connects: passing around newspapers, talking, laughing across wide stretches of floor as if no one was in between, moving easily among ourselves, comfortable, uninhibited, used to being in crowds and ignoring them.

But while ostensibly doing other things, it is a group waiting: Houle with a two-day-old *Wall Street Journal* he brought from home; Savard marking his *Racing Form*; Lapointe and Ruel arguing loudly over his shoulder; a few read newspapers, some have cottage thrillers, well-curled and folded in their hands, others just sit and watch. Shutt jabbers with Lafleur, then gets up, says something to Jarvis and Risebrough, laughs his quick laugh, walks to the front window, walks back, picks up a discarded newspaper, leafs through its sections, and finding no sports section puts it down, and sits beside Lafleur again. Out of an elevator, looking swollen and rumpled, Chartraw, the last to know, asks who won the Islanders game. The rest watch their watches, those without them often asking the time, passing the news along to others. Then, a minute or two before 12 noon, Lemaire moves. Those around him jump, and together they move up the escalator to the first-floor banquet room.

I come along a few minutes later. The tables are almost set but there is no food, and I find a seat between Shutt and Lapointe. With others at the table, they're talking about Bowman. Lapointe is angry.

"*Tabernac*," he growls, "did ya hear him last night? 'Pretty good effort, gang.' Pretty good effort!" he repeats, getting angrier at the thought. "We were horseshit."

Drinking their water, the team at the table murmur agreement.

"Those two goals they got near the end," Robinson adds, shaking his head, "*câlisse*, that used to drive him crazy."

Lapointe continues, still angry, "How the hell we gonna win

this way?" he snaps. "He's gotta start givin' us some shit out there," and we nod again.

Shutt has been waiting for an opening; he jumps in with the clincher. "Hell, in practice the other day," he chirps, "I'm skatin' around, he calls me over, 'How're ya feelin', Steve?'" His eyes widen, as ours do. "What kinda question's that?" he complains. "I tell ya he's losin' his marbles."

More murmurs.

It has been a curious season for Bowman. Since Pollock's departure and Grundman's appointment, he has often seemed passive and indifferent. We allow "unimportant" goals near the end of an easy win, we arrive at practice a little later and leave a little sooner, we do what we seldom did before, what we were afraid to do, then brace ourselves for the outrage we know is coming, and none comes. Now, late in the season, the pattern we knew would quickly change has not changed, and we're worried. He's mellowing, we say to ourselves, or he's having a bad year, or he's leaving next year and doesn't care any more, or maybe he just wants to make Grundman look bad. But Bowman, being Bowman, never explains. Except there are two things he said earlier this season that are beginning to make sense to me. I remember them now only because I am looking for an explanation myself. In a strangely sympathetic tone, he told a reporter that it wasn't easy playing on a team like ours. That winning three straight Stanley Cups, expected to win each year and every game, we had been under enormous pressure for a long time. Then, a few weeks later, talking to us about team rules and fines, as an aside he said that rules or not, a team must really discipline itself.

A team that knows it's the best, that proves it's the best, gradually stops listening. It knows best, and if it doesn't, it must find that out for itself. This season, we weren't ready to be perfect all the time. We didn't want to feel the need to win every game we played, or to win a special way every time we did. We wanted to be like everyone else, to know that if we won, everyone would be happy; and if sometimes we lost, to know that everyone—coaches, management, press, and fans included—would pretend to survive the experience. We wanted to relax a bit, to enjoy ourselves. We didn't want Bowman's smothering heavy hand any more, and clear from our attitude was that if he tried to lay it on us, we would throw it off as best we could.

Mostly we have gotten what we wanted. Bowman has eased off, we have been far from perfect, losing more often, rarely showing any special flair when we win. Everyone—coaches, management, press, and fans—has shown remarkable patience and

restraint, each reminding himself often that to win four consecutive Cups is difficult, that no one can win all the time, and that the
season is far from over. And for a time, we did the same. But no
longer. We have discovered that we aren't very good at being like
everyone else. We've tried to be happy whenever we won, and not
so unhappy whenever we lost, but we can't do it. We've tried to
relax and enjoy ourselves, but not playing the way we want to play,
the way we can play, far from relaxed, we have found we can't enjoy
ourselves at all.

Now nearing the playoffs, an important game with the
Islanders a few days away, we try to tighten up our game, to give it
the consistency and direction we know it needs. When we can't
quite do it, those who complained most about Bowman's heavy
hand now complain loudest at its absence. After most of a season
having it our way, we are finally ready for Bowman. Yet still he does
nothing. What is he waiting for?

Eaten with more energy than appetite, lunch is over in its
usual twenty minutes, and noisily we disperse: some to the lobby,
taking up positions that were left only minutes before, some
browsing in the newsstand or in hotel shops; others leave for
movies across the street or on walks in various directions, but all of
us at some time return to our rooms for game shows or soaps, for
cards or backgammon, but mostly to sleep or read.

It is six hours and forty-five minutes to game time and
counting, but slowly.

I go up to the room and call Lynda: "Hi, how're ya doin'?
You're kidding! How long's he been—not the flu? Brother! Sarah's
okay? On the steps again! Oh no, how's she feelin'? Mmm, um,
hmm—well, um, what've you been doin'—no, no, no, I know. I
mean what else have ya been—since Tuesday night? Did Luc shovel
the driveway? Brother! Huh? Oh, fine, er, not too bad. It was really
cold in Toronto. You wouldn't have believed how cold—huh? In
Boston? Oh, um, not too bad. A bit windy. Huh? Oh, nothing
much. Just um, oh, not much really. Oh, I dunno, probably just
more of the same. . . ."

I lie down and take a nap.

Late in the afternoon, bored with napping and reading, I go
down to the lobby for something to do. Outside, through its tall,
patchwork windows I see several players in the parking lot in front,
bent over, huddling around something, arguing, pointing here
and there, crouching lower, still arguing and pointing, then
straightening up, some of them laughing, a few still arguing, and
walking back to a white line painted on the pavement. The laughing and arguing continue, then one by one they turn and approach
the line, pause, and flip quarters against the curb several feet away.

I go outside and watch. Loud and mocking, the happy banter keeps up. Yet as each player steps to the line, his mood changes. Brows knit, lips draw tight across teeth, smiles disappear. Quarters arc through the air, hit, bounce, and stop; faces turn anxious, then hopeful, then angry or jubilant: hundred-thousand-dollar-a-year men, many-time Stanley Cup winners, playing a game and wanting to win.

Lapointe and Shutt have their quarters near the curb; only Cam Connor and Lemaire are left. As Connor winds up, like Meadowlark Lemon at a foul shot, Lapointe walks in front of him, excuses himself, and walks back. Several more times, he pretends to do the same and Connor stutters and stops each time. At the side, Shutt makes rude comments. With each aborted try, the tension builds. Connor has gone in the hotel several times for change, and down to his last quarter, he tries again. Lapointe and Shutt stay (more or less) quiet and still; Connor's left foot starts ahead, his right arm moves back in a pendulum swing, then smoothly forward, until just before the moment of release his thumb twitches and the quarter skitters noisily across the pavement, stopping halfway to the curb. There are screams of laughter and more rude comments. Connor, not completely surprised, borrows some money from Robinson and goes for more change.

It is down to Lemaire. The heckling increases as he steps to the line and grins into the sun. Short, balding, like the Pillsbury doughboy all round and not very firm, his soft, wide face a sea of crinkles when he smiles, his laugh a tickled squeal he can't control, he looks far from formidable. But don't be fooled.

Last summer, we played a softball game at Quebec's giant James Bay hydro-electric development. One of about ten such games we play each summer, they are strictly good-time, beer-on-the-bus, run-the-bases-the-wrong-way stuff. But this night, through forty feet of twilight, we faced a hot pitcher. Lemaire, "Co" as he is called, was our lead-off batter. As he stepped to the plate, the chatter on the bench began:

"C'mon Co, get us started."

"He throws 'em like you shoot 'em, Co. No sweat out there."

Hah hah hah.

Lemaire swung and missed at the first pitch.

"Oooh, close Co, close," someone yelled. "Try a little more to the right."

"Yeah, and about six seconds sooner."

Hah hah hah.

Looking into the remaining light, we could see Lemaire's eyes twinkle and his mouth in a grin and we knew he was enjoying this as much as we were. Two balls, then one more swinging strike.

"Hey, that's better, Co," another voice shouted, "at least you're on the same pitch."

Hah hah hah.

Another ball and it's three-and-two. Readying himself, he stepped toward the next pitch, then held up in time, the catcher short-hopping the ball out of the dirt. Lemaire started for first base. "Strike three!" the umpire said.

Lemaire swung around, his squinting eyes flying open. On the bench, we began to laugh.

"Attaboy, Co. That's the start we needed."

Hah hah hah.

He said nothing, and turned and walked back to the bench. That twinkly face, the one that always collapsed and crinkled, now tightened and ground out words we could scarcely hear.

"It was low," he said.

The grin has left his face, his quarter flips through the air, hits, bounces, and stops just short of the curb. There is a loud yell. Shutt and Lapointe dance up and down screaming insults. Lemaire says nothing, just pumps his right arm at his side as he does when he scores a goal, and walks to the curb to collect his money. On a team of experienced, distinguished big-game players, no one is a better big-game player than Lemaire. It's his face that fools you.

A few minutes later, the bus driver sounds his horn and it is time to go. Everyone starts for the bus, except Connor. It has been a hard year for Connor. A first-round pick the year the Flyers won their first Stanley Cup, he went instead to the WHA, where he played until this season. But though he arrived to considerable expectations, slowly it has become clear that he lacks the skating and puck-handling skills necessary to be a regular, yet needs to be a regular to make his tough, team-oriented game work. So, unhappily between stools, he plays infrequently, even less than he might otherwise because of a series of quirky illnesses and injuries that by now seem to us as if they can only happen to him. He seems genuinely star-crossed this season, not tragically, for, loose and friendly like an ambling cowboy, he seems always able to find the funny side of things.

With everyone else walking to the bus, Connor finally has his chance. Laughing, he yells after those who beat him so mercilessly, "Ah hah, I'm not gonna lose this time," and taking a quarter from his pocket, he flips it towards the curb. The quarter hits, bounces, and rolls in a long, slow arc, disappearing down a drain.

Lapointe sits down in his right front seat, Lambert beside him, where until a few years ago Pete Mahovlich sat. Across from them, the seat remains empty as it has for most of the year, as Cournoyer's back has kept him out of all but a few games. I walk towards the rear of the bus and, just past halfway, turn in to the left, in front of where Jimmy Roberts sat until he was traded two years ago. I sit alone. Others come onto the bus turning in right or left, apparently at random. But nothing is random. Just as it is in the dressing room, we each have a seat that is ours, that is no less ours because once, often many years ago, we assigned it to ourselves.

Like anything else about a team, where we sit on a bus is part of a routine, automatic and unnoticed unless the routine is broken. As so much of our life seems random and inexplicable to us— goalposts, or unseen saves, a bouncing puck, a three-goal game— each part of our routine gets associated with good times and bad, and becomes superstition. So we sit where we do because if we didn't, we might sit in a seat important to someone else. And sitting where we do as much as we do, gradually where we sit becomes important to us. This has been my seat for seven years, and if someone wants to talk to me, he can come here and sit next to me.

At training camp, and the few times each year when injuries bring two or three new players to the team, it can be a problem. For new players, unfamiliar with our habits, sit *anywhere*, and one person in the wrong seat means someone else in the wrong seat until a simple chain of confusion becomes a mess. While most of us hover near our occupied seats wondering what to do and where to go, not quite willing to admit that a particular seat matters to us, someone will usually come along and say something—"Hey, get the fuck outa my seat"—to straighten out the problem. Over time, the rest of us have simply learned not to make that mistake. If someone momentarily forgets, we remind him—"Hey, don't change the luck"—and he will move. He knows that if he doesn't, and we lose, it's his fault.

The bus is quiet but comfortable. Preoccupied with other things, we don't notice its silence. A few minutes later, gradually aware of it, we become self-conscious and uncomfortable, and make some noise, but still it is only conversation between seat partners or across aisles, nothing that can be heard more than a row or two away. Mostly we say nothing, because at times such as this, talk can seem an annoying distraction, taking us ahead in time, suspending our mood until it drops us abruptly closer to the game than we are prepared for. Only a few who need to talk as spillover for tensions that build too high do so, because anything too much, too loud, unrelated to the Bruins or to us, can and will be misconstrued as someone not thinking about the game, and not ready to play. We know that at the back, Bowman and Ruel watch and listen, noticing nothing until four hours, four days, four weeks from now when we lose, then remembering everything that happened in between.

The bus turns onto Causeway Street under the permanent shade and grime of the meccano-like elevated "Green Line" of the MBTA. On one side of the street are burger joints and shabby bars; on the other is a huge brick structure joined on the outside, divided inside into the derelict Hotel Madison, North Station (of the Boston and Maine Railroad), and Boston Garden. In front of the Madison, a tattered, weathered man, maybe forty, maybe sixty, staggers along the sidewalk, here and there raising a brown paper bag to his face and tipping it back. Stopped by traffic, we sit and watch. Finally tipping it back too far, he loses his balance and stumbles to the sidewalk. "Hey, must be an old goalie," a voice shouts, and everyone laughs. Several times a season, a spaced-out face singing in an airport, a patron passed out in a bar, someone in loud conversation with himself, anyone whose mental, physical, or emotional state seems the slightest bit shaky, it's always the same thing: "Must be an old goalie."

I have always been a goalie. I became one long enough ago, before others' memories and reasons intruded on my own, that I can no longer remember why I did, but if I had to guess, it was because of Dave. Almost six years older, he started playing goal before I was old enough to play any position, so by the time I was six and ready to play, there was a set of used and discarded equipment that awaited me—that and an older brother I always tried to emulate.

I have mostly vague recollections of being a goalie at that time. I remember the spectacular feeling of splitting and sprawling on pavement or ice, and feeling that there was something somehow noble and sympathetic about having bruises and occasional cuts, especially if they came, as they did, from only a tennis ball. But if I have one clear image that remains, it is that of a goalie, his right knee on the ice, his left leg extended in a half splits, his left arm stretching for the top corner, and, resting indifferently in his catching glove, a round black puck.

It was the posed position of NHL goalies for promotional photos and hockey cards at the time and it was a position we tried to re-enact as often as we could in backyard games. There was something that looked and felt distinctly major league about a shot "raised" that high, and about a clean, precise movement into space to intercept it. Coming as it did without rebound, it allowed us to freeze the position as if in a photo, extending the moment, letting our feelings catch up to the play, giving us time to step outside ourselves and see what we had done. In school, or at home, with pencil and paper, sometimes thinking of what I was doing, more often just mindlessly doodling, I would draw pictures of goalies, not much more than stick figures really, but fleshed out with parallel lines, and always in that same catching position. Each year when my father arranged for a photographer to take pictures for our family's Christmas card, as Dave and I readied ourselves in our nets, the shooter was told to shoot high to the glove side, that we had rehearsed the rest.

To catch a puck or a ball—it was the great joy of being a goalie. Like a young ballplayer, too young to hit for much enjoyment but old enough to catch and throw, it was something I could do before I was big enough to do the rest. But mostly it was the feeling it gave me. Even now, watching TV or reading a newspaper, I like to have a ball in my hands, fingering its laces, its seams, its nubby surface, until my fingertips are so alive and alert that the ball and I seem drawn to each other. I like to spin it, bounce it, flip it from hand to hand, throw it against a wall or a ceiling, and catch it over and over again. There is something quite magical about a hand that can follow a ball and find it so crisply and tidily every time, something solid and wonderfully reassuring about its muscular certainty and control. So, if it was because of Dave that I became a goalie, it was the feeling of catching a puck or a ball that kept me one. The irony, of course, would be that later, when I finally became a real goalie instead of a kid with a good glove hand, when I learned to use the other parts of a goaltender's equipment—skates, pads, blocker, stick—it could only be at the expense of what had been until then my greatest joy as a goalie.

I was nineteen at the time. It surely had been happening before then, just as it must before any watershed moment, but the time I remember was the warm-up for the 1967 NCAA final against Boston University. For the first few minutes, I remember only feeling good: a shot, a save, a shot, a save; loose, easy, the burn of nerves turning slowly to a burn of exhilaration. For a shot to my right, my right arm went up and I stopped it with my blocker; another, low to the corner, I kicked away with my pad; along the ice to the other side, my skate; high to the left, my catching glove. Again and again: a pad, a catching glove, a skate, a stick, a blocker, whatever was closest moved, and the puck stopped. For someone who had scooped up ice-skimming shots like a shortstop, who had twisted his body to make backhanded catches on shots for the top right corner, it was a moment of great personal triumph. I had come of age. As the warm-up was ending, I could feel myself becoming a goalie.

Goaltending is often described as the most dangerous position in sports. It is not. Race drivers die from racing cars, jockeys die, so do football players. Goalies do not die from being goalies. Nor do they suffer the frequent facial cuts, the knee and shoulder injuries, that forwards and defensemen often suffer. They stand as obstacles to a hard rubber disc, frequently shot at a lethal speed, sometimes unseen, sometimes deflected; the danger to them is obvious, but it is exaggerated—even the unthinkable: a goalie diving anxiously out of the way of a 100 m.p.h. slap shot, the shooter panicking at his own recklessness, the fans "ah"-ing at the near miss. Except for that one, feared time, the time it doesn't happen that way, when the puck moves too fast and the goalie too slow, and, hit in the head, he falls frighteningly to the ice. Moments later, up again, he shakes his head, smiling as others slowly do the same, again reminded that he wears a mask which at other times he sees through and forgets. The danger of playing goal is a *potential* danger, but equipment technology, like a net below a trapeze act, has made serious injury extremely unlikely.

From the time I was six years old, until as a freshman at Cornell I was required to wear a mask, I received fifteen stitches. Since then I have had only four—from a Dennis Hull slap shot that rebounded off my chest, hitting under my chin, in my first playoff year. I have pulled groins and hamstrings, stretched, twisted, and bruised uncounted times various other things, sent my back into spasm twice, broken a toe, and torn the cartilege in one knee. In almost eight years, after more than 400 games and 1000 practices, that's not much.

Yet, I am often afraid. For while I am well protected, and know I'm unlikely to suffer more than a bruise from any shot that is taken, the puck hurts, constantly and cumulatively: through the pillow-thick leg pads I wear, where straps pulled tight around their shins squeeze much of the padding away; through armor-shelled skate boots; through a catching glove compromised too far for its flexibility; with a dull, aching nausea from stomach to throat when my jock slams back against my testes; and most often, on my arms, on wrists and forearms especially, where padding is light and often out of place, where a shot hits and spreads its ache, up an arm and through a body, until both go limp and feel lifeless. Through a season, a puck hurts like a long, slow battering from a skillful boxer, almost unnoticed in the beginning, but gradually wearing me down, until two or three times a year, I wake up in the morning sore, aching, laughing/moaning with each move I make, and feel a hundred years old. It is on those days and others that when practice comes, I shy away.

The puck on his stick, a player skates for the net. Deep in my crouch, intent, ready, to anyone watching I look the same as I always do. But, like a batter who has been knocked down too many times before, when I see a player draw back his stick to shoot, at the critical moment when concentration must turn to commitment, my body stiffens, my eyes widen and go sightless, my head lifts in the air, turning imperceptibly to the right, as if away from the puck—I bail out, leaving only an empty body behind to cover the net. I yell at myself as others might ("you chicken"). I tell myself reasonably, rationally, that lifting my head, blanking my eyes, can only put me in greater danger; but I don't listen. In a game, each shot controlled by a harassing defense, with something else to think about I can usually put away fear and just play. But in practice, without the distraction of a game, seeing Tremblay or Lambert, Risebrough, Chartraw, or Lupien, dangerous, uncontrolled shooters as likely to hit my arms as a corner of the net, I cannot. In time the fear gradually shrinks back, manageable again, but it never quite goes away.

I have thought more about fear, I have been afraid more often, the last few years. For the first time this year, I have realized that I've only rarely been hurt in my career. I have noticed that unlike many, so far as I know, I carry with me no permanent injury. And now that I know I will retire at the end of the season, more and more I find myself thinking—*I've lasted this long: please let me get out in one piece.* For while I know I am well protected, while I know it's unlikely I will suffer any serious injury, like every other goalie I carry with me the fear of the *one big hurt* that never comes. Recently, I read of the retirement of a race-car driver. Explaining his decision to quit, he said that after his many years of racing, after the deaths of close friends and colleagues, after his own near misses, he simply "knew too much." I feel a little differently. I feel I have known all along what I know now. It's just that I can't forget it as easily as I once did.

Playing goal is not fun. Behind a mask, there are no smiling faces, no timely sweaty grins of satisfaction. It is a grim, humorless position, largely uncreative, requiring little physical movement, giving little physical pleasure in return. A goalie is simply there, tied to a net and to a game; the game acts, a goalie reacts. How he reacts, how often, a hundred shots or no shots, is not up to him. Unable to initiate a game's action, unable to focus its direction, he can only do what he's given to do, what the game demands of him, and that he must do. It is his job, a job that cannot be done one minute in every three, one that will not await rare moments of genius, one that ends when the game ends, and only then. For while a goal goes up in lights, a permanent record for the goal-scorer and the game, a save is ephemeral, important at the time, occasionally when a game is over, but able to be wiped away, undone, with the next shot. It is only when a game ends and the mask comes off, when the immense challenge of the job turns abruptly to immense satisfaction or despair, that the unsmiling grimness lifts and goes away.

If you were to spend some time with a team, without ever watching them on the ice, it wouldn't take long before you discovered who its goalies were. Goalies are different. Whether it's because the position attracts certain personality types, or only permits certain ones to succeed; whether the experience is so intense and fundamental that it transforms its practitioners to type—I don't know the answer. But whatever it is, the differences between "players" and "goalies" are manifest and real, transcending as they do even culture and sport.

A few years ago, at a reception at the Canadian Embassy in Prague, the wife of Jiri Holecek, former star goalie for Czechoslovakia, was introduced to Lynda, and immediately exclaimed, "The players think my Jiri's crazy. Do they [my teammates] think your husband's crazy too?" (No more of the conversation was related to me.) For his book on soccer goalies, English journalist Brian Glanville chose as his title *Goalkeepers Are Different*. It is all part of the mythology of the position, anticipated, expected, accepted, and believed; and in many ways real.

Predictably, a goalie is more introverted than his teammates, more serious (for team pictures, when a photographer tells me to smile, unsmilingly I tell him, "Goalies don't smile"), more sensitive and moody ("ghoulies"), more insecure (often unusually "careful" with money; you might remember Johnny Bower and I *shared* a cab). While a goalie might sometimes be gregarious and outgoing, it usually manifests itself in binges—when a game is over, or on the day of a game when he isn't playing—when he feels himself released from a game. Earlier this season, minutes before a game with the Rangers in the Forum, Robinson looked across the dressing room at me and asked, "Who's playing?" Before I could answer, Shutt yelled back, "I'll give ya a hint, Bird," he said. "Bunny's in the shitter puking; Kenny hasn't shut up since he got here." While teams insist on togetherness, and on qualities in their teammates that encourage it both on and off the ice, a goalie is the one player a team allows to be different. Indeed, as perplexed as anyone at his willingness to dress in cumbrous, oversized equipment to get hit by a puck, a team allows a goalie to sit by himself on planes or buses, to disappear on road trips, to reappear and say nothing for long periods of time, to have a single room when everyone else has roommates. After all, *shrug*, he's a goalie. What can you expect? Flaky, crazy, everything he does accepted and explained away, it offers a goalie wonderful licence. It was what allowed Gilles Gratton to "streak" a practice, and Gary Smith to take showers between periods. In many ways, it is also why my teammates accepted my going to law school.

Good goalies come in many shapes, sizes, and styles. So do bad goalies. A goalie is often plump (Savard, a defenceman, always insists "I like my goalies fat"), sometimes unathletic, and with reflex reactions surprisingly similar to those of the average person (recently at a science museum, with a flashing light and a buzzer I tested my eye-hand reactions against Lynda's; she was slightly faster). While most might agree on what the ideal physical and technical goalie-specimen might look like, it almost certainly would be a composite—the physical size of Tretiak, the elegance of Parent, the agility of Giacomin or Cheevers, the bouncy charisma of Vachon or Resch—with no quarantee that *supergoalie* would be any good. For while there are certain minimum standards of size, style, and agility that any goalie must have, goaltending is a remarkably aphysical activity.

If you were to ask a coach or a player what he would most like to see in a goalie, he would, after some rambling out-loud thoughts, probably settle on something like: consistency, dependability, and the ability to make the big save. Only in the latter, and then only in part, is the physical element present. Instead, what these qualities suggest is a certain character of mind, a mind that need not be nimble or dextrous, for the demands of the job are not complex, but a mind emotionally disciplined, one able to be focussed and directed, a mind under control. Because the demands on a goalie are mostly mental, it means that for a goalie the biggest enemy is himself. Not a puck, not an opponent, not a quirk of size or style. Him. The stress and anxiety he feels when he plays, the fear of failing, the fear of being embarrassed, the fear of being physically hurt, all are symptoms of his position, in constant ebb and flow, but never disappearing. The successful goalie understands these neuroses, accepts them, and puts them under control. The unsuccessful goalie is distracted by them, his mind in knots, his body quickly following.

It is why Vachon was superb in Los Angeles and as a high-priced free-agent messiah, poor in Detroit. It is why Dan Bouchard, Tretiak-sized, athletic, technically flawless, lurches annoyingly in and out of mediocrity. It is why there are good "good team" goalies and good "bad team" goalies—Gary Smith, Doug Favell, Denis Herron. The latter are spectacular, capable of making near-impossible saves that few others can make. They are essential for bad teams, winning them games they shouldn't win, but they are goalies who need a second chance, who need the cushion of an occasional bad goal, knowing that they can seem to earn it back later with several inspired saves. On a good team, a goalie has few near-impossible saves to make, but the rest he must make, and playing in close and critical games as he does, he gets no second chance.

A good "bad team" goalie, numbed by the volume of goals he cannot prevent, can focus on brilliant saves and brilliant games, the only things that make a difference to a poor team. A good "good team" goalie cannot. Allowing few enough goals that he feels every one, he is driven instead by something else—the penetrating hatred of letting in a goal.

The great satisfaction of playing goal comes from the challenge it presents. Simply stated, it is to give the team what it needs, when it needs it, not when I feel well-rested, injury-free, warmed-up, psyched-up, healthy, happy, and able to give it, but when *the team* needs it. On a team as good as the Canadiens, often it will need nothing; other times, one good save, perhaps two or three; maybe five good minutes, a period, sometimes, though not often, a whole game. Against better teams, you can almost predict what and when it might be; against the rest, you cannot. You simply have to be ready.

During my first two years with the team, for reasons none of us could figure out, we would start games slowly, outplayed for most of the first period, occasionally for a little longer. It happened so regularly that it became a pattern we anticipated and prepared for, each of us with a special role to play. Mine was to keep the score sufficiently close in the first period, usually to within one goal, so as not to discourage any comeback—their role—that otherwise we would almost certainly make. We were a good combination. I could feel heroically beleaguered the first period, all the time knowing that it would end, that we would soon get our stride, and when we did that I would become a virtual spectator to the game.

That has changed. It began to change the next season, and for the last four years, the change has been complete. A much better team than earlier in the decade, it needs less from me now, just pockets of moments that for me and others sometimes seem lost in a game. But more than that, what it needs now is not to be distracted—by bad goals, by looseness or uncertainty in my play. It needs only to feel secure, confident that the defensive zone is taken care of; the rest it can do itself.

It makes my job different from that of every other goalie in the NHL. I get fewer shots, and fewer *hard* shots; I must allow fewer goals, the teams I play on must win Stanley Cups. Most envy me my job, some are not so sure. Once Vachon, my predecessor in Montreal, in the midst of one of his excellent seasons in Los

Angeles, told me that he wasn't sure he would ever want to play for the Canadiens again, even if he had the chance. He said he had come to enjoy a feeling he knew he would rarely have in Montreal—the feeling of winning a game for his team—and he wasn't sure how well he could play without it. In a speech a few years ago, my brother talked about the heroic self-image each goalie needs and has, and is allowed to have because of the nature and perception of his position. "A solitary figure," "a thankless job," "facing an onslaught," "a barrage," "like Horatio at the bridge"—it's the stuff of backyard dreams. It is how others often see him; it is how he sometimes sees himself. I know the feeling Vachon described because I felt it early in my career, when the team wasn't as good as it is now. It is a feeling I have learned to live without.

But something else has changed, something that is more difficult to live without. Each year, I find it harder and harder to make a connection between a Canadiens win and me—nothing so much as my winning a game for the team, just a timely save, or a series of saves that made a difference, that arguably made a difference, that *might* have made a difference, that, as with a baseball pitcher, can make a win feel mine and ours. But as the team's superiority has become entrenched, and as the gap between our opponents and us, mostly unchanged, has come to seem wider and more permanent, every save I make seems without urgency, as if it is done completely at my own discretion, a minor bonus if made, a minor inconvenience, quickly overcome, if not.

A few months ago, we played the Colorado Rockies at the Forum. Early in the game, I missed an easy shot from the blueline, and a little unnerved, for the next fifty minutes I juggled long shots, and allowed big rebounds and three additional goals. After each Rockies goal, the team would put on a brief spurt and score quickly, and so with only minutes remaining, the game was tied. Then the Rockies scored again, this time a long, sharp-angled shot that squirted through my legs. The game had seemed finally lost. But in the last three minutes, Lapointe scored, then Lafleur, and we won 6-5. Alone in the dressing room afterwards, I tried to feel angry at my own performance, to feel relieved at being let off the uncomfortable hook I had put myself on, to laugh at what a winner could now find funny; but I couldn't. Instead, feeling weak and empty, I just sat there, unable to understand why I felt the way I did. Only slowly did it come to me: I had been irrelevant; I couldn't even lose the game.

I catch few shots now, perhaps only two or three a game. I should catch more, but years of concussion have left the bones in my hand and wrist often tender and sore, and learning to substitute a leg or a stick to save my hand, my catching glove, reprogrammed and out of practice, often remains at my side. Moreover, the game has changed. Bigger players now clutter the front of the net, obstructing and deflecting shots, or, threatening to do both, they distract a goalie, causing rebounds, making clean, precise movements into space—commitments to a single option unmindful of possible deflection or rebound—an indulgence for which a price is too often paid. What I enjoy most about goaltending now is the game itself: feeling myself slowly immerse in it, finding its rhythm, anticipating it, getting there before it does, challenging it, controlling a play that should control me, making it go where I want it to go, moving easily, crushingly within myself, delivering a clear, confident message to the game. And at the same time, to feel my body slowly act out that feeling, pushing up taller and straighter, thrusting itself forward, clenched, flexed, at game's end released like an untied balloon, its feeling spewing in all directions until the next game.

I enjoy the role I play—now rarely to win a game, but not to lose it; a game fully in my hands, fully in the hands of my teammates, and between us an unstated trust, a quiet confidence, and the results we want. Our roles have changed, but we remain a good combination, and I find that immensely satisfying.

Without Orr and Esposito, the Bruins, high-fliers for nearly a decade, play that way no longer. Brad Park, traded from New York, has taken on a more economical and more realistic style, and is once again one of the league's best defensemen. Jean Ratelle, also acquired from the Rangers in the Esposito trade, has had some of his most productive seasons. But unlike Orr and Esposito, they are quiet stars, most effective when supplementing the action, not commanding it themselves, letting it emerge past them, then acting as its necessary cutting edge. Playing a new frill-less but still combative style, the Bruins have become a team built from the bottom up, its personality and direction coming from a tough, hard-working, semi-skilled core—Stan Jonathan, Mike Milbury, Bobby Schmautz, John Wensink, Gary Doak, and especially Wayne Cashman, Terry O'Reilly and Don Marcotte—"Lunch Pail A.C." is what coach Don Cherry appropriately calls them. Once a team with the two great superstars of the sport, it is a team that now seems without stars, no longer a Stanley Cup contender yet intensely competitive in another way, and just good enough to fool you sometimes.

From the opening faceoff, the Bruins get possession, and send the puck into our left corner and pile after it. O'Reilly and

Marcotte slam Lapointe against the glass, the puck bounces between skates and sticks, out of the corners to the front of the net and back, until desperately Lapointe shoots it over the blueline to center. It goes to Milbury, who shoots it back in, and the chase begins again. Jonathan, Schmautz, Cashman, Wensink, O'Reilly, and Marcotte again, for five or six minutes it continues (it will be the same for three or four minutes at the start of the second period, for two or three minutes at the start of the third, a little longer if they score, a little shorter if they don't), for as long as they can keep up the pace. Now O'Reilly and Marcotte, Jonathan and Cashman slam Lapointe against the glass, but a little too late. The puck is already moving to the wing, to open men with open ice; and slowly we come to direct the game. Later, with penalties and random scoring chances, the game will swing again, but not for long, and always it swings back. Against the Bruins, a game never searches for direction; it is only its result that seems unsure.

The Bruins and Canadiens in Boston Garden is my favorite game to play: bursting with energy and commitment, our speed always threatening to break out, on the smaller ice surface their strength and muscle usually holding us back, making us be stronger, making them go faster, bringing out the fullest and best in both of us. Too cramped and bruising for pretty plays, too gut-involving, it is a game of players, not skills, and without such distractions, a game where you see *people*, unguarded and exposed, and come away thinking you know them:

• O'Reilly, racing, spinning, falling, everything faster, harder, than he can control; on his knees, on his back, usually with someone else, up again before the other guy is.

• Cashman, skating bent and stiff like an old man with a sore back, chopping ahead with effort and little speed, getting where he needs to go.

• Park, like a fire hydrant on a freeway, players moving quickly by on either side of him, but knowing the lanes that players use for skating and passing, intercepting them, then starting up with his quick windmill stride, moving thirty feet to another play.

• Cheevers, playing goal like a defenseman, playing the man instead of the puck, knowing the man, knowing the situation and moving first; like a high-roller in a crap shoot, knowing if he's wrong, his luck will change.

• Cherry, standing in back of the bench, on the bench, on top of the boards, screaming and gesturing ostensibly to the referee; standing down again, quiet, a tiny permanent grin on his face, like a ten-year-old kid holding a stink bomb behind his back.

• And the crowd, brawny and rough like its team, but without the meanness of crowds in Philadelphia or New York. Under it all, something good-natured and generous that shows through. It's a crowd expressive and involved, building with the action, suddenly swarming over you, shrill at first, then deep and resounding, making the exciting more exciting, fusing excitement into the game before it can escape.

• And the Garden itself: old and dirty, not unlike sports neighbor Fenway Park, but its quirks unsoftened, uneulogized by the romance of baseball, and what makes Fenway a cherished anomaly makes the Garden an embarrassment. For me it is special. It has to do with three ECAC championships and 2,000 Cornell fans sounding as people on pilgrimage sound. It has to do with the 1971 series, and with a game four years later, when, after a year out of hockey and struggling in a comeback, I was reminded that I still could play. It has to do with the Bruins, Boston University, Boston College, and Harvard, good, tough competition that makes seasons interesting, exciting, and worthwhile. It has to do with winning and rarely losing, and never losing an important game.

The Boston Garden ice surface is small enough to involve me in every game. Its steep, balconied seats bring intimate, exciting contact between the fans and us, and the game. And in an age when new arenas go up like modern cathedrals, often dramatic on the outside, usually uniform and dull inside, the Garden is engagingly maladroit: its huge scoreboard clock that hangs distinctly off-center; its commemorative banners, on one side of center ice, thirteen large "WORLD CHAMPIONS" banners, green and white for the Celtics—on the other in yellow and black those of the Bruins, one each for sixteen Division Championships and four Stanley Cups, all cluttered together, looking like the morning wash; its dull red seats that hide dirt and always look dirty; the ubiquitous flat yellow wash that covers its walls and balcony facings, the one great attempt to brighten it up, not glossy, not bright, looking at least one coat too thin. All of it together somehow fits, giving the Garden its unique personality. To me, Boston Garden is like a dishevelled friend.

First the Bruins, then us, but neither of us able to take the game in hand, finally it settles into its usual twisting, swinging equilibrium. Then, early in the third period, when we're behind 2-1, Robinson ties the game on a power play; and a few minutes later, Tremblay wins it.

We pile onto the bus in a winner's high, loud and loose, full of ourselves, full of a feeling beyond our control. At the back, strangely playful, Bowman and Ruel argue about the game, Bowman looking around, smiling, winking at those who turn to listen,

Ruel arguing on. But beneath the noise and energy, there is something else. At the front, a bus-length away from Bowman and Ruel, a voice whispers to each of us as we pass to our seats, "Need any?" and the whispered answers vary.

From two or three duffel bags almost out of sight on the floor, passed with the invisible randomness of a sidewalk spy exchange, slipped quickly under coats, into pockets or bags—beer, still chilled and sweating, dispensed like precious contraband. At our seats cans are taken out, smothered over by coats to muffle the tiny explosions as they're opened, then elbows unraised, heads untilted, chins tuck, wrists turn, and bodies slide out of sight down the backs of seats, lower as the cans empty. Finally as each is drained, it is stuffed back into pockets or bags to be disposed of later. Officially, there is no drinking on the bus; unofficially, the same rite is performed after every game.

The bus starts up, the beer spills down, and words begin to flow. One by one, laser-like reading lights extinguish; one by one tiny orange discs appear, glowing brightly with each languorous breath, as cigar smokers, with the world by its tail, settle into their mood. And slowly, as the bus turns from dusk to dark, the talk softens and runs out of steam. It is now when a game feels best, when bodies and minds clenched all day suddenly release and feelings gently wash over you. Lying back in my seat, my eyes wide open, I let it happen.

Nearing the airport, the bus bounces to an abrupt halt. Left unsecured on a seat, an empty beer can jumps to the floor and shatters everything. Backs settled in comfortably spring upright and freeze, and wait; and there is more silence. But when the driver starts up again, the can begins to roll. And roll. Under seats, between feet dancing to get in its way, on and on for long, anguished seconds. "Jesus Christ," we murmur and scream at the same time, "somebody stop it!" But no one can. Then, just as abruptly as it all began, it stops, and is silent again. Our shoulders still hunched, our heads unmoving, we wait. But the voice at the back says nothing. Relieved and excited, we can't believe our luck. We've gotten away with it again.

Of course, at the back of the bus, Bowman and Ruel know exactly what's going on. They know about the beer, they can guess at the duffel bags, the coats, and everything else. But by being discreet, we have made it seem possible that they don't know. We've allowed them to avoid the uncomfortable position of having to accept what they feel they cannot, or reject what they know they should not. Instead, far from the action, they can officially "not know." And they will continue not knowing until indiscreetly we lose a few games. Then, what went so long unseen will mysteriously flare to their attention—"That's it, drink up," the voice at the back will say. "Ya forget we lost, Tremblay?" But tonight we played our parts well, and so will they. Officially, it must have been a pop can.

Last Sunday, the Sabres reminded us that we could still play the way we need to play; tonight, we confirmed to ourselves that nothing much has changed. Though almost the same thing, there is in fact an important difference. For the Sabres game, bringing with it no special expectations, need not have happened, at least not then. But tonight could have been no other way, no other time. In the career of any player, there is a time when he will not get any better, when he can only work and struggle, and hope not to get worse. In the cycle of any team, it is the same. For the team and me, it is that time now. Disappointed that we've shown our special skills so rarely, excited here and there when we do, frustrated again when they go away, none the less we can be optimistic that tomorrow or the next day or next week those skills will return for good. For we have seen them and felt them, we know they are there. But other things can't be passed off until tomorrow. They must be met as they come, as they always had been met, and if they aren't, it will mean something is undeniably different, something which now cannot be reversed. We might have played poorly and lost to the Sabres, for we often do. We can't play poorly against the Bruins and not know something has changed. So moments ago, in the sound of words and laughter streaming loudly through the bus, there was excitement, and immense relief.

Like a stop-watch to a sprinter, it is the reliable opponent that tells a team where it stands. The Bruins are not as good as we are, and so in Montreal we win, and in Boston we tie or win; but the difference between us is small, and by playing their best as they always do, they force us to play our best, so each time we play them we find out what our best is. And I find out mine. It is an important thing to know, and year after year, only the Bruins do that for us.

As a senior at Cornell, I was co-winner of Boston University's "most honored opponent" award, given for games against BU through a college career. Though I had won other, more prestigious awards, it was one that meant much to me, for BU had meant much to me as a player. Our closest Eastern rival, they were the necessary other side in many of my most fundamental moments, the inspiration and competitive prod for them, irrevocably and fondly associated with them. My first season, starting because of an injury to the team's senior goalie, I played through several promising but undistinguished games, on the verge of something more, yet timorously waiting. After a 3-3 double overtime tie with BU, I suddenly felt I could make it the way I wanted to make it. I had broken through. A few months later, we played twice within a week: in the first period of the ECAC final, I survived great pressure to learn something about myself I needed to know; then, during the warm-up for the NCAA championship game, feeling skates, pads, gloves, and stick move the way they never did, I could feel myself a real goalie for the first time. There were other games other years with lesser BU teams, not quite good enough to expose new strengths or weaknesses in us, but good enough to make us confirm what was already there, which games against other teams seldom did.

What BU was, what the Bruins are now, is a good opponent, a rare and treasured thing for any team or player. For a good opponent defines a player or a team. By forcing you to be as good as you can be, such an opponent stretches the boundaries of your emotional and playing experience, giving you your highest highs and lowest lows; your best and worst and hardest moments. When you get to an age or to a moment that causes you to look back, you realize how important that is. After years of games and feelings, it is only those boundaries, those special highs and lows, that remain; the rest, with nothing special to distinguish them one from another, gradually just disappear.

It is why good teams and good players, good enough to stand alone, stand straighter and more vividly with a good opponent: the Yankees with the Dodgers, Borg with McEnroe, Ali and Frazier, names permanently linked because in fact they needed each other. After days and weeks of Red Sox and White Sox, Wepners, Nastases, and Mildenbergers, each needed a good opponent to make him best, to make him memorable, to give him cherished lifelong feelings. So, when a career ends, when the passion of the game subsides, towards a good opponent you feel only gratitude.

Friday

MONTREAL

EDDY PALCHAK LEFT THE FORUM AT 3 O'CLOCK THIS MORN-
ing. When our charter from Boston landed, as we walked to cars
that would take us home, Palchak, with assistant Pierre Meilleur,
was unloading equipment bags from the plane into a van that
would take them to the Forum. There, he and Meilleur unpacked
the bags, hanging the equipment to dry, piling underwear, socks,
jocks, and sweaters in the laundry room to be washed by a Forum
assistant when he arrived early this morning. Then, with only a few
hours' sleep, at 9:30 a.m. he was back, setting out a second set of
underwear, sharpening several pairs of skates for the noon practice.
By 3:30 this afternoon, more than an hour after the last player has
left, he will leave the Forum again. Tomorrow, with a game at
night, he will arrive for our morning skate an hour earlier than
usual, at 8:30, leaving again at 1, arriving back at the Forum at 5,
finally finding his bed in a Philadelphia hotel, after the game, after
the plane ride, after unpacking the bags and hanging up the wet
equipment at the Spectrum, some time after 3 a.m.

For Palchak, a friendly, conscientious man with a round
pillow face and wonderful Buddy Hackett-like smile, it is a familiar
routine. In the 250 days between mid-September and mid-May, he
will work every day but Christmas and two or three others that he
won't know about until the day before. For more than twelve

years, first as assistant trainer, now as trainer, of the Canadiens, it has been his life-style, and now, late in the season, he is beginning to feel it as he always does.

He is tired. It happens to him slowly, but with next week always worse than the week before, until about now, listless and drained, he hits bottom. Tomorrow, he thinks, with a good night's sleep he'll feel better, so today's work is put off until tomorrow, and by mid-afternoon he's back in his apartment for the sleep he knows will never come. A few hours later, still awake, he goes to a nearby restaurant for dinner. Then, instead of a movie or going to the race track as he might have done in October, he returns to his apartment, watching TV until he falls asleep. Tomorrow, he wakes up one day more tired, with more than one day's work to do. A bachelor, Palchak has a girlfriend, but working during the week she finds it hard to go out on week nights; Palchak, occasionally free during the week, works weekends. Friday was once their night, the night their schedules brought them together. But now, for Palchak, nearing forty and feeling it, Friday is a night to rest up for the weekend.

Though he never complains, for the last few years he has found each year a little harder. The travel seems worse, though it probably isn't, the equipment bags, trunks, and everything else have come to feel heavier, and they aren't. And though he suffers none of the back problems beginning to plague some of his veteran NHL colleagues, since dropping a portable skate-sharpening machine on his left knee last season he's had trouble with all the lifting his job requires. But mostly what gets him down, when anything does, is the hours: every day for most of the day, for much of the year, a life-style that allows little else to intrude. When others eat, when others sleep, when others go to the movies or to the track, Palchak can't. Instead, he gets by on snacks, sleeping when he can, eating on the run, everything else waiting for the season to end. On planes, sitting in the middle of a card game—asleep; working through lunch and dinner, eating mid-afternoons and midnights, a life even farther from the mainstream than our own. Yet it's a life he enjoys. For he knows the feeling he has now will soon disappear, that as playoffs draw close, energy systematically drained away by a season will mysteriously reappear, the feeling forgotten until next year at this time. He may get tired at times of acting as nursemaid and general "go-fer" for twenty high-strung athletes, and easily forget that he is part of a team, but tomorrow, Sunday, Tuesday, soon, he knows there will be a big win, an excited "My skates were super, Eddy," and everything will feel different again.

Neither management nor player, Palchak inhabits the delicate middle ground, getting along with both at the expense of neither, trusted by both even when sometimes we don't trust each other. Quiet and unobtrusive, he enjoys the background and manages the role with instinctive ease. When either side tries to gain quick advantage, as each sometimes does, and looks for his help— Bowman by asking him the off-ice habits of players; the players about travel schedules which Bowman keeps to himself—Palchak hasn't heard anything, he hasn't seen anything. And if it's clear he has, he will skillfully avoid the question, without confrontation, without hard feeling, or direct it to where it more properly should go. He knows that if he compromises the dual trust he holds and becomes a "player's man" or a "coach's spy," he can never reverse the compromise, and cannot do his job. For it's up to him to be the unseen man, to do what needs to be done, without flash, without fail, without disturbing the players or coaches from what they must do. He is a survivor in a survivor's job. Palchak has gone through four coaches, four sets of owners, and two generations of players; he will go through more.

Sick and tired of being sick and tired. It is how February feels and it's how I feel this morning. I wake with a cold I didn't have when I went to bed a few hours ago, my body sore like the second day of training camp, stiff and tight like eggshells, breaking apart with brittle pain each move I make. A few years ago, it was a feeling I almost enjoyed, the pain a reminder of what I had gone through to feel that way, feeling old, and knowing I wasn't; knowing that the pain would soon go away to make me feel even better. But now, though it will go away and be gone when it must be gone, it stays longer, just long enough to make me wonder if this time it might stay.

After I park in my usual place, I shuffle slowly down Atwater, past Sherbrooke and Lincoln, changing from limp to limp until finding one more comfortable. It is mild enough to feel warm, and I open my ski jacket. Remnants of Tuesday's snowfall melt into sudden pond-like puddles, dirty and ankle deep, that will be frozen again by tomorrow. Up ahead, partly obscured by a high-rise apartment building, are the back and side of the Montreal Forum. Counterpart to baseball's Yankee Stadium, to soccer's Wembley, the Forum is hockey's shrine, a glorious melting pot of team, city, and sporting tradition. Yet from this angle, from any angle, it seems a little disappointing. It is not elegant, not dramatic, not exciting or controversial; it is a cautious, box-like mix of browns and beiges, pebbled concrete, glazed brick, and aluminum that but

In Dryden's eight years with the Canadiens the team won six Stanley Cups.

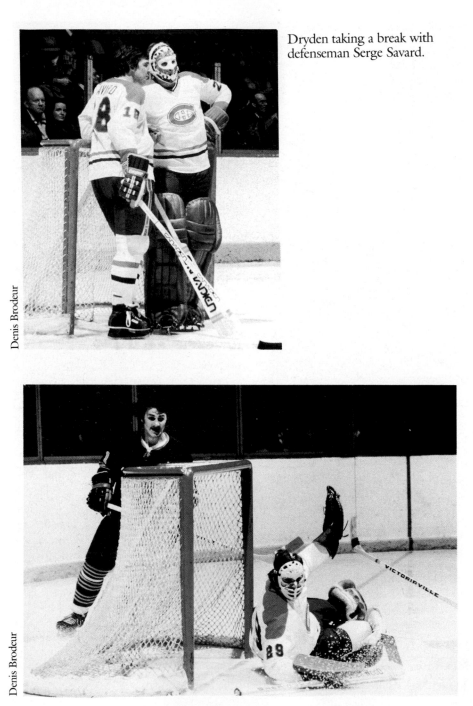

Dryden taking a break with defenseman Serge Savard.

Gilbert Perreault watches from behind as Dryden makes the save.

Dryden scrambles along the boards trying to keep Philadelphia Flyer Gary Dornhoefer from the puck. In the second game of the 1976 Stanley Cup finals in Montreal, Larry Robinson drove into Dornhoefer, hitting him so hard that his body dented a section of the boards.

Dryden defends his net against Jerry Korab of the Chicago Black Hawks. The Canadiens defeated the Hawks in a 4-2 series for the 1973 Stanley Cup.

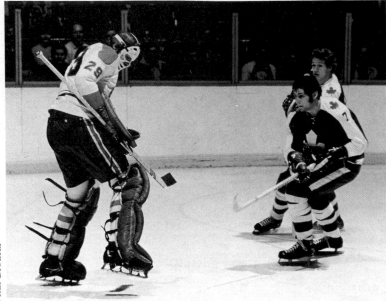

Darryl Sittler (27) and Jim Harrison (7). In the mid-1970s, Dryden writes, the Leafs always seemed poised for a final breakthrough, but never became real contenders. And all the energy and excitement they felt at being promising finally just wore away.

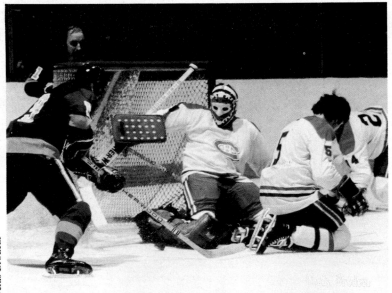

L.A. Kings Butch Goring behind the net and Mike Corrigan in front, with Canadiens Guy Lapointe (5) and Don Awrey (24).

Denis Brodeur

Referee Bob Myers watches Boston Bruin Wayne Cashman fighting with Dryden for the puck. The Bruins and Canadiens in Boston Garden was Dryden's favourite game to play: "bursting with energy and commitment [it was] a game of players not skills."

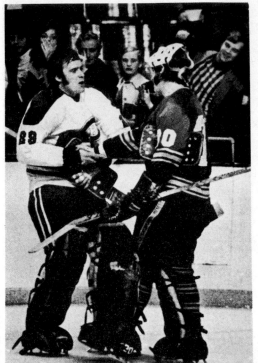

Denis Brodeur

Dryden had been called up from the Voyageurs only two weeks before an injury to Rogie Vachon sent him into the game. Seeing this, Sabres coach Punch Imlach motioned goalie Joe Daley off the ice and sent Ken's brother, Dave, in his place— the only time in the NHL two brothers played against each other in net.

Denis Brodeur

Teammate Serge Savard and Terry O'Reilly of the Bruins. To Dryden, the Bruins were a treasured thing for any team or player—a good opponent. Good opponents make you your best. They give you your highest highs and your lowest lows, your best and worst moments.

Denis Brodeur

Alexander Bodunov skates into Team Canada's zone during the historic 1972 Team Canada vs. the USSR matchup.

With famed Russian goalie Vladislav Tretiak.

Denis Brodeur

By the end of his career, Dryden was catching fewer shots. Years of concussion had left his hand and wrist often tender and sore. Learning to substitute a leg or a stick to save his hand, his catching glove, reprogrammed and out of practice, often remained at his side.

Denis Brodeur

Denis Brodeur

Goaltending requires "a certain character of mind, emotionally disciplined, one able to be focussed and directed, a mind under control. Because the demands on a goalie are mostly mental, it means that for a goalie the biggest enemy is himself."

Denis Brodeur

"A good 'good team' goalie cannot focus on brilliant saves—the only things that can make a difference to a poor team. Allowing few enough goals that he feels every one, he is driven instead by something else—the penetrating hatred of letting in a goal."

Denis Brodeur

Dryden says that leaning on his stick wasn't just a rest position, but a way to appear indifferent. After making a save it said to players on the other team, "It wasn't that hard a shot." If he let in a goal, to the fans it said, "You can't get to me."

Dryden wasn't even technically a rookie when he won the Conn Smythe Trophy as the Most Valuable Player in the 1971 Stanley Cup playoffs. (He won the rookie award the following year.) With only six NHL games behind him, Dryden led an underdog Canadiens team to a Stanley Cup.

Denis Brodeur

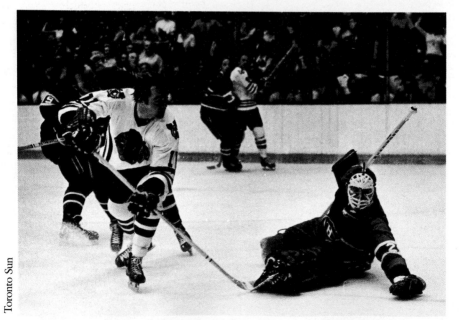

Toronto Sun

Dryden saves a shot from Danny O'Shea during the 1971 Stanley Cup finals against Chicago.

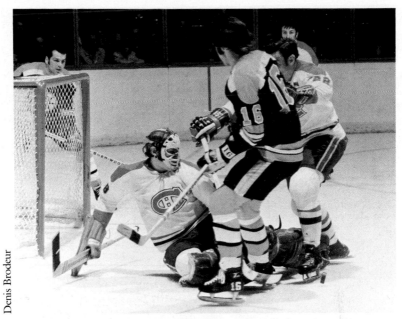

Dryden's first game at the Boston Gardens in the 1971 Stanley Cup quarter finals. Derek Sanderson (16) and John Ferguson (22) vie for the puck in front of Dryden as Don Marcotte (behind the net) and Guy Lapointe look on.

Dryden had a 2.24 goals against average over 8 years.

Denis Brodeur

Steve Vickers of the New York Rangers won the Calder Memorial Trophy for best rookie in 1973, the year after Dryden.

Ken and his brother, Dave, in "Dryden's backyard." Ken's backyard inspiration came from Julian Klymquiw, an assistant trainer with the Red Wings, who was the goalie for the penalty shot contests staged during CBS's pre-game shows in the 1950s.

As a kid, Ken never thought he would be an NHL goalie; he couldn't see the way from his backyard to the dressing rooms of the NHL.

A melée in front of the net: Savard (far left), Guy Lafleur (10), and Larry Robinson (back right).

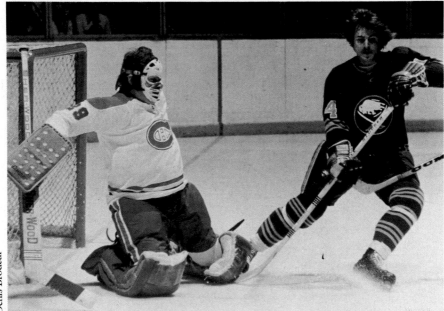

René Robert of the Buffalo Sabres.

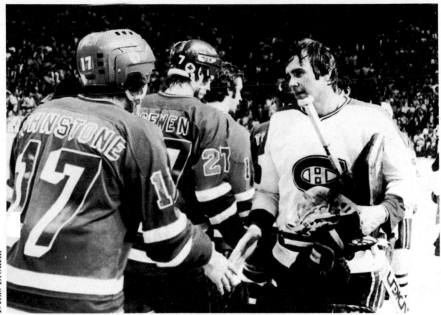

Denis Brodeur

Montreal Canadiens played the New York Rangers in Ken's last playoff and last game in 1979.

Denis Brodeur

Montreal fans surround Ken at the parade following the Canadiens' Stanley Cup victory in 1979.

"The happiest picture I have."—Ken Dryden

for its height might look more at home in a suburban industrial park. Indeed, it makes but one compromise to architectural packaging. In its lobby, four escalators cross, and when lighted they can be seen through tinted glass windows to form two enormous crossed hockey sticks.

Inside, at first it seems little different: an elongated bowl of red, white, and blue seats, richly enamelled, its ice a glacial blue, here and there touches of neon, bright, attractive, a nice building to be sure, but with nothing to dominate your eye—no dramatic color schemes, no wagon-wheel ceilings, no giant replay screens. Yet, in its unassuming elegance, it offers the right environment for hockey in Montreal. On the ice and off, it's an environment that doesn't try too hard, that doesn't need to, where everything fits—fans in stylish winter furs, usherettes in bright, tasteful uniforms, an operatic tenor, a special team, a style of play, and most of all a game. It is the Forum's unique achievement. Expansive yet intimate, exuberant yet unselfconscious, it supports and complements a game, never competing for your attention. And when a game ends, fading away, it gives you nothing to detail the impression it leaves—just a memory of the game and the unshakable feeling that you've watched it in its proper place.

Six or seven tiny, parka-ed figures meet me at the corner, none of them Peter. He has been absent from school lately and no one seems to know where he is. Shaking their heads, they think he must be sick. Inside, a Forum workman straightens up from washing an executive car and flashes a thumbs-up sign, as others near him smile and nod the same. I smile back, trying to think of something to say, when suddenly "Doc" appears. At least fifty, a tiny white-haired sprite not much more than a hundred pounds, Doc works in the purchasing office by day, and by night helps the visiting team's trainers for home games, always dressing up in one of their emblemed shirts, calling them "my team," roguishly playing the part. Playing theirs, the visiting players scream "spy" at him when he walks in their dressing room the first time; playing our part, we scream "traitor" when we see him in ours, threatening all manner of consequences if he ever comes back. Doc, stiffening as if for a fight, just threatens back, snarling that we're going to lose, that his team is ready. Then we chase him out of the room, Doc laughing as he goes.

Now he skips down the Forum steps and is past me before he can stop. "Good game, sir," he rasps with his usual mock formality. "Better watch my team tomorrow though." Then, quickly looking around to see if anyone is watching, he leans over to me. "They're hot," he whispers, and knowing it's the Wings and knowing they're not, with a raspy "heh heh heh" he's gone. He's the kind of Runyonesque character traditionally associated with race tracks and boxing gyms, the guy on the fringes who gives sports its flavor, the guy who is now disappearing.

The Forum is disturbingly empty: just a few players sit quietly cocooned away in a dressing room; twenty-five or thirty staff work in distant upstairs offices; throughout the rest of its vast insides a few dozen men are busy washing, painting, fixing, tidying things up. There is one other person. Entering the corridor to the dressing room, I hear muffled, reverberating sounds from the ice, and before I can see who it is, I know it's Lafleur. Like a kid on a backyard rink, he skates by himself many minutes before anyone joins him, shooting pucks easily off the boards, watching them rebound, moving skates and gloved hands wherever his inventive instincts direct them to go. Here, far from the expedience of a game, away from defenders and linemates who shackle him to their banal predictability, alone with his virtuoso skills, it is his time to create.

The Italians have a phrase, *inventa la partita.* Translated, it means to "invent the game." A phrase often used by soccer coaches and journalists, it is now, more often than not, used as a lament. For in watching modern players with polished but plastic skills, they wonder at the passing of soccer *genius*—Pele, di Stefano, Puskas—players whose minds and bodies in not so rare moments created something unfound in coaching manuals, a new and continuously changing game for others to aspire to.

It is a loss they explain many ways. In the name of team play, there is no time or place for individual virtuosity, they say; it is a game now taken over by coaches, by technocrats and autocrats who empty players' minds to control their bodies, reprogramming them with X's and O's, driving them to greater *efficiency* and *work rate*, to move *systems* faster, to move games faster, until achieving mindless pace. Others fix blame more on the other side: on smothering defenses played with the same technical sophistication, efficiency, and work rate, but in the nature of defense, easier to play. Still others argue it is the professional sports culture itself which says that games are not won on good plays, but by others' mistakes, where the safe and sure survive, and the creative and not-so-sure may not.

But a few link it to a different kind of cultural change, the loss of what they call "street soccer": the mindless hours spent with a ball next to your feet, walking with it as if with a family pet, to school, to a store, or anywhere, playing with it, learning new things about it and about yourself, in time, as with any good companion, developing an *understanding.* In a much less busy time undivided by TV, rock music, or the clutter of modern lessons, it was a child's diversion from having nothing else to do. And, appearances to the contrary, it was creative diversion. But now, with more to do, and with a sophisticated, competitive society pressing on the younger and younger the need for training and skills, its time has run out. Soccer has moved away from the streets and playgrounds to soccer fields, from impromptu games to uniforms and referees, from any time to specific, scheduled time; it has become an *activity* like anything else, organized and maximized, done right or not at all. It has become something to be taught and learned, then tested in games; the answer at the back of the book, the one and only answer. So other time, time not spent with teams in practices or games, deemed wasteful and inefficient, has become time not spent at soccer.

Recently, in Hungary, a survey was conducted asking soccer players from 1910 to the present how much each practiced a day. The answer, on a gradually shrinking scale, was three hours early in the century to eight minutes a day today. Though long memories can forget, and inflate what they don't forget, if the absolute figures are doubtful, the point is none the less valid. Today, except in the barrios of Latin America, in parts of Africa and Asia, "street soccer" is dead, and many would argue that with it has gone much of soccer's creative opportunity.

When Guy Lafleur was five years old, his father built a small rink in the backyard of their home in Thurso, Quebec. After school and on weekends, the rink was crowded with Lafleur and his friends, but on weekdays, rushing through lunch before returning to school, it was his alone for half an hour or more. A few years later, anxious for more ice time, on Saturday and Sunday mornings he would sneak in the back door of the local arena, finding his way unseen through the engine room, under the seats, and onto the ice. There, from 7:30 until just before the manager awakened about 11, he played alone; then quickly left. Though he was soon discovered, as the manager was also coach of his team Lafleur was allowed to continue, by himself, and then a few years later with some of his friends.

There is nothing unique to this story; only its details differ from many others like it. But because it's about Lafleur it is notable. At the time, there were thousands like him across Canada on other noon-hour rinks, in other local arenas, doing the same. It was when he got older and nothing changed that his story became special. For as others in the whirl of more games, more practices, more off-ice diversions, more travel and everything else gave up solitary time as boring and unnecessary, Lafleur did not. When he moved to Quebec City at fourteen to play for the Remparts, the ice at the big Colisée was unavailable at other times, so he began arriving early for the team's 6 p.m. practices, going on the ice at 5, more than thirty minutes before any of his teammates joined him. Now, many years later, the story unchanged, it seems more and more remarkable to us. In clichéd observation some would say it is a case of the great and dedicated superstar who is first on the ice, last off. But he is not. When practice ends, Lafleur leaves, and ten or twelve others remain behind, skating and shooting with Ruel. But every day we're in Montreal, at 11 a.m., an hour before Bowman steps from the dressing room as signal for practice to begin, Lafleur goes onto the ice with a bucket of pucks to be alone.

Not long ago, thinking of the generations of Canadians who learned hockey on rivers and ponds, I collected my skates and with two friends drove up the Gatineau River north of Ottawa. We didn't know it at the time, but the ice conditions we found were rare, duplicated only a few times the previous decade. The combination of a sudden thaw and freezing rain in the days before had melted winter-high snow, and with temperatures dropping rapidly overnight, the river was left with miles of smooth glare ice. Growing up in the suburbs of a large city, I had played on a river only once before, and then as a goalie. On this day, I came to the Gatineau to find what a river of ice and a solitary feeling might mean to a game.

We spread ourselves rinks apart, breaking into river-wide openings for passes that sometimes connected, and other times sent us hundreds of feet after what we had missed. Against the wind or with it, the sun glaring in our eyes or at our backs, we skated for more than three hours, periodically tired, continuously renewed. The next day I went back again, this time alone. Before I got bored with myself an hour or two later, with no one watching and nothing to distract me, loose and daring, joyously free, I tried things I had never tried before, my hands and feet discovering new patterns and directions, and came away feeling as if something was finally clear.

The Canadian game of hockey was weaned on long northern winters uncluttered by things to do. It grew up on ponds and rivers, in big open spaces, unorganized, often solitary, only occasionally moved into arenas for practices or games. In recent generations, that has changed. Canadians have moved from farms and towns to cities and suburbs; they've discovered skis, snowmobiles, and southern vacations; they've civilized winter and moved it indoors. A game we once played on rivers and ponds, later on streets and driveways and in backyards, we now play in arenas, in full team uniform, with coaches and referees, or to an ever-increasing extent we don't play at all. For, once a game is organized, unorganized games seem a wasteful use of time; and once a game moves indoors, it won't move outdoors again. Hockey has become suburbanized, and as part of our suburban middle class culture, it has changed.

Put in uniform at six or seven, by the time a boy reaches the NHL, he is a veteran of close to 1,000 games—30-minute games, later 32-, then 45-, finally 60-minute games, played more than twice a week, more than seventy times a year between late September and late March. It is more games from a younger age, over a longer season than ever before. But it is less hockey than ever before. For, every time a twelve-year-old boy plays a 30-minute game, sharing the ice with teammates, he plays only about ten minutes. And ten minutes a game, anticipated and prepared for all day, travelled to and from, dressed and undressed for, means ten minutes of hockey a day, more than two days a week, more than seventy days a hockey season. And every day that a twelve-year-old plays only ten minutes, he doesn't play two hours on a backyard rink, or longer on school or playground rinks during weekends and holidays.

It all has to do with the way we look at free time. Constantly preoccupied with time and keeping ourselves busy (we have come to answer the ritual question "How are you?" with what we apparently equate with good health, "Busy"), we treat non-school, non-sleeping or non-eating time, unbudgeted free time, with suspicion and no little fear. For, while it may offer opportunity to learn and do new things, we worry that the time we once spent reading, kicking a ball, or mindlessly coddling a puck might be used destructively, in front of TV, or "getting into trouble" in endless ways. So we organize free time, scheduling it into lessons— ballet, piano, French—into organizations, teams, and clubs, fragmenting it into impossible-to-be-boring segments, creating in ourselves a mental metabolism geared to moving on, making free time distinctly unfree.

It is in free time that the special player develops, not in the competitive expedience of games, in hour-long practices once a week, in mechanical devotion to packaged, processed, coaching-manual, hockey-school skills. For while skills are necessary, setting out as they do the limits of anything, more is needed to transform those skills into something special. Mostly it is time— unencumbered, unhurried, time of a different quality, more time, time to find wrong answers to find a few that are right; time to find your own right answers; time for skills to be practiced to set higher limits, to settle and assimilate and become fully and completely yours, to organize and combine with other skills comfortably and easily in some uniquely personal way, then to be set loose, trusted, to find new instinctive directions to take, to create.

But without such time a player is like a student cramming for exams. His skills are like answers memorized by his body, specific, limited to what is expected, random and separate, with no overviews to organize and bring them together. And for those times when more is demanded, when new unexpected circumstances come up, when answers are asked for things you've never learned, when you must intuit and piece together what you already know to find new answers, memorizing isn't enough. It's the difference between knowledge and understanding, between a super-achiever and a wise old man. And it's the difference between a modern suburban player and a player like Lafleur.

For a special player has spent time with his game. On backyard rinks, in local arenas, in time alone and with others, time without short-cuts, he has seen many things, he has done many things, he has *experienced* the game. He understands it. There is *scope* and *culture* in his game. He is not a born player. What he has is not a gift, random and otherworldly, and unearned. There is surely something in his genetic make-up that allows him to be great, but just as surely there are others like him who fall short. He is, instead, *a natural*.

"Muscle memory" is a phrase physiologists sometimes use. It means that for many movements we make, our muscles move with no message from the brain telling them to move, that stored in the muscles is a learned capacity to move a certain way, and, given stimulus from the spinal cord, they move that way. We see a note on a sheet of music, our fingers move; no thought, no direction, and because one step of the transaction is eliminated—the information-message loop through the brain—we move faster as well.

When first learning a game, a player thinks through every step of what he's doing, needing to direct his body the way he wants it to go. With practice, with repetition, movements get memorized, speeding up, growing surer, gradually becoming part of the muscle's memory. The great player, having seen and done more things, more different and personal things, has in his muscles the memory of more notes, more combinations and patterns of notes, played in more different ways. Faced with a situation, his body responds. Faced with something more, something new, it finds an answer he didn't know was there. He *invents the game.*

Listen to a great player describe what he does. Ask Lafleur or Orr, ask Reggie Jackson, O. J. Simpson, or Julius Erving what makes them special, and you will get back something frustratingly unrewarding. They are inarticulate jocks, we decide, but in fact they can know no better than we do. For ask yourself how you walk, how your fingers move on a piano keyboard, how you do any number of things you have made routine, and you will know why.

Stepping outside yourself you can think about it and decide what *must* happen, but you possess no inside story, no great insight unavailable to those who watch. Such movement comes literally from your body, bypassing your brain, leaving few subjective hints behind. Your legs, your fingers move, that's all you know. So if you want to know what makes Orr or Lafleur special, watch their bodies, fluent and articulate, let them explain. They know.

When I watch a modern suburban player, I feel the same as I do when I hear Donnie Osmond or René Simard sing a love song. I hear a skillful voice, I see closed eyes and pleading outstretched fingers, but I hear and see only fourteen-year-old boys who can't tell me anything.

Hockey has left the river and will never return. But like the "street," like an "ivory tower," the river is less a physical place than an *attitude*, a metaphor for unstructured, unorganized time alone. And if the game no longer needs the place, it needs the attitude. It is the rare player like Lafleur who reminds us.

There is a sense of destiny about Lafleur that is present only in a great player, and Lafleur has been a great player most of his life. A national figure at ten as star of the Quebec pee-wee tournament, moving up to Jr. A at fourteen, he amassed unprecedented scoring totals with the Remparts, and by seventeen was the kind of unmistakable star that a team will plan for and scheme for years ahead if it can. In May 1970, with two lower draft picks already acquired from other teams, the Canadiens traded Ernie Hicke and their first-round pick to the California Golden Seals for François Lacombe, cash and the Seals' first pick in the 1971 draft. In a draft that included such prospects as Marcel Dionne and Rick Martin, the Canadiens, with the first pick, selected Lafleur.

It was a propitious moment. Days before, with a triumphant tenth Stanley Cup, Béliveau, captain, aging hero and idol to Lafleur, had played his last game, announcing his retirement some weeks later. The torch was passed, the line of pre-eminent French-Canadian superstars beginning with "the Rocket," Maurice Richard, more than thirty-five years before would continue unbroken. For a poor boy from a small pulp-and-paper town on the Ottawa River, the world was unfolding as it should—destiny calculated, manipulated, controlled by others; destiny none the less.

Now, eight years later, it is in a sense no less evident. He is a dazzling star, the best of his sport, his team more dominant than any since the last years of the Rocket. Wealthy, celebrated, emerging off-ice as a poised if not wholly polished public person, he has years of success ahead of him. Béliveau, the institutional embodiment of the team now elegantly blue-suited in upstairs offices, will eventually retire; Lafleur will retire and replace him, the torch will pass again.

It is an old story, now a rare one, confined mostly to the pages of adolescent fiction; a player, a team, and his sport. But now, with free-agentry to tempt him away, a player's loyalty and self-interest divide, then collide, the rift wider, the collision more destructive, self-interest the winner at an ever younger age. Still, Lafleur seems untouched. No well-placed tattoos, no self-promoting blood of Canadiens' *bleu*, *blanc*, *et rouge* coursing in his veins, you can hear it in simple, uncoaxed words—"hockey's my life," he says often; too young to know, he knows, and no one argues. It's a life immutable; not my life, not one I would want, still a life *someone* should live, pure, simple, romantic—after all, what's wrong with adolescent fiction?

I have known Lafleur for nearly eight years. In that time, I have been to his home only once, for a team party; he has never been in mine. We have never been roommates on the road; we have never talked for more than a few coincidental moments at a stretch; only twice have events stripped away teammates and left us alone and together. In the playoffs three years ago, an RCMP informer told of threats he had overheard to kidnap Canadiens players, somehow interpreted as Lafleur and me. Advised to tell no one else, we nodded and smiled to each other our common plight, alarmed, amused, with gumshoes looking unmistakably like gumshoes behind newspapers and potted palms, in driveways and rearview mirrors twenty-four hours a day for several days. Then, early this season, with Lafleur looking to renegotiate his contract, an erroneous report of my salary in a Montreal paper became his public ammunition, and, uneasy, we came together again. Still, watching him from three dressing room seats away, stuttering, stumbling through early career disappointments, suddenly in glorious triumph, I should have known better. But for nearly all that time, I have misread him.

For there is a life there, and in destiny and romance there is no room for life. Painted as they are with broad brush strokes, vivid and lush, they find shape and pattern only with distance. The person who lives them is too close. He feels sweat as well as triumph. He understands what others see, but feels none of it himself.

In the 1971 playoffs, as a 23-year-old law student with only six NHL games behind me, I led an underdog team to a Stanley Cup. Romance? Destiny? Not to me, though at times I've tried to make it so. "It'll hit me in the morning," the celebrant gushes, apologizing at the same time. "It hasn't sunk in yet." Tomorrow it sinks in—satisfaction, immense pleasure, but no romance. For what is romantic about life between the highs, the plane rides and bus rides, the crushed hopes and fears, the morning-to-morning headaches every bit a part of the same experience? Even now, eight years later, I can't forget enough to get outside my story and see it as others do. Instead, remembering just enough from along the way to know the boundaries of the rest, I stifle the imagination that makes romance possible.

Yet, anxious to find destiny and romance in others, Lafleur included, I find it, and assume that they find it too. So when Lafleur says, "Hockey's my life," I hear his wide-eyed words and supply a tone which belongs to me, which isn't his. For, like most of us, Lafleur is no romantic about his own life. Where is the romance in beginning life poor, except if you didn't? Romantic dreams may send you beyond ghettoed walls, but with nothing else, they send you crashing back. Wanting never to return to that childhood life, with desperate hopes and desperate fears, what is romantic about coming face to face with success, knowing you could blow it all? Sensitive and awkwardly shy, where is the romance in making it, only to find obligation, tradition, and responsibility, and a long, hockey-less future at its end? Béliveau, a towering figure, seemed always aware, always certain, of his legacy, as if once having perfected it, he had decided never to risk it again; a figure of destiny. No disembodied presence, Lafleur still struggles in the game like the rest of us.

Not long ago, I asked him to explain the unquestioning direction to his life he so often expresses in interviews—playing a little longer, retiring, staying on with the team, travelling the country as its ambassador as Béliveau has. He looked at me, surprised. "What else would I do?" he asked. "When you play as a kid, you have no time to learn or study anything. After fifteen or twenty years, what else do I know?" To the Canadiens, to Béliveau, his attachment is more than sentimental. Lafleur knows what he wants and has known since he was young, quietly setting out to build it—a hockey *life*, a life he knows and enjoys, one he is secure in. As much as his on-ice performance, it was this quality about Béliveau that first attracted Lafleur to him. *Béliveau had secured his future.* And so would Lafleur.

Yet his life will be different from Béliveau's. His game, built on speed, will not age so well. He is not a fatherly, elder-statesman type. He will fight age, unsuccessfully, while Béliveau, with an elegant touch of gray in his game since he was young, eased comfortably into it. And when he retires, he will be a very different ambassador. The fiery Richard was a hockey player, primitive and unsophisticated by today's standards, who understood the game only on the ice. Unwilling to accept an often cosmetic role, he left. Béliveau, understanding the role better, enjoying it, believing in it, performs it with customary elan. The sometimes intemperate Lafleur will cope. They come from different generations.

In what he now, with a roll of his eyes, calls "my hockey first" interview, last year Lafleur told Robin Herman of *The New York Times*, "I really love my family and kid, but first of all it's my hockey, my career. Sometimes my fans go second, and my family is third. It's turning all the time." Then twenty-six years old, four years an NHL superstar, he was merely expressing the reality of most career-directed, cause-directed men. But in his characteristic candor, his tone, flat and unrepentant, was more revealing, the tone of a contented victim, resigned to the future he wants.

I hang up my coat and go to the trainers' room. There is already a line-up to the door. Houle, naked, stands on the treatment table where he often stands, Meilleur wrapping his upper thigh and abdomen with a rubber groin-strap. In a corner chair, Lemaire reads a newspaper, a hot pack on his shoulder. Hughes, Lupien, and Mondou wait. Tremblay pushes in, gathers some tape and pre-wrap, Risebrough takes two hot packs from the hydrocollator, and both leave. Coughing, sniffling, grimacing here and there, Lapointe hovers at the back, trying to look as bad as he feels. Feeling as I do in an emergency ward, my bruised shoulder no longer so important, I leave.

It has been a fairly routine year. Brian Engblom broke his jaw in training camp, Lafleur his nose. Robinson and Napier broke their noses at other times, Shutt his wrist; Lemaire dislocated a shoulder, Risebrough and Hughes (twice each) and Lapointe separated theirs. Add an assortment of back sprains, knee sprains, hip pointers, groin pulls, cuts, bruised ribs and knees; colds, flu, bronchitis, pneumonia, even dermatitis; nothing very serious, things that come and seem to go, except in knees, shoulders, and backs, except when you are older. But while good health may be the equilibrium state for others our age, for us it is recovery and repair. Only at the opening of training camp, when we're brimming with rested, tanned, robust summer-health, does everything feel right. Then, as things begin slowly to break down, it's ice packs, heat packs, tape, pills, ointments, machines, the sports ethic, and us to keep us going.

And we do keep going. It's what is expected of us, it's what we expect of ourselves. "Out ten days," the press release reads, although we're certain to be out longer. "When'll you be back?"

teammates, coaches, fans, and press wonder in our ears, and we're back in eight. For injuries hurt the team, and only later, much later than we can ever imagine at the time, when their residue has settled in for a long, uninterrupted stay, do we realize that they hurt us too. But even if we had known, it might not matter, for we want to play, as another test to be met and won, as an important message to the team. Always in each other's hands, we need to know who we can count on, who can suffer the random misfortune of injury and come through unaffected when needed. In time, we know. For the player too easily distracted by injury, it is a problem. Bill Nyrop, an important if mostly overlooked fourth defenseman to the "Big Three" of Robinson, Lapointe, and Savard, was good enough to have played a larger role on the team, but he was genuinely bothered by illness and injury—when we joked obliquely about it, he would pass it off, explaining he was a "thoroughbred." We could never be sure which game he wouldn't be able to play, so gradually we looked to someone else. Hockey, like all professional sports, demands plow-horse resiliency and resolve, a day's work done no matter the circumstances, before thoroughbred flair can work.

There is nothing romantic in the way we view our bodies. Used and abused through a grinding season, aesthetic only to those who watch, like a plumber's wrench or a carpenter's hammer they are our instruments pure and simple; a collection of disembodied parts—legs, hands, head—that work well or not so well, that are built up, fuelled, and conditioned, that get broken and cut. They are parts we know and understand; parts that wear out—sometimes from injury, sometimes from cumulative injury and age, suffered in private for a while, later as an object of public sympathy/disdain/ridicule ("his legs are gone").

Yvan Cournoyer was the first Canadiens player I ever met. At training camp in 1970, he took his physical examination ahead of me; stripped to his shorts, short and cherub-faced, he looked like a muscle-bound *putti*, his thighs rolled taut like two enormous roasts spilling over his knees. When I saw him, I thought everyone must look that way, and I wanted only to go home and keep my legs to myself. Cournoyer was a great natural goal-scorer with a hard, wickedly effective shot, but his game was based on speed. Cruising right wing without the puck, he would dart here and there, then suddenly explode into an opening for a pass, powering to the net, leaving everyone behind—he was called the "Roadrunner." But by the mid-1970s, though it was apparent to no one else, he could feel himself slowing down. Deciding he could no longer play his former way, he tried carrying the puck more often, playing the defensive zone with greater interest, doing things not instinctive to him, in the end becoming less effective. He had been suffering back problems for some time, and finally underwent tests where disc trouble was diagnosed. His first back operation was in 1977, and instead of being depressed by it, he felt relieved and not a little excited, for now he knew the speed that had left him had gone for a reason, and with an operation seemed recoverable. But it was not, and this year, his back pains returning, he had a second operation, this time facing it with no relief or excitement. A few weeks ago, before he went to Florida to recuperate, I asked him about it. He paused, his bright face suddenly darkening, and as if reliving the moment in the operating room he said slowly, "When you see that big light for the second time...," then the words stopped. At that moment, he had known his career was over.

Tremblay sits at his seat rubbing ointment over much of his body, winding pre-wrap where he has just rubbed, and finally tape. Then, as if part of a routine familiar to him, he goes right into dressing for practice. Within two months of joining the team a few years ago, his skin began to turn red and blotchy, gradually scaling, itched into open sores, oozing, bleeding, sticking to longjohns, clothes, bedsheets, to whatever it touched, reopening again and again. It caused him frantic discomfort at first, and he has since seen numerous dermatologists and used a wide variety of creams and ointments, but to no avail. He is now no better than he ever was. Only one thing makes the rash go away—the end of the season. Within weeks it has vanished, only to reappear in the same inverse pattern of days and weeks at the start of the next season. In a bar, on a plane, as he listens to Bowman's pre-game talk, unpreoccupied with anything else, he scratches, but mostly now he seems not to notice that he's doing it. Tremblay has learned to cope. Rubbing the sores, wrapping them for each practice and game, he has simply come to accept it as another part of his season.

Almost next to him, his back against the wall, Risebrough sits vacant-eyed, a hot pack on his knee, another on his shoulder. When he was twenty, playing junior hockey, he tore the ligaments on both sides of his right knee. Since then, wearing a brace when he plays, he has managed a successful and mostly injury-free career. But now when he awakens in the morning, he feels stiffness in his knee that takes time to work out. And once or twice a year, he re-injures it, not seriously, just enough to remind him how close he remains to the edge he has never quite left. This year he has added a new problem, his right shoulder. He separated it in November, and coming back after Christmas, he separated it again a few days later, returning only a week ago, the shoulder still bothering him. Today, after two games in two nights, he is stiff and sore and I see worry in his face. For though only in his mid-twenties, he can see a clear, disquieting pattern emerging to his career, and he's just beginning to know that from now until he retires, it won't change much.

For each of us, it's a race, a short, quick race we don't know we're in until we start to lose. We build up our bodies, break them down, and build them up again; it is the natural, unconcerned rhythm of our careers, until one day they break down faster than we can build them up and the end is not far away. Though we know that it's coming and can feel its symptoms, the effects, we pretend, are much less clear, and the time always seems months and years off, except for others. I'm not there yet, at least I don't think so, but what every other year was a slump can suddenly become the irreversible status quo. And, desperately preoccupied with redeeming myself and proving others wrong, like everyone else I would be the last to know.

"Eddy! Boomer! Where are those fuckin' trainers?" a voice bellows. It is almost noon, and in the final panic of getting ready, laces get broken, tape and cotton are urgently needed, and it's a question we're all asking. In an eminently reasonable, hide-and-seek voice, Robinson calls out, "Oh Ed-dy, Boo-mer, you can come out now. We give up."

A few moments later, punching his glasses back from the end of his nose, Palchak walks in looking harried as usual. There's no sign of Meilleur.

"*Ta-berr-nac*," Lapointe exclaims, "il vive!"

Tremblay looks up as if he's not so sure, and looks down again.

"Hey Eddy," Houle shouts, "where's our checks?"

Every seventeen days, ten times a season, Palchak goes to the upstairs offices during practice and returns with our paychecks. Today is the day. In his heavy nasal voice, sounding as if someone is pinching his nostrils, Palchak tells us that we'll get our checks after practice. Pinching their nostrils, several players repeat what Palchak says, and everyone laughs.

Chartraw looks across at Houle. "Hey Reggie," he shouts, "what d'ya want your check for? Ya got another hot tip?" and there's more laughter.

"Lemme guess," Shutt interrupts, "you and Bunker Hunt are gonna corner the silver market again." There is loud laughter. Then, in a voice sounding vaguely like the TV commercial, Robinson says solemnly, "When E. F. Houle speaks..." and perfectly on cue a chorus shouts, "not one fuckin' person listens," and there's more laughter.

Sitting almost next to me, quieter than usual, is Pierre

Larouche. He looks a little embarrassed and almost isolated from everything going on around him. Last night, on the plane back from Boston, not having played for the third straight game, he couldn't hold back any longer. He found himself, not unintentionally, next to a reporter for *Le Journal de Montréal*, and started talking. As the reporter listened, nodding, writing, offering no argument in return, Larouche grew more and more sure of himself, and gradually more angry. This morning, above the headline that reads, "Canadiens battent Bruins, 3-2," it says that Larouche demands to be traded.

It hasn't gone the way it was supposed to for Larouche. Traded here from Pittsburgh less than two years ago for Pete Mahovlich, just twenty-two years old at the time, already with one 53-goal season and more than a hundred career NHL goals, he had been too good, too young, for a mediocre team not to spoil, and the Penguins had spoiled him. But coming to the Canadiens, a team good enough to use what he could do, and strong enough to discipline, improve, and otherwise mask what he couldn't, it would be different. In his first game, in the Forum against his former Pittsburgh team, he earned three assists and excited everyone with what we knew would happen next.

But it never did, and today, sitting in a corner of the room wearing only his jock, he looks like a disillusioned little boy. Slender, with dark pop-star good looks, in a room of slab-muscled bodies, he looks immature and unused, like a hand without calluses. But Larouche, a luxury player in the best and worst sense of the term, plays with his mind, not his body. He is a goal-scoring prodigy able to score with humiliating ease; without the puck, away from an opponent's zone, he stands separate from the play, cruising the middle of the ice, lazy, uninvolved, an indifferent spectator to the game. But as each of his coaches has reminded himself, more than once, goal-scoring is a gift that cannot be taught. The rest can be learned. But he scored so often in minor hockey, in junior, and finally in the NHL, that he made what he couldn't do seem like a quibble, and never had to learn. Until he got to Montreal.

After a trade, an old slate impossibly cluttered and complicated gets wiped clean, and a traded player, with the help of the management who made the trade, of new coaches, teammates, press, and fans who know no better, is able to pretend that old problems, the ones that brought on the trade, were not of his own making. That in fact they were the result of a former coach who didn't understand him, a former city that didn't appreciate him, a former team with the wrong style of play. Sometimes it happens to be true; most of the time it isn't. Shortly after Larouche's trade, the old patterns of his game reappeared and finally were noticed. In Montreal, in wide-open games where defense meant little to winning, Larouche scored impressively, then rode his statistics through uneventful, do-nothing road games until he was back in Montreal again. Later, when it became clear that his pattern wouldn't change, a conscious decision was made *not* to play him in Montreal, to force him instead to earn his self-sustaining points on the road, in order to *earn* games in Montreal. But late in his first season and now into his second, Bowman has begun using him as one of his discretionary players, inserted into a game when additional offense is needed, taken out when it isn't.

Yet every so often, waiting for the breakthrough we all know is coming, we see it happen: a practice when he skates with surprising energy, anxiously involved all over the ice; a game, like one a few months ago, when he rushed back into our zone to cover up for a defenseman who was trapped up ice. They are just moments, random and isolated, but indicators that he can do what he needs to do, that prove to him, and to us, that he can do it. He is so close. He needs nothing extraordinary, for the extraordinary is already there. And a step away from being a regular, in Larouche's case, means a step away from being a star.

But nothing changes, except gradually everything becomes harder and harder for him. For he is a star. He has been a star all his life, and everything about him is based on being a star. Cocky like a star, extravagant like a star, he talks with a swagger that comes from goals, that needs goals to work. Now every so often, as if to remind himself and others of something, he demands to be traded, and gets a star's attention.

It seems remarkable, even to us, but on a team of specialists that succeeds and prospers with Gainey's fifteen goals and Jarvis's eleven, Larouche, a fifty-goal scorer, is too much of a specialist. Giving up a goal in one game to get one or two in another, less important game, is not a Stanley Cup-winning rate of exchange. There are still some games when he does something so extraordinary that you change your mind and decide never to change it again, that anyone so offensively talented simply *must* play, that any defensive problems *must* be accepted, but then something happens and you change your mind again, not for the last time. For always he tempts you, tantalizing you with his skills, fooling you because you want to be fooled, because you want those fifty goals. So always you wait a little longer. And though he demands to be traded, he won't be traded, at least for a while. Bowman and Ruel know that when one goal is needed there are few players better able to score than Larouche. On a team as strong as we are, a team so strong he cannot be a regular, Larouche is a luxury we can afford, and need, if only a few times a year.

I have never been traded, nor do I think I've ever been in much danger of being traded, though of course I can't be sure. A few years ago, while negotiating my return to Montreal after a one-year absence, I asked Sam Pollock for a no-trade clause in my contract. Pollock, a short, roundish man, who always seemed in great physical agony when non-physical things bothered him, contorted his face and began breathing audibly, gradually talking on about something else. He believed strongly that championship teams couldn't be built on trades and consequently rarely made them, but he always insisted on retaining the right to trade as a means to improve his team should it be necessary. I quickly realized that to win such a clause, *if* I could win it, would take a long and destructive fight, something I wasn't prepared for at the time, and I decided not to pursue it. And so, like every other Canadiens player, at any time, any season, I might be traded.

It has never seemed right to me that someone should have that power over me, or over anyone. That someone can simply call me up and tell me that if I wish to continue in my profession, I will have to pack up my family and move to Detroit or St. Louis or wherever the voice on the phone tells me to go. I don't like the idea of being "swapped" or "exchanged," though the words hold no exaggerated meaning for me. I simply find it demeaning. And whenever I've lingered with the thought long enough to confront myself, I've always come to the same conclusion—that if I were ever traded, no matter where, I couldn't accept the helpless, shabby sense of manipulation I would feel, and would retire.

Yet, in every player, myself included, there resides a closet general manager willing to wheel and deal in teammates and opponents, a lifelong fan who, when notified of his own trade, will ask, "Who for?" As a player, I know that I'm unwilling to play out a season as a competitive lame duck, patient, hoping that next year's draft picks will make things better. In my whole career, I will have fewer than ten chances to win a championship, and I want a real chance every year. So at least a few times each season, I persuade myself that a "superstar" is overrated, "old reliable" simply old, the "young phenom" simply young, and that each must be traded. Yet I've learned, and continue to learn, that trading is never as simple as it seems.

You should always know what you're giving up; you can never be sure what you're getting—it is the general manager's dictum. But a trade involves change, and the effect of change can never be easily predicted. Each team, each player on a team, is a web of dependencies, personal and professional, positive and negative, many of which can only be guessed at beforehand: the small player who needs the protective confidence he gets from a big player, the big player who needs a small player's quickness to open up the ice; the younger player who needs an older player as a model, the older player who needs a young player to excite him and motivate him through his late-career ennui; the teammate who translates a difficult player to the rest of the team, the secondary star who leads only where there's a pre-eminent star to follow, the older player who blocks the development of a younger player, the player who makes a team enjoy being a team. A trade disturbs these relationships, many of which the team intends to disturb by making the trade, and in doing so, the personality, character, and chemistry of a team will be affected, both on and off the ice. Just how a trade changes things often takes some time to emerge—Phil Esposito in Chicago, Boston, and New York was three different players—but two things are certain: If a team doesn't agree with a trade, it will feel let down, using the trade as a crutch whenever it needs it, often before; and even when anticipated, a trade is a wrenching personal experience for a team.

When I was a teenager playing for Humber Valley, Pete Mahovlich was a teenager across the city playing for St. Mike's. The younger brother of one of hockey's great players, Frank Mahovlich, then a star with the Leafs, Pete was a big, gangly kid who tried to play the way his brother did—taking the puck at center, circling back into his own zone, "winding up" as Foster Hewitt would say, then leaving everyone to watch as he powered his way up ice for a shot on goal. But in his adolescent awkwardness, Pete couldn't play that way, and when he tried, we would chase after him with two and three players, stopping him more often than not before he reached center ice. And each time we did, it seemed a moment separate from the game. For, because of who he was and who he pretended to be, when we stopped him we had stopped *Mahovlich*.

After a disappointing junior and minor pro career, when he was traded from Detroit to the Canadiens, things began to change. He came under the influence of John Ferguson, a tough, fiery "enforcer" then late in his turbulent career. "Get mad, Pete. Get mad," Ferguson would exhort constantly, and Mahovlich would get mad, if never for long. But gradually, he put an edge on his flouncing, puppy-dog style and became a star, if not a superstar, though he might have. Tall, strong, a wonderfully adept puck-handler, at times he could take the puck from end to end and score. In his first full season with the Canadiens he scored 35 goals; in his next five seasons, as his point totals soared, he scored 35 (again), 21 (in 63 games), 36, 35, and 34 goals. Curiously, he seemed content there, just underrated enough to encourage others to overrate him, not entirely happy in the shadow of his linemate Lafleur, yet unwilling to emerge on his own. It was as if he understood the torment his brother had once felt, scoring 48 goals one season early in his career with the Leafs, then unable to surpass himself, treated as a nagging disappointment for much of the rest of his career. Later, not quite joking, he said to his linemate Shutt, "struggling" through a 49-goal season, having scored 60 goals the year before, "I told ya, Shutty. Ya get 60 [goals] one year, they want 65 the next."

More than a superstar, Mahovlich wanted to be a character. I played with him for nearly six years and saw him score many memorable goals, including a short-handed, end-to-end goal against the Soviets in 1972 which few who saw it will ever forget. But if I have one lasting image of him, it is from off the ice— wearing a patchwork sports jacket, the kind Heywood Hale Broun might wear, a rough, tweed fedora on his head, pushed up and punched around to look a certain way, a cigar in his teeth, a day's growth of beard, a big picket-fence grin, and saying in a too-loud voice with a too-loud laugh, "Hey, who has more fun than people?" (In all the years I heard him say it, I never had an answer.)

He was a big, handsome, talented man who wouldn't play it straight—the guy who wears lampshades at parties, the perennial conventioneer in desperate search of a good time. Off the ice, *he* was the original Mahovlich, competing against no one except, as he would later discover, himself.

Holding court in the dressing room, on a plane, in a bar, he was a little louder, a little funnier, a little more uninhibited than the rest, always the first to buy a round—throwing out crumpled bills, stuffing smaller ones back into whichever pocket was closest—always quick to buy another to keep the feeling going. He said that he always knew if he had had a good time the night before when he checked his pockets the next morning. If he found crumpled bills in his shirt pocket, in all five of his jacket pockets, in all of his pants pockets, he knew he must have had "a helluva time." His brother was often distant and moody; Pete was the gregarious one, the life of every party. Yet, in fact, both were deeply sensitive and very much alike, Frank keeping everything inside, Pete letting it out, and steamrollering it before it could bother him. More than any of his teammates, he was affected profoundly by the mood and spirit of the team. He needed to like, and be liked, intensely in order to play well. He needed a coach he could "play for," a coach for whom he would do what was asked not because of personal pride or threat, but because he liked him. He had liked Al MacNeil, but he didn't like Bowman, and gradually it became a problem for him. And he needed the same kind of mutual feeling within the team.

On the road, Pete was our social director, ambassador, and guide, his role to make sure that everyone was happy, and he always did his best. Whenever we were looking for something to do, we always looked for him—"Hey Pete, what're ya doin' tonight?"—then followed along. If he said he was tired, which he rarely did, and was going to bed early, we would react as if he was letting *us* down, spoiling *our* fun. But we knew that he didn't like to say no, and could never say it for long, so we kept asking until we knew with a laugh he'd relent. But it was a life-style that couldn't last. Competing with himself, always needing to be funnier and more outrageous to seem as funny and outrageous as he had been the day before, he finally burned out. His skating grew labored, he complained to Bowman that he needed more ice time to "get [himself] going." Instead he got less. The worse things got, the more he tried to right them with one dramatic play, usually an end-to-end rush that would leave his linemates Lafleur and Shutt as spectators. When it didn't work, when he'd be stopped at center or lose the puck at an opponent's blueline, it became more and more annoying. Then one morning, after sitting two seats away from him for more than six years, I found that he was gone. That night, he showed up at the Forum in a Penguins sweater.

While he had talked of being traded off and on for some time, it seemed it would never happen. When it finally did, when he left, the dressing room changed. Everything we had come to expect of him—the hats, the jackets, the laughs, the outrageous stories—we couldn't count on any more. Even the few things we told ourselves we wouldn't miss, we did. Each had become something we could depend on, something we could fit in with and organize around, something that was part of him, that had become part of us. For while sameness can be deadening, it is also comforting. Like George Burns's awful songs or Johnny Carson's double-takes, when you like someone there is something quite nice in knowing what's coming next, in knowing that nothing has changed; that when laces are cut, when petroleum jelly is smeared on the earpiece of a phone, we will all look at Lapointe, and he'll say, "Hey, get the right guy"; that when interest rates go up and the Dow Jones goes down, Houle will complain of inflation and taxes, and if he forgets, someone will remind him; that when Lemaire giggles and squeals and collapses to the floor, someone will say, "There goes Co again"; that when Savard has a "hot tip," Houle and Shutt will be interested, and if it pays off, Ruel will have backed away at the last minute; that before a game Lafleur will take out his teeth and grease back his hair, oil the blades on his skates, set off an alarm clock, smash the table in the center of the room with his stick, then laugh and say, "Wake up, *câlisse*"; and that when the room goes suddenly quiet, someone will bring up Larouche's checking, Risebrough's shot, Chartraw's spinouts, Houle's breakaways, something, *anything*, to keep the feeling going. In a life that changes with the score, this is our continuity, our security. When Mahovlich was traded, the room felt lousy for a while.

The room empties slowly at first, then with its usual urgent rush. Chartraw, Lapointe, and I are left. Chartraw doesn't make it. At 12:01 (a minute late), he slips onto the ice into the invisible shelter of twenty others. Except when we see him, we laugh and slap our sticks to the ice, exposing him. But Bowman isn't out yet. Curiously late, a moment later he emerges from the dressing room, apparently unaware of what has happened.

I'm in a contrary mood; I don't feel like practicing today. I skate around faster than I want to, slowing down here and there until the fun goes out of it, my arms and shoulders drooping theatrically. As I look around, at Lapointe and Robinson, Shutt, Lambert, and Houle, their arms and shoulders drooping the same, I recognize what I feel. This will not be a good practice.

Behind me, I hear a shout.

"Jee-sus Christ, *the pylons*!"

I look up and see Bowman with an armful of orange plastic pylons, planting them at various spots on the ice. Instinctively, I look into the seats and find what I'm looking for—a group of about thirty or forty men scattered over several rows in one corner. While it doesn't always happen this way, it happens often enough that we think we've found a pattern—whenever our otherwise closed practices open up for even a small group to watch, the pylons come out and it becomes "Scotty's Show."

Bowman blows his whistle and brings us down to one end of the ice. We form into a shapeless huddle, some kneeling, others propping themselves on sticks or on top of the net, and Bowman talks to us about last night's game. Within seconds, as the group in the stands watches intently, we stop listening: Shutt fingers the tape on his stick, Tremblay stares into the empty seats; I tighten a strap already tight. Then suddenly, in a loud, earnest baritone, Bowman explains something about the pylon drill, and gets us back. Not certain that we understand what he's said, he decides to demonstrate. Pretending to be the centerman, he breaks around the first pylon diagonally over the blueline for a pass, shouting back to us and gesturing as he goes. The seriousness of his tone, however, is not helped by his quirky skating stride, or by the pass he calls for from Lemaire that goes behind him and down the ice. A little flustered, with the group in the stands now back in their seats, Bowman blows his whistle for us to begin.

The drill doesn't go well. Not used to its patterns, not very good at being mechanical, quickly we turn it into a shambles. And though Bowman, now speaking in a Tiny Tim falsetto, apparently believes that we should have had our heads up to see the pylons, we didn't, and we don't. After the second or third one has bobbled across the ice, and after a pregnant "I'm in charge here" pause, he collects the pylons and we begin our regular drills.

Unable to sustain our funk, gradually we compete against ourselves, and the practice picks up. A short hour later, Bowman blows his whistle, "Okay, that's it," and we let out a satisfied roar, then stay on the ice. With his irrepressible "Who's got a good shot?" Ruel coaxes most of the players to his end of the ice for shots on Larocque.

I go to the other end with Lapointe, Lambert, and Risebrough. Larocque and I are competing again. Though we've won our last three games, with games against the Flyers and Islanders coming soon—games I will almost certainly play—a good, enthusiastic, hard-working practice might get him the Detroit game, and he knows it. So today he is among the first on the ice, and will certainly be the last one off. It is bound to be noticed. I don't really want to play against the Wings, an inept, uninteresting team, especially in the Forum—but I don't want *not* to play either. So I compete back, staying out for shots I don't want and today maybe don't need, staying out just long enough that not staying long enough cannot be a factor.

Lapointe lines up fifteen or twenty pucks near the blueline and slaps them at me one by one; then Lambert and Risebrough do the same, but from closer. Unsure what to do next, with boasts and bets and great enthusiasm we decide on a penalty-shot contest, which Risebrough inexplicably wins. Running out of ideas, Lambert and Lapointe leave the ice, and Risebrough joins Ruel. Larocque is still in goal. I skate around, turning backwards and forwards, dropping to my knees for stretches, skating from board to board several times. Still Larocque hasn't moved. I skate down the ice and stand next to him, waiting a turn. When I get it, he stands next to me, waiting his turn.

Crack-crack, *crack-crack*, like a snare drum in a roll, the pucks jump from Ruel's stick to a line of sticks across the blueline. "C'mon my Ricky," Ruel shouts to Chartraw, "shoot the puck! Shoot the puck!" and Chartraw, then Tremblay ("my Mario"), and Napier ("my Mark") take two or three strides from the blueline, wind up for a slapshot, and *crack-crack*, the next puck shoots from the corner to the next stick in line, again and again until gradually the numbers dwindle. Finally, with only Ruel and Lupien left, there seems no great need for two goalies, yet neither of us will leave. Ruel puts us through a short skating drill, then we go back for more shots. The net is empty. Larocque and I skate towards it, easily at first, then like two kids reaching for the last piece of cake, with disinterested single-mindedness. When I realize that only an embarrassing sprint will get me there first, I angle away and skate to the dressing room. Larocque has won. But by leaving the ice first, I have reminded him that I am still the number one goalie.

Palchak distributes the checks. Houle looks at his and shakes his head. "How come my contract says I'm so rich and this check says I'm not?" he wonders, knowing the answer.

"*Câlisse de tabernac*, taxes!" Tremblay growls and storms to the shower. Shutt watches him go.

"That goddamn Lévesque," someone snarls, not for the first time. "Why the hell doesn't he do something about that instead of the fuckin' referendum?"

There are loud murmurs of agreement.

Suddenly Shutt goes to the skate room, picks up a plastic cup, fills it with ice, and returns to the room. Then, as we watch with squeamish, open-mouthed glee, he urinates in the cup until it's almost full, tops it with Coke for color, puts it down beside him, and walks to the shower. Undressed and ready for our showers, we decide to stay put. Moments later, water dripping from his body, Tremblay reappears and sits down. We watch him from the corners of our eyes. He dries himself slowly, then turns his head to one side and sees Shutt's Coke. He looks around for Shutt, then, sharing smiles with those around him, grabs the Coke and sips from it—no laugh, no wink, no devil-may-care leap this time.

The laughter dies down, and one by one we become aware of some short, quick screams, like those of a passing racing car—it's Palchak sharpening skates. Robinson stands up, puffs out his cheeks, sticks out his belly, wrinkles up his nose like an accordion, punches imaginary glasses back into place with his middle finger, and, stooped over like an old-world shoemaker, his hands in front of him as if holding a skate, he waits for the sound to begin again. Then, pursing his lips,he moves his hands back and forth as if across a sharpening stone, while others make the quick guttural scream of a passing racing car. When the sound stops, wrinkling up their noses like accordions, punching imaginary glasses back into place with their middle fingers, in heavy nasal voices several chorus, "Hey Eddy, leave some for us," and there's more laughter.

Laflcur has left, Risebrough and Lemaire disappear back into the trainers' room, and Larouche heads out the door in the direction of Bowman's office. The room gets quiet. Suddenly Lambert disappears around a corner and returns with the hard, heavy beat of rock music blaring from our stereo. "Aw-right Lambert," we scream, "play that funn-ky music!" and the mood that seemed tired finds life again. His hair pushed up and back in a pompadour like a dry-look Little Richard, Lambert dances, his body jerking to the rhythm, his mouth sneering with feeling. "Ooh Lambert," we shout, "make me *feeeel* it," and, eyes closed, he hovers across the floor, loose and fluid. A few moments later, the stereo turned lower, then off, no one protests.

The room quickly empties. We are on the road from Sunday until the middle of next week, and with banking to do, and tax decisions by the end of the month, mid-afternoon downtown meetings with lawyers and accountants await. Going out the door, Houle yells back that he'll be across the street at the pub. Dressing quickly in more three-piece suits, more suits and sport coats than usual, few seem to hear him.

Last year, many years after being traded by the Canadiens to Los Angeles, Bob Murdoch took me for a long, undistracting drive along freeways and beaches, and as we drove, we talked of our future plans and of contracts we had both just signed. Several years before in Winnipeg, we had been roommates together while playing for Canada's National Team, both of us just out of college and playing one step higher than we ever thought we could play, both of us planning non-hockey careers, yet wondering if there was one step higher we could go. But in the middle of that year, Canada withdrew from the World Championships it was scheduled to host, and the team was disbanded. Adrift, our plans of playing until the 1972 Olympics gone, we talked of quitting; and we talked of continuing on. A few months later, we both began negotiating with the Canadiens, the team holding our NHL rights. With matter-of-fact excitement, we would dream out loud of contract and bonus figures we had heard for others, wondering if Sam Pollock would go as high as "10 and 10" ($10,000 signing bonus, $10,000 a year in salary), "10 and 12," or maybe "10 and 15." In May 1970, we both signed contracts and the following September began together with the Voyageurs.

Eight years later, as we drove around Los Angeles that day, the tone of our conversation had changed. No longer wide-eyed, we talked of our contracts and big jaded numbers spilled easily from us—"a hundred thou," "two hundred thou," individual bonuses, team bonuses, signing bonuses. Then, after continuing this way for several minutes, we suddenly stopped, looked at each other, and started laughing.

Remarkable though it might seem, as recently as ten years ago, it was possible to watch a hockey game and never once think how much its players were paid. For while salaries had moved up till they were nearly compatible with those in other sports, they were not so high as to seem relevant to what was happening on the ice. So good players were "all-stars" or "trophy winners," and good players in bad seasons were "overrated," not "overpaid." It began to change late in the 1960s. As sports and entertainment moved closer together, as sports turned from pastime to business, partnered and propelled by TV, leagues expanded, new money appeared with new expectations and styles, lawyers and agents emerging in its wake. Salaries went up, hold-outs increased. Comfortable with their historic upper hand, many general managers fought back, refusing even to negotiate with agents, turning negotiations and their resulting settlements into newsworthy events, turning money from an occasional issue to an incessant one.

But though that was a dramatic development at the time, the real change came a few years later when the courts struck down the "reserve clause," opening up free-agentry, giving a new competitor—the World Hockey Association—its chance. Between May and September 1972, as WHA teams signed players for their initial season, the "going rate" on a new contract more than doubled. Bobby Hull received a million-dollar bonus for signing with the Winnipeg Jets; Brad Park, Rod Gilbert, Vic Hadfield, Walter Tkaczuk, and many of their teammates signed WHA-size contracts with the Rangers. Gradually, as old contracts became due, other teams fell into line.

From a private, almost inconsequential matter, money moved front and center, where mostly it has remained. New teams in new hockey cities, hard pressed to sell goals and assists to fans used to ERAs and yards per carry, sold price tags as performance, and sold both as celebrity, overnight turning 25-goal scorers like the Bruins' Derek Sanderson into "million dollar" superstars. Agents, happy to use old clients to publicly solicit new ones, came up with creatively inflated figures and sold them to the media as news. The story became money, lots of it, all the time: ticket prices, TV contracts, free agents; day after day rumors, denials, speculations about who is going where, when, and mostly for how much.

"Sports" had become "Sports Inc." With big money now to be made in sports, big money *would* be made, and the attitude changed. "Cities" became "markets," "games" became "products," "sports" part of the "entertainment business," fighting for "entertainment dollars." Owners sold civic pride, appealed to civic vanity, got civic concessions, moved into civic monuments; blamed civic pride, left. Players adopted pin-stripe suits and permanented hair. Money, once only a practical imperative, a vehicle to let them as adults play what as little boys they could play for nothing, was now a reason itself to play. Sports became a means to something else, a player's commitment distracted and suspect; money *a* motivation, so *the* motivation.

It is something far different from what I expected nearly nine years ago. Coming to Montreal as a part-time goalie with the Voyageurs while completing law school, I thought the Canadiens would simply take over from my parents for a time, paying my tuition and books, my room and board and little else until I graduated. Then, after giving them one more year as I was obliged to do, I would merely stop playing and they would stop paying. But I was better than we both thought, and with the team winning most of the time, and the WHA to compete implicitly or explicitly for my services, my salary has increased many times. In most ways, nothing has really changed. The cars I rode in as a child are the cars I drive now, the house I live in is the same, the food I eat, the clothes I wear the same; my bank account is larger, but quantitatively life seems little different.

Still, there have been changes. An agent, an accountant, a tax lawyer, and an investment counselor now ease and complicate my life. When I talk to old friends who earn a thirty-year-old's average wage, they seem uncomfortable, or I do. For me, money, which seemed always a by-product, distant, even unrelated to the game, has taken on new importance. A cause of great bitterness and division, it brought me to retire for a year; a cold-eyed standard against which I judge my relationship with the team, and against which I am now in turn judged.

It is the other side of the Faustian bargain. For when a high-priced player, especially a free agent, comes to a team, he comes with a price tag—the "million dollar" ballplayer. It was the market that created the price tag, but now it's the price tag that he must live up to. So, with nothing more than a bigger bank account to make him a better player, he must play better, like a "million dollar" ballplayer, or be bitterly resented. For many, it's too much of a burden. Surrounded by goodwill at one moment, feeling immense satisfaction at exceeding others' expectations; then signing a new contract so large that performance is no longer relevant, for expectations cannot be reached, a shutout, a home run being simply what you're paid to do. And while once you were allowed such motivations as personal or team pride, such post-game feelings as satisfaction or sadness, that no longer applies. With all that money, all other feelings, all other motivations, are relinquished. Nothing else can feel good or bad, nothing else can matter; nothing else is relevant. What was always a business transaction, but never seemed so, can seem like nothing else again. It sounds like a small price to pay, except to the athlete it doesn't feel that way.

I have never been able to justify the amount of money I earn. I can *explain* it, but that's not the same thing. I know it has to do with the nature of the entertainment business, that, as with actors, dancers, musicians, and others, thousands will attend an arena and pay to watch me work, and millions more will stay at home to do the same on TV. I know that large revenues are produced, which in turn get shared among those who produce them, that indeed using strict economic argument, my teammates and I, more important to producing those revenues, more irreplaceable in their production than most owners or executives, should probably be paid more. I also know that I'm as skilled at my job as most senior executives are at theirs, that I've trained as long and hard as they have, that my career is short, with risks and life-lingering side effects not present in other jobs, that soon I will retire and earn less than others my age with my training and experience earn.

Still, that is not enough. And if someone asks me why I *should* earn more than a teacher, a nurse, a carpenter, a mechanic, I have no answer. I can simply say that, offered money for something I always did for nothing, and would have continued to do for whatever the "going rate" was, with no obvious strings attached I take it, which, if eminently human, doesn't come without its own psychic downside.

In his fine book, *Life on the Run*, former basketball star Bill Bradley relates overhearing another player explain, "Money alone makes you more of what you were before you had money." I would like to think it does, but I'm not so sure. Because money buys you a return ticket from anything you do, it may only make you less sure of what you really are. But I suppose that's the kind of nice intellectual distinction I can afford to make.

For a player, money is also important another way. To many, it means respect, and ultimately self-respect, offering a new life-style, new surroundings, new friends—doctors, lawyers, professional people many years older—a new self-image. The kid who never seemed too smart is suddenly a businessman, *un homme d'affaires*, for the first time in his life feeling like more than a jock.

He is dressed up in expensive suits, briefcase and agent in hand, riding elevators to skyscraper offices, listening to smart people use words that never made sense, but that coming from their mouths almost do (though trying to explain them later to his wife he will become angry at *her* when he can't quite do it).

But nothing comes free and clear. With more money than you can handle yourself, you hire others to do it for you, and so you never learn. Budgets, tax returns, the disagreeable facts of other people's lives, are passed on and out of yours because of money. Only later, gradually disoriented by all you have, feeling helpless before the costly infrastructure needed to support it, do you realize there was a price; that in its freedom, money can be a trap. For what happens later? What happens to the life-style, the expectations, the lawyer, accountant, and investment counselor, the respect and self-respect when the money stops. And it will stop. What then? Like an oil-rich third-world country, an athlete, beginning with little, finding himself with great unplanned-for riches, is suddenly aware that in him is a finite resource fast running out. Without the broader sophistication to deal with it or to build something lasting from it, surrounded by others too anxious to try, he lives with one desperate, nagging fear—this is my chance, *don't blow it.*

So, torn between extravagance and tomorrow, it means a Corvette with the signing bonus of your first contract, then agents, lawyers, accountants as partners to the rest, instead of the taxman, hoping the ledger works out right. In the first few years, it seems like more money than can be spent in a lifetime. In the last few, married, with a family, a house and two cars, you wonder where it went. It was money you once had spread in your mind over thirty years or more, but you forgot the price of beer would rise. And now, while the pile looks much the same, it is filled with 80¢, 70¢ inflation-weakened dollars, and you can see the years ahead shrink agonizingly back. It is like living through an Arctic summer for the first time. Arriving in May or June, and feeling the wonderful, endless sunlight, knowing, but forgetting, that sometime it will end. Then one day in July, long after it began to happen, five, six, eight minutes a day, you feel the sun slowly hemorrhaging away. And unable to stop it, suddenly you know what's ahead.

Before it can happen, you retire, your problems disappearing with you, later to be uncovered by some inquiring journalist. It is in no way a remarkable story, though the celebrity of the names involved makes us think it is. Rather it is simply the universal story of having something before you can appreciate it, then having it go away when you can. And as Roger Kahn discovered in his accomplished book *The Boys of Summer*, and as others have discovered since, it's an easy story. Like nursing-home abuses for an investigative reporter, it is one that's always there, you only have to decide to find it.

But there's one more thing. What does money do to the game on the ice? How does it affect a player? In playoff games, does Guy Lapointe put aside his shot-blocking phobia because of money? And what about Lafleur and his relentless brilliance? What about Robinson and Gainey and Lemaire? What about the so-called money players? Do they play the way they do because of money? No amateur would believe it, nor would many fans, nor indeed many players, but on the ice, in a game, more money, less money, playing for team or country, a blocked shot, a body-check, a diving save comes only from instinctive, reflexive, teeth-baring competition. Money, like other motivations, comes from the mind and has nothing to do with it. More money can't change that.

After practice, I cross the street to the bank. Though it's almost 2 p.m., a line of people remains, winding in and out between makeshift barriers, waiting their turn at the scattering of tellers' windows still open. I stand near the door, away from the line, scanning the off-duty tellers at their desks. One looks up, catches my stare, and I walk past the line to a section marked "New Accounts." There, a woman beside me fills out forms for a new account. As many in line watch absently, assuming I'm doing the same, I fill out a deposit slip, hand it to the teller with some checks, and get back a receipt. In five minutes, while those in line have only moved three or four places closer to the front, I am done and leave the bank.

Once I used to wait in line like everyone else. Then one day a teller motioned me out of line, and I haven't been back since. Feeling a bit guilty each time, I continue none the less, unwilling to give up its convenience. For the tellers and me, it has become routine and normal. They treat me the way they think people like me expect to be treated. And I accept.

It is the kind of special treatment we have grown accustomed to, and enjoy. We have been *special* for most of our lives. It began with hockey, with names and faces in local papers as teenagers, with hockey jackets that only the best players on the best teams wore, with parents who competed not so quietly on the side. It will end with hockey. But in between, the longer and better we play, the more all-encompassing the treatment becomes, the more hockey seems irrelevant to it. For we are special, *period*. Others understand that—*they know*. We know. They give, easily and naturally: slippers, sweaters, plant holders, mitts, baby blankets, baby clothes knit and sent in the mail; paintings, carvings, etchings, sculptures in clay, metal or papier mâché; shirts, slacks, coats, suits, ties, underwear; cars, carpets, sofas, chairs, refrigerators, beds, washers, dryers, stoves, TVs, stereos, at cost or no cost at all. A hundred letters a week, more than 3,000 letters a year—"You're the best," all but a few of them say. On the street, in restaurants and theaters, you are pointed out, pointed at, talked about like the weather. Your picture is hung from a boy's bedroom wall, appears in magazines and newspapers, on radio and TV; hockey cards, posters, T-shirts, and curios, everywhere, anywhere, name, face, thousands of times, flashed to an audience that waves into TV cameras, that writes to editors to have proud yellowed clippings in their wallets.

And we love it. We say we don't, but we do. We hate its nuisance and inconvenience, the bother of untimely, unending autographs, handshakes, and smiles, living out an image of ourselves that isn't quite real, abused if we don't, feeling encircled and trapped, never able to get away. But we are *special*, head-turning, chin-dropping, nervous, giggly, forget-your-own-name special, what others buy Rolls-Royces and votes and hockey teams for, what others take off their clothes and kill for, we have. All we have to do is play.

We are *celebrities*. Like actors, musicians, politicians, writers, famous people, we are common threads between husbands and wives, parents and kids, friends. And once a celebrity, always an ex-celebrity; in thirty or forty retirement years here and there we are bound to be dredged up and recalled, if briefly. Until then, our images and names are reported on, gossiped about, carried over great distances by cable or wave—and we renew our celebrity each time we play.

But if exposure is the vehicle of celebrity, *attention* is what separates one celebrity from another. Guy Lafleur and Yvon Lambert are both celebrities, yet on the same ice, on the same screen, Lafleur is noticed, Lambert is not. Lambert, methodical and unspectacular, has nothing readily distinctive about him; his image is passed over, his name unheard. Lafleur *is* distinctive: the way he skates, the sound of the crowd he carries with him, the goals he scores. And so too are others for other reasons: Tremblay for his fiery, untamed spirit; Gainey for his relentless, almost palpable will; Tiger Williams, Eddie Shack, Ron Duguay, each colorful and exciting; and Dave Schultz.

More and more as sports coverage proliferates beyond games, as it becomes entertainment and moves to prime time, as we look for the story behind the story to put performance into a context, and drama into life, then off-ice, off-field performance becomes important. Personas are born, and sometimes made, cameras and microphones there as they happen. The crazies, the clowns, the "sports intellectuals," the anti-jock rebels, Jim Bouton, Bill "Spaceman" Lee, the playboys, Joe Namath, Derek Sanderson, Duguay, all are distinctive *personalities*, some real, some not so real, but getting our attention, each bigger celebrities because of what they do away from the game.

But while few can be virtuoso performers, TV has given us a new minimum off-ice, off-field standard. *Articulateness*. The modern player must be articulate (or engagingly inarticulate, especially southern style). It is not enough to score a goal and have it picked apart by the all-seeing eyes of replay cameras. A player must be able to put it in his own eloquent words, live, on-camera words that cannot be edited for the morning paper. *How did you do it? How did you feel?* If the answers contain grammatical errors or profanity, the magic is broken for the fan at home. For celebrity is a full, integrated life, earned on-ice, performed, sustained and strengthened, re-earned off-ice. As writer Roger Angell once put it, we want our athletes to be "good at life," role models for children, people we like and commit to, people we want to believe earned what they have, every bit as good at things off the ice as they are on. But if players are inarticulate, suddenly harsh and pejorative, they're *jocks*—less likeable, less good at life, less celebrated; finally, seeming even less good *on* the ice.

At its extreme, it creates the category of professional celebrity, those "famous for being famous," so accomplished at being celebrities that their original source of celebrity is forgotten (does anyone remember what Zsa Zsa Gabor was?). At the least, it encourages learning the *skills* of the public person: how to look good, how to sound modest and intelligent, funny and self-deprecatory. It's a celebrity's short cut to the real thing, but it works. Walter Cronkite *looks* trustworthy, Ronald Reagan *seems* like a nice guy, Steve Garvey and Denis Potvin *sound* intelligent. Or are they only articulate? Good enough at something to be a public person, or simply a good public person? From where I sit, in front of a TV or a newspaper, I can't tell the difference, and I'll never get close enough, long enough, to know.

And if that isn't enough, all around are battalions of people anxious to help us look better. Not just flacks and PR types, but a whole symbiotic industry of journalists, commentators, biographers, award-givers. There are ghost-writers who put well-paid words under our names, then disappear; charity organizers, volunteers giving time and effort so that "honorary chairmen," "honorary presidents," "honorary directors" may look even better. Kids in hospitals, old folks in old folks' homes are merely props as we autograph their casts and shake their hands to demonstrate our everlasting generosity and compassion. And never far away, photographers and cameramen to record the event. It is the bandwagon momentum and industry of celebrityhood. In the end, for us, is one *image*.

Years ago, I saw writer David Halberstam on the Dick Cavett show after the release of his landmark book, *The Best and the Brightest*. With time running out, he allowed Cavett to play name association with him. Robert McNamara? "...brilliant, incisive..." and then a trail of three or four more adjectives, and a short, clipped phrase. McGeorge Bundy? "...brilliant, complex..." and again a similar trail, skipping from name to name. His subjects were fifty-year-old men who had lived long and complicated lives, full of twists and contradictions, things irreconcilable, all exhaustively chronicled in his book, but here they were reduced on TV to ten or fifteen words, sometimes fewer. That was all. An image.

For me it is concrete and yet disembodied, what agents call "Ken Dryden"—*What is "Ken Dryden" like?* Recently, I asked an acquaintance, a senior executive at an advertising agency, to pretend he was trying to persuade a client to use me as commercial spokesman for his company. Having met only two or three times several years before, my acquaintance knew me mostly as others do. He wrote the following memo to his client: "...Historically I know you have had some concerns about using athletes...either because of potential problems developing out of their careers and public life, or due to simply their lack of availability. I think Ken is quite different from the rest. He is known as a thoughtful, articulate and concerned individual. I think it would go without saying he would not participate in any endorsement unless he was fully committed to and satisfied with the product. (His Ralph Nader exposure would assure that.) He is serious, respected and appears to be very much his own man. I don't think we could ever consider using him in humorous or light approaches (like Eddie Shack) unless it would be by juxtaposition with another accompanying actor or player. He has good media presence....His physical presence is also commanding. He is quite tall and impressive.... Other encouraging things would be his intelligence and educational background. He would be more in tune with our target audience with his credentials as a college graduate (Cornell) and a fledgling professional person (law). Also, during production, I think this intelligence and coolness would help in case of commercial production as well as helping to keep costs under control due to mental errors...."

My image. Right? Wrong? It doesn't matter. It is what people think, it presupposes how they'll react to me, and how they will act, and for the ad man and his client that is what matters. Being told what others think means if I don't like it I can do something about it. I can do things that are "good for my image." They aren't hard to find, or to do. I can stop doing things "bad for my image." Or, as actors and actresses remind us casually and often, I can do things to "change my image." Too serious? If I run around the dressing room throwing water *at the right moment*, someone is bound to notice—a journalist with a deadline to meet and space to fill, a new angle, *news*: "Dryden misunderstood."

And though some things take longer, others less central do not. Want to be known as an antique collector? Collect an antique. A theater-goer? Go. Once is enough. Tell a journalist, sound enthusiastic, and above all, before you go, play well. Then stand back and watch what happens. Clipped and filed around the league, it spreads like a chain letter, to other journalists themselves without time to check it out, and *presto*, it is part of your standard (authorized) bio. And your image. It is really nothing more than selling yourself like everyone else does, at home, at the office, just trying to make yourself look better. But it is easier. As in a singles bar, everything is taken at face value, everyone is willing, *if you play well*.

If you change the word "image" to "reputation," as you might have done a few years ago, you would have something quite different. For a reputation is nothing so trifling or cynical. Rather, it is like an old barge. It takes time to get going, then, slow and relentless, is difficult to maneuver and manipulate, even harder to stop and turn around. An image is nothing so solemn. For us, it is merely a commercial asset, a package of all the rights and goodwill associated with a name—"Ken Dryden"—something I can sell to whomever I want. But it is a sticky question. For the image I'm selling is *your* image of me, and the goodwill, though it relates to me, is your goodwill. Whatever commercial value there is in my name, my image, it is *you* who put it there, for you *like* me or *trust* me or whatever it is you feel about me, and any prospective buyer, anxious to put my name alongside his product, knows that, and is counting on that to make you buy. And you might buy, even though it may not be in your best interests to buy what I endorse, even to buy at all. So, by selling my name, I have taken your trust and turned it against you. You like Robert Young as an actor, you trust him, you buy his coffee. Thanks, and thanks again.

I did a commercial once, six years ago. I had decided that I never would, but this one was different enough to start me into a web of rationalizations until I forgot the point, and accepted.

A fast-food chain was looking for a winter promotion; Hockey Canada, the federal government hockey advisory board, wanted a fund-raiser and a way to deliver a message to kids and their parents that minor hockey can be approached and played differently. The idea was a mini-book done by Hockey Canada, then sold through the restaurant chain to its vast market. I was to be a collaborator on the book, and its public spokesman. But after doing the TV and radio ads (for the book, but with a corporate jingle at the end), and seeing the point-of-purchase cardboard likenesses of me in the restaurants, I understood what I had done. It is a mistake I haven't repeated. Since then, among others, I have turned down endorsements for a candy bar ("...the way I see it, a full body shot of you in the net, mask up, talking, then we draw in tight on your catching glove, you open it, the bar's inside..."), for a credit card company ("...You may not know me without my mask, but..."), and, with several unnamed others, their names all beginning with the sound "dry" (*Dry*sdale? *Dry*er? *Dri*nan? *Drei*ser?), for a roll-on deodorant whose slogan was "It keeps you *dry*."

It is a game—an *ad* game, an *image* game, a *celebrity* game. Everyone needs someone to talk about, right, so why not about us? Everyone needs heroes and villains. We earn a little money, get some exposure, the commercials are going to be done anyway. Besides, it doesn't last long. A few years and images change, celebrity cools, and it's over. It all evens out. But it doesn't, and we all lose, at least a little.

We lose because you think I am better than I am—brighter than I am, kinder, more compassionate, capable of more things, as good at life as I am at the game—and I'm not. Off the ice, I struggle as you do, but off the ice you never see me, even when sometimes you're sure you do. I am good at other things because I'm good at being a goalie, because I'm a celebrity and there's always someone around to say I am, because in the cozy glow of success, of good news, the public—or the media—want me to be good. It is my angle, and so long as I play well the angle won't change. I am bright and articulate because I'm an athlete, and many athletes are not. "Like a dog's walking on his hind legs," as Dr. Johnson once put it, "it is not done well; but you are surprised to find it done at all." But the public doesn't believe that, just as I don't believe that about celebrities I don't know. Taller, brighter, more talented, more compassionate, glittering into cameras and microphones, awarding each other awards for talent and compassion, "great human beings" every one of them—wet-eyed I applaud, and believe. And all of us lose. The public loses because it feels less worthy than it is; I, because once, twenty-three years old and trying to learn about myself, I wanted to believe I was everything others said I was, or soon would be; instead, older and having learned much, I feel co-conspirator to a fraud.

We are not heroes. We are hockey players. We do exciting, sometimes courageous, sometimes ennobling things like heroes do, but no more than anyone else does. Blown up on a TV screen or a page of print, hyped by distance and imagination, we seem more heroic, the scope of our achievement seems grander, but it isn't, and we're not. Our cause, our commitment is no different from anyone else's, the human qualities engendered are the same. Instead, we are no more than examples, metaphors because we enter every home, models for the young because their world is small and we do what they do. But by creating celebrity and mistaking it for substance, too often we turn celebrity into hero, and lose again.

Joe McGinniss, author of the acclaimed *The Selling of the President*, *1968*, later wrote a book called *Heroes*. Unsatisfying in many ways, it sketched McGinniss's own tormented trail from being *the youngest*, to *the highly acclaimed*, to *the former* all before he was thirty, at the same time ostensibly searching for the vanished American hero. He finds no hints in traditional sources, in mythologists or philosophers, in critics or poets, he gives us none in the theories he offers. But along the way, he makes some discoveries, and so do we. He travels to talk to George McGovern and Teddy Kennedy, to anti-war priest Daniel Berrigan, to General William Westmoreland, to John Glenn and Eugene McCarthy, to author William Styron, playwright Arthur Miller, and others, some of them heroes of his, all of them heroes to many. But, like chasing a rainbow, he finds that as he gets closer, his heroes disappear. In homes and bars, on campaign trails, jarringly out of heroic context, they are all distinctly, disappointingly normal. They are not wonderfully, triumphantly, down-to-earth normal, as normal appears from a distance. Up close, breathing, drinking too much, sweating, stinking, they are unheroically normal. *Normal.* And for heroes, to McGinniss, normal isn't enough.

We are allowed *one* image, one angle; everything must fit. So normal in one thing begins to look like normal in the rest. Unlike the Greeks, who gave their gods human imperfections, for us every flaw is a fatal flaw. It has only to be found, and it will be found. For in moving from celebrity to hero, there is a change. It's the difference between a city and a small town. In a city, the camera's eye is always proximate, yet distant; in a small town, it peers, leers, offers no place to hide. John Glenn, astronaut, first American to orbit the earth—at home with his wife he is friendly, likeable, to an interviewer's prying eyes only "the next junior senator from Ohio," seeming as if he could never have been anything else. A hero? Or not? It doesn't really matter.

"Whom the gods would destroy, they first oversell," as Wilfrid Sheed wrote in *Transatlantic Blues*. Superficially created, superficially destroyed, for the hero, for the celebrity, it all evens out. Except along the way a price is paid. So still we lose. The public because, saddened and hurt by heroes who turn out not to be heroes at all, it turns cynical and stops believing. I, because I'm in a box. For what is my responsibility? Is it, as I'm often told, to be the hero that children think I am? Or is it to live what is real, and be something else?

Recently, a friend asked me to speak to his college seminar. Near the end of two hours, we began to talk about many of these same questions. A girl raised her hand. She said that a year or two earlier on the Academy Awards, she had seen Charlton Heston receive a special award for his "humanitarian" work. Heston had made the same point, the girl said, that thousands of volunteers had done far more than he, and that they deserved the award, that in fact his own contribution was quite small. I asked her, then the class, what the story had told them about Heston. Several hands went up; that he's even modest, they decided. A few of the students laughed; then one by one others did the same.

Saturday

"O body swayed to music, O brightening glance,
How can we know the dancer from the dance?"

—W. B. Yeats, "Among School Children"

MONTREAL
PART I

THE TALK HAS LOCALIZED AND QUIETED. ON OUR WIDE GRAY bench, on the floor, in identical white longjohns shrunk identically up our calves and forearms, we sit or lie and wait for Bowman. At 6:31 p.m. he enters. Instinctively we straighten, our heads turning as one, following him across the room. Short, with bull-like shoulders and neck, his head tipped back, his prominent jaw thrust ahead of him as both lance and shield, he strides purposefully to a small blue chalkboard. We wait quietly. With his back to us, he looks to one side of the board, then to the other, turns, turns again, and screams,

"Eddy! Pierre! Where's the chalk?"

We blink; the mood breaks. There is surprised laughter all around.

Bowman writes the Detroit Red Wings' line-up on the board, grouping defense pairs and forward lines together, adding three or four unconnected names at the bottom. Turning, he looks at us briefly, then throws out his jaw, his eyes jerked upward to a row of white cement blocks directly above our heads, where they remain. He's ready.

"We had a guy watch [the Wings] in Boston last week," he begins quietly, "and these are the lines they went with," reading off what he's just written. "But they've had a lot of guys in and out of the line-up, so there may be some changes."

His tone is calm and conversational, even subdued, and while he often begins this way, we're never quite prepared for it.

"What we gotta do is work on some of these guys," he continues slowly. "McCourt," he says, pointing to center Dale McCourt's name, "this is a real key guy. He likes to hold onto the puck and make plays, a lot like Mikita." His voice picks up speed as if he is suddenly interested in what he's saying. "If ya give him the blueline, he can hurt ya." Then it slows and deepens to a rich baritone, in his eyes a look that wasn't there before. "We gotta get on this guy!" he blares, his right palm hammering the point into his open left hand. "Right on him!" Then, just as suddenly quiet again, "We gotta skate him," he says gently, still talking about McCourt. "This guy doesn't like to skate," and as that thought triggers another, his lips curl and tighten over his teeth. "We gotta *make* him skate!" he roars.

With only the slightest pause but with another change in tone, he discusses Vaclav Nedomansky, the former great Czechoslovak player ("He handles the puck well, but he'll give it up," Bowman says flatly, "specially in his own zone"), hard-shooting defenseman Reed Larson ("We gotta play him like Park or Potvin," he insists. "You left-wingers, play him tight"), Errol Thompson, Willie Huber, penalties and power plays, the Wings' defense, on and on like a never-ending sentence; and my attention span collapses. I look around and see bodies dancing on the benches from buttock to buttock, eyes ricocheting around walls, off ceiling and floor—Bowman's lost us. Then something he says reminds him of something else, and he gets us back again, "...and for crissake," he shrieks, his voice a sudden falsetto, "somebody do something about that squirt Polonich," referring to the Wings' pesky little goon Dennis Polonich. "I'm tired of him running around thinkin' he runs the show." Then more slowly again, his voice an angry baritone, "*Put that guy down!*" But before his last message can completely register, he quickly mentions Dan Labraaten's speed, interrupting himself to talk about Thompson's shot, then Jean Hamel and Nick Libett. He loses us again.

It's as if his mind is so fertile and alive that each thought acts as a probe, striking new parts of his brain, spilling out thoughts he is helpless to control, each with its own emotion. A transcript might read garbled, frustratingly short of uninterrupted thoughts, but his message is clear. It is attitude more than information. And though he drones on about the Wings, the message is about us. For the Wings, nearly a last-place team, are irrelevant if we play well, and Bowman won't pretend otherwise. So every few seconds, triggered by nothing in particular, he throws out a new thought, in an angry, insistent tone, and gets our attention back.

Some nights he talks only ten minutes; a few times, to our wound-up agony, twenty-five minutes or more. When he finishes, we mock what he says for most of an hour after he says it, until just before game time. Then as we panic to cram in all the last-minute thoughts and emotions we suddenly feel we need, we throw back at each other what he told us an hour before, this time in *his* tone.

Restless, bored out of our own private daydreams, we discover each other. Under cover of hanging clothes, we make jungle sounds, stick fingers up our noses, laughing wildly, silently, Bowman continuing as if unaware. Lapointe, his face loose and denture-free, stares at Lemaire innocently fingering the tape on his stick. Knowing what's coming next, we watch one, then the other: Lemaire looks up; Lapointe grins dementedly. Grabbing a towel, Lemaire buries his giggle and covers up. Then, like a slap in the face, Bowman interrupts himself and gets us back. "... and that Woods," he says, referring to Paul Woods, a small, quick center, who once played with the Voyageurs, "is there some reason we can't touch that guy?" he asks pleasantly. Then angrily, "Is there? For crissake, I see Lupien pattin' him on the ass," and before he can go on, we start to laugh. Startled, at first he seems not to understand the laughter; then, enjoying it, he begins to camp it up, "And Mondou," he continues, hunching over, wrinkling his nose, "sniffin' around him, 'Hiya Woodsie. How are ya, Woodsie?' and the guy's zippin' around havin' a helluva time." Unable to hold back, we scream with laughter. We're with him now. Then the look in his eyes changes. The joke's over. "You're not playin' *with* him!" he roars. "Hit him!"

He has been going nearly fifteen minutes. The periods of calm now longer, the emotional bursts more infrequent, he has just one left. Telling us to tighten up defensively, particularly the Lemaire line, he reminds himself of something very familiar: "And when we got the puck in their zone," he yells, "for crissake, don't just dump it out in front blind. That's the worst play in hockey." Mouthing the last few words with him, we look at each other and smile.

He pauses for a breath, and his tone changes one last time. Calm and conversational, as he was when he started, Bowman sums up: "Look, don't take this team lightly. They've had their problems, but they've had injuries and they're getting some of their guys back. And now they're comin' on a bit. They've only lost one of their last three, so we gotta be ready for a good game. We gotta think of our division first. This is a four-pointer, and we got 'em back in Detroit next week. Let's put 'em down now and we won't have to think about 'em the rest of the year."

His eyes leave the row of blocks above our heads and move to the floor in front of him, "Okay, that's all," he says quietly.

We leap up clapping and shouting. When he's out the door, the room goes quieter. Leaning back, Shutt carefully folds his arms. "Scott was very good tonight," he offers cheerily. Then, looking at the clock, "Cut in on my backgammon time though. That's gonna cost me some bucks." Standing, he looks over a room now busily in motion, "Okay, who's my pigeon?" he asks. Several heads pop up, then, seeing who it is, turn away, ignoring him. He tries again, "C'mon, who'll it be?" Seated beside him, as if tugging on his master's pant-leg, Lafleur mutters a half-hearted challenge. Though he beats him less often than he likes to admit, Shutt, a look of disdain on his face, turns and pleads, "Come on, Flower, give it a rest. Think what you do to my conscience," and looking around, he asks again. Nothing. His point now made, "All right, Flower," he sighs theatrically, "let's go," and with a grin and a board under his arm, he walks from the room, Lafleur shaking his head behind him.

With Robinson and Tremblay, I go to the weight room. Nearly as big as the dressing room, a few years ago when the Soviets showed they were good enough on the ice to make what they did off it seem important, the room was renovated and packed tight with weight equipment to encourage off-ice training. But since we have won so often without it ("don't change the luck"), the equipment has been forgotten or ignored by all but a few. Instead, we use the room in other ways: after games, Lafleur and his pack of interviewers come here to unburden the clutter of the dressing room; before games, it is a place to go when the game is far enough away it can still be escaped, when a roomful of players with nothing to do, anxious and uneasy, builds up the mood of a game before it wants to.

Lafleur and Shutt set their board on a bench. I lie on the carpeted floor near Risebrough, easing into some exercises. Across the room, eyes extruded, Engblom reddens from the weight of a bench press, Lambert reads a newspaper, Robinson glances at some mail, Chartraw here and there bangs at the heavy bag, Houle and Tremblay, half seated on a pop cooler, stir their coffee and talk. It is like a Sunday afternoon at the club—easy, unconcerned, the game still far away. Lying on my back and barely conscious, I stretch through old, well-worn routines, nothing new, nothing unexpected, counting holes in ceiling tiles until the holes and tiles disappear, nothing to jar me into remembering where I am and what I'm doing it for, moving only enough to blank my mind.

Some minutes later, aware of a sound, I stir. "Seven o'clock!"

a voice cries again. "Everybody in the room." It is trainer Meilleur, and hearing him this time, I look up, and everyone is gone.

I walk back to the room, the game inescapable.

Shin pads, shoulder pads, socks, pants, and sweaters cover the floor. The random movement in and out of the room has stopped. Voices that can't shut up rebound from its walls—the build-up has begun.

"Need this one, guys. Gotta have it."

"Yessir gang, gotta be ours."

"Big one out there. Big one."

But still twenty-two minutes until the warm-up, it's too serious, too soon, and, feeling uncomfortable, we back off. The mood changes.

"It's a four-pointer, gang," Houle reminds us, unaware of the change.

"You're right, Reggie," Savard says absently. "If they beat us they're only forty-seven points behind us."

"Yeah, then we gotta think about 'em the rest of the year," mocks Shutt, and there's loud laughter.

Risebrough looks across at Chartraw: "Hey Sharty, you think about 'em?" There's no answer. Chartraw, lying on the floor, a towel over his head, didn't hear the question. Risebrough asks again. The towel moves. "Who?" Chartraw asks.

"The Wings," he is told.

"The Wings," he repeats, and says nothing more.

Feeling the mood swing too far, something in all of us becomes panicky.

"Hey, c'mon guys, gotta be ready."

"Goddamn right, guys. These guys are playin' well."

"That's right, that's right. They only lost one of their last three."

But still too early, again it breaks.

"Yup, only one of their last three, only eleven of their last thirteen," chirps Shutt, and there's more laughter.

"I hope you were listening, Tremblay," Robinson shouts, thinking of something else. "Ya don't just dump it out in front blind. You heard him, 'It's the worst play in hockey.'"

Gainey looks at Lapointe. "Hey Pointu, what number we up to now?" he asks.

Lapointe, who knows such things, shrivels his eyes. "Uh, lemme see," he says, thinking aloud, "'the worst play in hockey,' number 117, I think," then, more sure of himself, "Yeah, 117."

"Hey, what was 116?" someone asks.

"Shootin' it in your own net," a voice shouts, and there's more laughter.

Every practice, every game, more than 150 times a year, every year, I put on my equipment the same way—inner jock first, then longjohns, sweat socks (the left ones first), outer jock, garter belt, hockey socks (the left one first), pants (left leg first), skates and pads (left ones first), arm vest, and finally sweater (left arm first). Dressing in layers as we do, the order can't vary much, but when it does, when I put on my right skate before my left, it doesn't feel right and I take it off again. It isn't superstition, it's simply habit and what feels right.

When I put on my equipment, it must go on at a steady, preoccupying pace: by 7:07, pants; 7:12, skates; 7:17, pads; 7:20, arm vest and sweater. After each is put on, as if reaching a checkpoint, I look back at the clock behind me: too fast, and with time and nothing to do I think about the game or whatever else crosses my mind; too slow, and I rush, and by rushing wonder if somehow I've affected how I will play. Not wanting to wonder, not wanting to think about the game or something other than the game, I keep rigidly to schedule. After a somnolent day of newspapers, naps, walks, TV, ceiling holes, and hypnotic exercises, I want to arrive at game time undistracted, my mind blank, my emotions under control. I know that if I can, the rest of me is ready.

It never quite happens, of course, and after this long I know that when a game begins, none of it matters anyway. Still, to keep worried, nagging voices under control, it is a routine I won't give up.

Suddenly remembering something he's heard, Shutt blurts, "Hey, ya hear Pit [Pete Mahovlich] got into a fight at a Penguins team party? Yeah, some guy knocked him down."

He gets murmurs of interest, but no surprise.

"Hell, doesn't take much to knock Pit down at a party," a voice mumbles.

"Or anywhere else."

"Poor old Pit," Robinson laughs, shaking his head, "no wins, eighty-four losses."

Waiting his chance, Tremblay jumps in before he is ready. "That's like you, Robinson," he growls, and, startled, we look up. Houle stifles a grin.

"Ooh Larry, that's a shot. You're not gonna take that, are ya?" Houle asks, doing his best to see that he doesn't. Before it can go any further, Lapointe steps in. "Hey, c'mon, let's be fair," he says, sounding suspiciously fair. "When has Bird *ever* had a fight?"

There is silence.

Happily back into something he started, Tremblay repeats the question, "When *has* Bird ever had a fight? Anybody remember?" We look blankly at each other. "Anybody?"

Robinson can't hold himself back any longer. "*Câlisse*, listen to that," he snaps with pretended outrage. "You guys're pretty brave startin' something, but ya sure disappear fast."

Suddenly contrite, Tremblay hangs his head. "Yeah, you're right, Bird. You *do* help us a lot," he says almost apologetically. "I mean, the way you stand up to 'em, threatenin' 'em, pointin' that finger of yours at 'em," and, standing up, hunching up his shoulders, he glowers at an imaginary face inches beneath him, his right index finger jabbing frighteningly at the air.

"'Hey, don't do that to my buddy,'" Tremblay warns in a not quite deep voice, "'don't *ever* do that. If I catch you breakin' his jaw again, *point point point*,'" he says, jabbing three more times. Pausing as if something further has happened, he goes on, this time more excited: "Hey wait a minute. Wait a minute!" he shouts, his voice pitching higher. "'Ya did it again. I told ya not to do it, didn't I? Didn't I?'" he repeats, now really excited. "'Jesus, now ya got me mad. I can't believe how mad I am. Boy, am I mad,'" and finally pushed to the limit, anger exploding out of him, "'and if you *ever ever* do that again, *point point point* . . .'"

There is loud laughter.

Gradually, hearing each other laugh, we become scared and quickly stop. "C'mon, we're too loose. We got a game tonight," a voice shouts. Then another.

"That's right, that's right. Gotta pick it up, guys."

But with the slightest pause, the spasm breaks. Savard turns to Lambert. It happens at almost the same time each time we play the Wings. "Hey, Lambert," he taunts liltingly, "you should be mad, Lambert," and with that, and knowing the rest, Lambert begins to laugh. He had been drafted originally by the Wings, a year later left unprotected and claimed by the Canadiens. "They didn't want you, Lambert," Savard needles with great delight. "They just shit on ya. Come on, Lambert. Get mad. Get mad."

And when Savard finishes, Robinson, Gainey, or one of several others starts in on him, "You too, Sarge," the voice will say, and with that we begin to laugh. Nine years ago, the Wings, already in the playoffs, eased through the final game of the season, losing 9-5 to the Rangers, putting the Rangers in a tie with the Canadiens, and, after the Canadiens lost to Chicago, into the playoffs on total goals; the Canadiens, Savard, Cournoyer, and Lemaire included, were eliminated. "Come on," the voice taunts, "they quit on ya. They made ya look like assholes, Sarge. You owe 'em something. Get mad, Sarge. Get mad." And with that, as abruptly as the subjects came up, they go away until the next Wings game.

Ten minutes. I strap on my right pad. Preoccupied with time and equipment and not yet the game, the room is quieter, if no more serious. Too quiet. Uneasy, thinking of Cournoyer, the team's captain, at home, his distinguished career probably over, Lapointe says, "Hey, let's win this one for Yvan," and instantly the room picks up. "Poor little guy," he continues, "his back all busted up, probably just lyin' at home . . ." and as he pauses as if to let his words sink in, Shutt and Houle jump in before anyone else can.

". . . havin' a little wine . . ."

". . . a little Caesar salad . . ."

". . . poor little bastard," Lapointe muses sadly, and we all laugh.

I'm not sure what I thought the Canadiens' dressing room would be like before a game, though in me there was certainly a lingering image and a Marty Glickman-like voice that went with it:

"Here we are inside the dressing room of pro sports' greatest franchise, the Montreal Canadiens. See and hear the majestic Béliveau, the lion-hearted Richard, the enigmatic Mahovlich. Watch as a team of proud, aging veterans readies itself for one more crack at hockey's top prize, the coveted Stanley Cup."

The first time was almost eight years ago, in Pittsburgh before my first NHL game. I remember being surprised, even disappointed, that it seemed so like every other dressing room I had been in: players undressing, dressing, no special words spoken, no mood of a different quality, no solemn rituals that set it apart. Then about ten minutes before the warm-up, it changed. The powder sock appeared. An ordinary sweat sock filled with talcum powder and taped shut at its open end, though uncommon today, it was used by many at the time to turn tacky black stick-tape a more pleasing shade of gray. This time, it appeared for a different reason.

"Hey, nobody get Fergie's new suit," a voice shouted, and before the fractious Ferguson could move, the powder sock splattered against his dark blue jacket, leaving it a not-so-pleasing powder blue. Amid laughter, a sympathetic voice cried, "Oh Fergie, that's terrible. Here, lemme help." The helper rubbed at the powder with a large ball of cotton, plastering it over with a thick cotton mat. Furious, laughing, Ferguson grabbed the sock; others, their skate laces dragging, ran from the room with their clothes, the sock pinballing here and there after them. When it disappeared about five minutes later, five minutes before the warm-up to my first game, a heavy talcum cloud filled the room.

I can never sense the mood in the room before a game. Noisy, or quiet, each can be read a different way; both can mean the same.

Some players use noise like exciting mood Muzak, riding it, building with it until game time; others need noise to blurt out the oppressive tension they feel, others to comfort themselves that all is well. I used to worry at the one-liners and frequent laughter before a game. Not my way, not a goalie's way, it seemed an incompatible distraction from what we were doing. But now I worry less. For a one-liner, a burst of encouraging chatter ("C'mon *this*" or "C'mon *that*"), an earnest gem of information, even a powder sock, can come from the same state of mind, depending on the way a player deals with pressure. Only for important regular-season and playoff games does the room sound different: a little more quiet, a little less laughter, as if noise is unneeded, laughter too easily misunderstood.

With only a few minutes left, Shutt suddenly remembers and looks across at Lupien. "Hey Loopie," he says with an unconcealed grin, "you and Mousse [Mondou] gonna get Woods?"

We begin to laugh, then laugh even harder thinking of what's coming next.

A chorus of mocking, adolescent-high voices fills the room.

"'Hiya Woodsie. How are ya Woodsie?'"

"'...How're the wife and kids, Woodsie?'"

"'...Hey Woodsie, I got a new boat. It's a real beauty.'"

Laughing at first, Tremblay looks at Lupien. "Hey, Lupien," he snarls, "why don't ya give him a kiss?" Lupien sets his chin, then smiles. The routine is done.

"*Tabernac*," growls Robinson, breaking a skate lace. "Eddy, Eddy, I need a lace!" he shouts.

"Left or right?" a voice asks.

"Ri—," he starts, then stops angrily. "Eddy!" he tries again, "Boomer! Gaetan! Peter!" No one appears and he's run out of names.

"Oh Ed-dy, Boo-mer, you can come out now." Nothing. A moment later, Lafleur appears. He's been at the Forum since 4:30 p.m., was fully dressed at 7 when I first noticed and probably long before that. He's been in the room at times, other places other times, and now he's back—his hair greased flat to the sides of his head, combed straight up in front, his teeth out, a toothbrush in his hand, brushing furiously at his gums. Lemaire sees him first.

"*Ta-berr-nac* ..." he exclaims.

We look up; amid laughter, as if reading from a newspaper, a voice intones, "'...he waits as if in a trance, his only thought the game still four hours away....'"

"*Câlisse*, you got *them* fooled, Flower," Savard laughs.

"Hey Shutty," Lapointe taunts, "there's your meal ticket." Shutt, who has made a career feasting off his linemate's rebounds, is typically nonplussed. "Ah, that's the way I like to see him," he says, "ready, but not too ready. There'll be rebounds tonight."

Five minutes.

"Good warm-up, guys. Good warm-up."

Laces get tied, straps tightened, last-minute shoulder pads slapped into place. The clock eases forward with each anxious glance: two minutes, a minute, thirty seconds.

"Here we go, guys. Here we go."

Messages get shorter, louder, more urgent, and are unheard. Risebrough and Tremblay pace the room, then Mondou, Napier, Hughes, and one by one several more. Palchak hands me the game puck. Everyone's standing; we're ready.

Bowman enters.

"Okay, let's go," he says quietly, and with a shout we spring for the door.

The Forum is almost empty. A few hundred fans cheer as they see us in the corridor to the ice, but with no support from 16,000 vacant seats around them, suddenly self-conscious, they go quiet. Grim-faced, my eyes on a spot always a few feet in front of me, when I hear their fragile sound I look up, and, remembering this is the warm-up, I look down again. The Wings are on the ice. I skate around, glancing back to look for Vachon, but, out of sync, when I'm at center he's a hundred feet away circling his net. Skating faster, cutting each corner as I come to it, a few laps later I pass him at center, and we smile and nod as goalies do. Gilles Gilbert winks, Tony Esposito and Chico Resch skate by as if preoccupied with other things, Bernie Parent hovers near the centerline, reluctant to be anywhere else until the ritual is done. A few times, eyeing each other up opposite sides of the ice and certain to pass at center, I looked suddenly away just to make him wait. But each time it bothered me more than it did him, and a few laps later, smiling and nodding I would play out my part.

I used to look for Joyce. A Forum usherette behind the visiting team's bench, Joyce met me on the street one day, and we stopped to talk like old friends. A few days later at the Forum, when I skated by in warm-up, we smiled and nodded to each other. We won; and I played well. From then on in each warm-up, skating counter-clockwise so I had the width of the ice to get ready, I would smile and nod to Joyce. Then last year, losing more often and playing poorly in the Forum, I stopped, and haven't said hello to Joyce since.

I still have the puck that Palchak gave me. Free of the dressing room, the team dances and cuts happily by me, but without a puck for nearly a minute, they're getting impatient. When I was seven or

eight years old, the Toronto Marlboros, then a junior farm team of
the Leafs, had a goalie I liked named Johnny Albani. Small, with a
short black crew-cut, when Albani led his team onto the Gardens
ice he would drop the puck he held in his catching glove and shoot
it off the protective glass to the right of his net. *Clink.* It was a
sound we heard only at the Gardens, for at the time only the
Gardens had protective glass, and a sound more special because a
goalie, using his awkward paddle-like stick, had made it. So when I
got home, grabbing my goalie stick and puck I would go out to the
backyard and try to emulate Albani. There, time after time, I would
draw the puck back, pivot, and power forward, at the critical
moment of release feeling my wrists roll over, my arms and stick
slam into slow motion, the puck slithering away in an arc, never
leaving the ground.

Years later, wrists firmed up, hours of practice behind me,
Albani-like I would lead my team onto the ice with a shot off the
glass, but too often it was an unsatisfying shot off the boards,
sometimes one that never left the ice. So, in time I tried something
else. Turning joy and achievement to humorless superstition,
*before each game, I must take the first shot; it must strike the boards to
the right of my net between the protective glass and the ice. If it doesn't,
I will play poorly.* So, as the team waits anxiously, I look for an
opening, fifteen to twenty feet of uncrowded space to take my
important shot.

It's one of many superstitions I've come to burden myself
with. I don't tell anyone about them, I'm not proud I have them, I
know I should be strong enough to decide one morning, *any*
morning, no longer to be prisoner to them. Yet I seem helpless to
do anything about it.

Sports is fertile ground for superstition; crossed hockey sticks,
lucky suits, magic stones, and things more bizarre, it comes from
the mystery of athletic performance—the unskilled bat that goes 4-
for-4, a goalpost, a bad hop, a *move*, brilliant and unconceived, that
happens, and never happens again. *Luck*, we call it, and coming as it
does without explanation, leaving the same way, when it comes we
desperately try to hold onto it, isolating it, examining its parts and
patterns, if never quite to understand them, at least to repeat them
by rote. What did I do yesterday different from other days? What
did I eat? What did I wear? Where did I go? Who did I talk to? and
each answer becomes our clue, not a serious clue, of course (of
course!), but still the best we have. So we use them—don't change
the luck.

But I use superstition in another way. I don't want Joyce or
the first shot to be the reason I play well. It may be "better to be

lucky than good," as we're often reminded (for a loser can be good, but only a winner is lucky), but I want to feel connected to what I do, I want the feelings a game gives unshared, undiminished by something separate from me. So, instead, I use it as a focus for the fear I feel. Afraid of a bad game each game I play, I use Joyce and the first shot to distract me from the fear of a bad game, which I can't control, to the superstition, which I can. I have turned it into a straw game, one with no other opponent, with standards and requirements *I* set, which I know I can meet. So when I *do* meet them, when I successfully smile and nod to Joyce, when my first shot hits the boards to the right of the net, I give myself reason not to fear a bad game. If things change, if Joyce quits or turns away when I look at her, if my shooting deteriorates, I simply change the game and set new, *achievable* standards. For me it's a way of controlling the fear I can't eliminate, a way to blank my mind and keep it blank when other ways fail. Off the ice, there are no lucky horseshoes, no four-leaf clovers, I need no superstitions; on the ice, older and more insecure, I need more each fearful year.

I see an opening, not as large as I would like, but cutting sharply for it, I drop the puck. Eager skaters dart after it—I shoot. The puck wobbles badly, but strikes where it must. Feeling a tiny surge of pleasure, I skate around mindlessly.

Round and round, and each lap the clock is eighteen seconds closer to zero. Over the glass, fans shout, reaching pens and programs toward me, but looking down at the ice, readying myself to play, I pretend not to hear. I glimpse usherettes, ushers, photographers; Eddie, behind the penalty box, a small, shy, older man who once a year gives me a wrinkled brown bag containing pajamas for Sarah and Michael that he made at work; Lennie, in the same corner where Pete Mahovlich, reaching his stick over the glass, would regularly sprinkle him with snow, laughing, grateful, with hundreds of fans as his witness, a *friend* of the team. Tonight Lennie stands in the exit talking, waiting.

Round and round we go. Gainey stops, the team stops and turns the other way. Larocque goes in net. I keep skating, glancing at the clock, aware of nothing else. At 15:00, I stop in front of the penalty box for stretches; at 10:10, my mask is in place; at 10:00, I skate to the net.

Like skippers in a fast-turning rope, Larocque jumps out, I jump in, the rhythm uninterrupted. But I am cold and unready, the pace is too fast, and shot after shot goes in. Before I can worry, Robinson skates to the middle of the ice, motioning everyone to the blueline. Facing only a single shooter, gradually I gain control. At Cornell, I tried to stop every shot in the warm-up; each one I didn't stop represented a goal I would allow in the game. With faster, better shooters, I have no chance, so I changed the game. Now I must stop only enough shots that the ones I don't stop disturb neither me nor the team. Like every other part of my game day, unworried, untired, uninjured, I want only that the warm-up come and go without trace.

With about three minutes left, I begin to think about *it*. Since I was young, a practice couldn't end until I had stopped *the last shot*. It was someone else's ritual first, probably my brother Dave's, but for every practice and warm-up since, as the proper end to something and the base on which to build something else, it has been mine. But sometime during twenty-five years, the ritual got complicated. It remains unchanged for practice, but for a warm-up *I must catch cleanly (no juggling or trapping) a shot from a player unaware his shot must be caught (no gratuitous flips). And then I must leave the net. If I don't, I will play poorly.* It is not so easy as it seems. Undefended shooters come in close and try to score, and I must stay in net long enough to get warmed up. Yet I have help, at least I think I do—Robinson. We have been teammates for more than four hundred games, and Robinson seems to understand. I have never told him, nor has he ever asked, nor have I told anyone. But as the clock flashes down, as I dance about my crease anxiously, he seems always to get the puck, and with it to take a shot I can catch.

With less than a minute remaining, as Robinson moves slowly into position, I catch Lapointe's shot and leave the net.

Tremblay rips off a skate, "Eddy! Eddy!" he yells. "*Câlisse*, I'm slidin' all over the place."

"Good warm-up, guys," says a voice coming through the door. "Good warm-up."

A few steps behind, another, "*Câlisse*, we gotta be sharper than that. We're dead out there!"

It's quieter than before. Ready or not, we have fifteen minutes. Nothing can be put off any longer. Skates, some sweaters, shoulder pads, and elbow pads come off, sticks are re-examined and taped, helmets adjusted, bodies slouch back against cool concrete block walls. An ice pack behind my head, now and then I sip at a Coke, looking at the program, putting Wings' names to numbers and faces I didn't recognize in the warm-up. Three seats away, Shutt does the same. Everything is slow, almost peaceful, each of us unconnected one from another, preparing in our own separate ways; as the game approaches, we reconnect. Against the Islanders or the Bruins, the room can be quiet or loud, it makes no difference. We know we are ready. Tonight, we aren't so sure, about each other, about ourselves. So sometimes we're quiet, and sometimes we make ourselves loud.

"C'mon, big gang," Houle exhorts, breaking the silence, "an early goal and they'll pack it in."

"Yessir, guys, they don't want any part of it." But again nothing.

"*Câlisse*, where's the life?" Robinson yells. "We're dead in here. C'mon, c'mon...."

Houle looks at Lapointe taping his wrists, turns and shouts in the direction of the toilets, "Hey Pointu, you in the shitter?" Then louder, "Can't hear ya, Pointu. Can't hear ya."

Lapointe looks up, then down again, saying nothing.

Lemaire, who, with Cournoyer injured, is the senior player on the team, tapes a stick, minding his own business. "C'mon, Co," Savard interrupts pleasantly, "this might be your last game. Never know, Co, at your age you might die out there."

Another routine begins. Lemaire giggles convulsively. Tremblay shrugs, "Who'd notice?" and there's loud laughter. But set to jump in, Shutt stops himself, then Robinson, and suddenly it ends.

"C'mon, c'mon, we're not ready!" a voice shouts. There is a pause, a change of tone, then another shout, more pleading this time.

"Hey, c'mon, let's be good homers, guys." Nothing. With a deep breath, Robinson tries something different.

"Hey, c'mon guys," he says casually, "gotta play it, might as well win it."

We know why we want to win. We know how a win can make us feel; we know how we feel when we lose. We know that we are better than the Wings, that we're expected to win, that we expect ourselves to win; that we *should* win. Still, before every game we worry that this isn't enough, that reasons unchanging from game to game have become wearied and clichéd, so we try others: seasonal reasons—"Let's start [finish] the season [the second half] off right, guys"; "Two points now is the same as two in April"; pride—"Need it for the division [Conference, overall], gang"; money—"Forecheck, backcheck, paycheck, guys"; "C'mon, might mean fifteen Gs [two Gs]"; home reasons—"Let's be homers, guys"; road reasons—"Let's not be homers, guys"; "Let's start [finish] the trip off right"; practical reasons—"It's a four-pointer, guys"; "C'mon, they've been hot [cold] lately"; "Two points against these guys [Wings, Canucks, Capitals] is the same as two against the Islanders [Bruins, Flyers]"; "Let's not give 'em [Bowman/Ruel, the fans, the press] anything to give us shit about"; others—"Hey, let's win this one for —— [an injured player]."

The reasons interchangeable, the logic and emotion invariable, it is usually to no effect. Still, every so often, something is said that reminds us of something we believe in, that is important to us. At the start or end of a season, when I hear, "Let's start [finish] the season off right," it means something to me. Before a game on the way to the West Coast, already dreaming of the peace and freedom a win and the weather can give, when I hear, "Let's start the trip off right," it pumps me up a little. Others have different things they react to, and in filling quiet times this way, occasionally we say the right thing for someone who needs it.

The mood is beginning to change. Programs are down, ice packs, Cokes put away; equipment is taped up, snapped up, laced up; bodies are twitching, coming off walls, eyes narrowing, tightening; moods, still separate, are building, and coming together. It's like a scream about to happen. Suddenly, it all comes crashing down. *Whaack.* Lafleur is back. With heads down retying our skates, we didn't see him enter, slamming his stick on the table in the center of the room. Tape, gum, laces, ammonia sniffers, eighteen shocked and angry bodies bounce violently in the air.

"*Maudit tabernac*, Lafleur!"

"Wake up, *câlisse*," he laughs, and is gone again.

At 7:53, Palchak walks over to Lapointe, Lapointe looks at the clock, and a little upset tells him he's early and should come back in four minutes, when he's supposed to. Watching the clock another minute, at 7:54, Lapointe goes to the toilet. A minute later, he's back. Two minutes later Palchak arrives to stone first his right skate, then his left. Finished, he does the same to Robinson's and Engblom's skates. It began with Cournoyer a few years ago—"the magic stone."

Four minutes remain. All day, bodies and minds have been fighting for control, and now, finally, bodies have won. Metabolisms in slow idle scream louder, and higher. Words grunt from mouths unable to hold them, and crush up against each other.

"Need it! Need it, gang."

"On that McCourt, guys."

"Nedomansky too."

"Don't let Polonich get 'em goin'."

"Gotta have it! Gotta have it!"

"Who's got the first goal?"

"I got it!"

"I got it!"

"That's it! That's it!"

The buzzer sounds three times—three minutes to go.

"Wake-up call! Wake-up call!"

"Three minutes to post-time, gang."

Mondou gets up, walks around the room slowly, stopping in front of each of us, tapping both our leg pads with his stick.

"Gotta have it! Gotta have it!"

"They're hot, guys!"

"C'mon, put 'em down! Put 'em down!"

"Gotta watch Larson!"

"Good start! Good start!"

"Get on Woods, guys!"

"Skate 'em! Skate 'em!"

"Four-pointer, guys. Four-pointer!"

One by one, we're standing. Pacing, slapping pads, kicking kinks away, revving up.

Bowman enters. He starts to talk, but we've nothing left to hear. The buzzer sounds again, once. It's time.

"Okay, let's go," Bowman says, and with a shout we break for the door.

I go first, then Larocque, then Lapointe. Lafleur, to the right of the door, taps my left pad, then my right, with his stick, jabbing me lightly on the right shoulder with his gloved right hand. He does the same for Larocque and Lapointe, then squeezes into line, ahead of Robinson. One by one the tight-faced line continues, to Napier, second to last, and Lambert, last. As we come into view, the noise begins and builds.

"*Accueillons*," the announcer shouts, "let's welcome, *nos Canadiens*, our Canadiens!"

The organ rumbles, the crowd lets out a surging roar. I swivel past the players' bench; my padded legs shuffle in single file through the narrow open door—*don't fall*, I think to myself—and I jump onto the ice. The others burst past me. Round and round and round they go. Eyes down, staring at a series of imaginary spots always twenty feet in front, I glide to the net. I clutch the top bar with my bare left hand. I scrape away the near-frictionless glare ice of my crease. From goal-line to crease-line, my skates like plows, left to right, right to left, sideways eight to ten inches at a time, I clear the ice.

The clock blinks to zero; the horn sounds, the whistle blows, the players spasm faster.

...gloves in front, stick to the side, watch for Lemaire, don't forget Robinson....

They file past.

"Let's go, Sharty, Bo, Mario," I roll-call the names as they go, my pads tapped, slapped in return. Lapointe approaches slowly, his stick in his right hand, tapping the left post, both my pads, then the right. Risebrough slashes hard at my left pad. At a distance Lemaire

winks, then taps my blocker. Circling slowly, waiting for the others
to go, Robinson, stick in his right hand, taps the left post, both my
pads, then the right. *Don't change the luck.*

"*Mesdames et messieurs*, ladies and gentlemen, *les hymnes
nationaux*, the national anthems."

A cherubic silver-haired man steps onto the ice—Roger
Doucet, his tuxedoed chest puffed like a pigeon's. I stiffen, then
drift in and out as he sings; between anthems I shift my skates so as
not to wear ridges in the ice. When he finishes, there is loud
applause, the mood two anthems closer to the game.

I take a deep breath. My chin tucked to my chest, my eyebrows
like awnings hooded over my eyes, I put on my mask. Referee
Wally Harris, turning to his right, holds his right arm in the air, the
goal judge to his right flipping on his red goal-light. Turning to his
left, Harris does the same. I don't see him. Years ago, I decided that
if I saw a red light before a game or before any period, I would see
many more behind me during the game. So I look away, earlier,
longer, than I need to, just to be sure. Then slowly I peek
upwards—to the faceoff circles, to Robinson's legs and Savard's, to
Jarvis's, McCourt's, and Harris's legs at the center-ice circle. They
are bent, set in faceoff position. I look up.

With a rhetorical nod, Harris asks Vachon if he's ready;
Vachon nods back. Harris turns to me, and nods.

I've made it—through a purposely uneventful day, mostly
unworried, unbothered, uninjured, undistracted by me or the
game, ready to play. Others may sit in darkened rooms staring at an
image—of opponents, of themselves—rehearsing movements or
strategies, rehearsing hatreds; I keep moving, physically, intellectu-
ally, to keep moving emotionally. For if I let myself stop, I wonder,
and if I wonder, I worry, and gradually grow afraid. But fear, like a
landscape seen from a passing train, blurs with speed and proxim-
ity, becoming nonrepresentational, and unrecognized. So each
year I move a little faster, until now, moving so fast for so long, I
find that I can almost forget fear, unaware even of the ingrained
superstitions, rituals, newspapers, naps, and walks that let me
forget. Finally, they are just natural, unnoticed parts of my game-
day routine.

I nod back.

SATURDAY
PART II Montreal

For us, this is just another game in a long schedule. It is one of
about fifty or sixty such games a season, anticipated with routine

emotion, played routinely to an almost certain result. It brings with it no special feeling, and except for the player who scores two goals or more, it will leave nothing special when it ends. Because we are the best, because a long, numbing season rarely permits one team to set an emotional trap for another, our games reduce almost to formula: physical readiness plus emotional readiness equals victory. Only rarely, when everything and everyone feels *right*, when nothing else seems to matter, does the game ever become pure fun.

Tonight, it won't happen. Thoroughly inferior and playing in Montreal, the Wings are waiting to lose. Watching us, they are deciding whether to contest the loss or to pack up emotionally and prepare for the next game. In Detroit, they take the initiative from the beginning, using energy drawn from the crowd to drive them on, to disorient the referee and us, in turn to give them more energy. In Montreal, trying to win with most of the game left to play, they would only rouse us into something they know they can't handle. So they wait, and hope that we'll wait. And we do.

And as we wait, we play as if distracted by other things. For us the Wings represent an opportunity: for Shutt, who must score fifty goals, and Lafleur, who must score more; for Robinson, who competes with Potvin and Salming; for Jarvis and Gainey, Tremblay, Lambert, and everyone else who has public and private expectations to meet. When hoped-for, planned-for goals don't come against the Leafs or the Bruins, two or three against the Wings can save a contract bonus, an all-star team place, or a scoring title. So, until the Wings make it a game, until winning and losing seem important, we play with other things in mind. I want a shutout.

The puck goes from Jarvis to Robinson, and quickly into the Wings' zone. For thirty seconds, a pack of four or five players chase it from side to side inconclusively. First Huber has it, then Gainey, then Thompson and Jarvis, then Chartraw, Hamel, and Chartraw again, only to lose it, only to get it back, only to do nothing with it. One hundred and seventy feet away, I watch from a deep crouch, inching ahead, turning, flexed in readiness, playing out each play until slowly I realize the game that has occupied me all day is still far away. Straightening, I wait; and keep moving. I sweep away ice shavings I swept away before. My eyes rebound from the puck to our bench to their bench to the clock to the puck to the clock, until I can't move them fast enough, and my legs begin to stiffen— *c'mon, gotta be ready, gotta be ready.* It's been more than a minute. Their first shot, which once seemed only a perfunctory moment, is building up in me as an event. I shake my legs—*c'mon*, *c'mon*—and suddenly, they come.

McCourt intercepts a pass inside his blueline, hits Thompson breaking at center, and together with Libett they come upon a fast-retreating Savard and Robinson. A jolt of panic goes through me. Quickly tightening into my crouch, winding tighter and lower as they get closer, my body is telling my mind I'm ready. But I'm trying too hard, winding too tight, too low. Thompson shoots the puck into the corner to my left. I chase back to the boards, but too slowly; the puck hits my stick, flips, and rolls past me. Scrambling for the net, I run into Robinson, knocking him away from the play. Libett shoots the puck in front. My head snaps after it. For a dawdling, tortured instant, I see only blurred bodies—then the puck, on Lemaire's stick, moving slowly out of our zone.

I breathe a deep breath but feel no relief. I pace my tiny crease, turning, turning again, sweeping away ice shavings no longer there, screaming at myself like the worst cheap-shot fan. I wanted a good start, to send a message to my teammates and the fans, to the Wings, to *me*. A solid "thumbs up" indicating I was ready and couldn't be beaten. I wanted to put away my nagging mind and just play. I wanted teammates undistracted, unafraid that what they would do, I might undo. As for the Wings, I wanted to tighten some already painfully tight screws, to force on them the kind of cruel question no one should have to answer: am I willing to go through what surely I must, for something I will surely never get? But with an uncertain start, I've delivered another message, and the game will be harder for us.

From ragged play near our blueline, the puck pops loose, Lafleur racing with it for the Wings' zone, Woods and Miller after him. Quickly out of room he slows, looking for Lemaire and Shutt, but they are forty feet behind, and he dumps the puck in the corner and goes for a change. Labraaten is open at center, but Larson's pass is high and behind him; Risebrough steals the puck from Harper, then overskates it; Hamel, Huber, Lapointe, and Robinson bang the puck off the boards to center, Hamel, Miller, and Lapointe bang it back in.

For several minutes, the game stutters on, searching for a rhythm it doesn't have, seeking a commitment that isn't there. It won't come easily. Against the Islanders or the Bruins, one player, *any* player, can do something special and the others, sharing the feeling and needing only an excuse, will excitedly follow. But against the Wings, against any poor team, all the signs, all the shared feelings, lie on the other side of the emotional threshold— on the bored, listless downward side where good plays come and go with no emotional coattails; where bad plays forgive the ones that came before, reinforcing a deadening mood, encouraging others to come after. For the handful of players who start a game with this commitment, the game will beat them down. Their mood is too different ("What's got into them?" we wonder), the gap between them and us so large that the emotional point of contact necessary to inspire others to follow isn't there. Lafleur and Gainey, our emotional constants, who in big games set the mood and tempo we want, are almost irrelevant. They are simply *Lafleur* and *Gainey*, playing the way Lafleur and Gainey always do. Tonight, and in games like it, it's the swing players—Robinson, Lapointe, Shutt, Tremblay, and one or two others—who will give the team its mood. Sometimes they feel the game, sometimes they don't. They are our emotional bellwethers.

Bowman paces up and back, saying nothing. His chin is forward, his mouth arching up and down in a gentle sneer, his eyes stare vacant and expressionless. Here and there he reaches for an ice cube to chew, lifting his head to the clock, keeping it there for long seconds as if looking through it, its numbers smudging, fading, never seen. Moving along the bench, he taps the backs of those he wants next; on and off, twenty-five seconds, twenty seconds, changing every whistle, miming the pace he's looking for. But the game bogs deeper. McCourt jumps over the boards; Jarvis, Gainey, and Chartraw follow. They are our stoppers; and starters. They work hard, unfailingly, visibly hard, and in moments of confusion or trouble they give us forty-five seconds of solid ground, and a standard of effort and control for the rest to follow. For them it means few goals, but fewer against; in more graceful hands, for Lafleur, Lemaire, Shutt, and others, it will mean goals.

From a flash of sticks, Jarvis gets the faceoff to Robinson. He waits unpressured, the game moving before him. First, in safe, prearranged patterns, it flows to the boards or behind the net; then, as he moves slowly up the ice, it cuts and curls into open spaces, Robinson to Savard, back to Robinson, to Jarvis, who quickly passes to Gainey as he breaks clear at center. Larson, set for a slow-developing play, backpedals, then turns and sprints after him. For two or three frozen seconds, the game stops. It's just Gainey and Larson, a private duel of speed and muscle, and finally of will. Straightening from my crouch, I watch Gainey—his body bent parallel to the ice, relentless, driving, like a train across an open field, an enormous *force*. Watching him the crowd moans. Larson angles sharply across the blueline, meeting him at the faceoff circle. They come together, bumping, straining at each other. Slowly, then suddenly, Gainey powers by. A hard, low shot that hits the middle of Vachon's pads is no anticlimax. The crowd settles back, a little flushed.

Sometimes a game offers such little gems, brief inspired moments, unplanned, unconnected to anything else in the game, meaningless to its outcome, that make a game better. They represent something more basic than goals or assists, something pure, something treading close on the *essence* of a game and those in it, something unmeasurable, unrecorded, quite unforgettable.

I remember another such moment a few years ago. It was early in the third period in a game against the Los Angeles Kings and Henri Richard, nearing forty but still a brilliant skater and puck-handler, took the puck near our blueline and started up the ice. In three or four strides, sensing someone behind him, he glanced back and saw the Kings' Ralph Backstrom, a former teammate and himself a great skater, only a stride behind. Richard speeded up, turning, twisting, turning back on himself several times, but Backstrom stayed with him. What had begun as an undifferentiated moment among hundreds in a game was becoming their special moment, and they knew it. For long seconds it continued, and though they wound in and out of other players, no one intervened. Later, an emotional Toe Blake, who had coached them for many years, remembered it as how it had been in Canadiens practices so often before. I don't know how it ended; it didn't seem important at the time.

Now Tremblay runs at Huber, then Hamel. Lambert finesses the puck along the boards, Risebrough digs it out for Lapointe, but his shot is blocked, a scramble ensues, and the game breaks down again. The whistle blows, the teams change, forty seconds later the game starts up, twenty seconds later the puck goes over the boards, the whistle blows again. More than thirty seconds later when a new puck is dropped, the game's uncertain momentum is gone.

About eighty times a game it stops—for offsides and icings, for penalties, for pucks frozen under bodies, along boards, in goalies' hands, the number varying little from game to game, though to a player or a fan it never seems that way. For when a game is exciting, it never stops, continuing through whistles and commercials in painful expectation of new excitements. But when a game has trouble, when it has only a fragile momentum on which to build, every whistle conspires against it, interrupting it, making it start and restart again and again, stopping it dead.

Greeting the game with routine excitement, the fans move slowly back in their seats, watching, waiting, nothing to cheer, too early to boo, uncomfortable in their patient impatience. The whistle blows, the organist pounds out a rollicking tune—life for the fans to give to the players to give to the game—coaxing only spiritless clapping in return. When the puck drops, the music stops, the clapping stops, and the rhythmless game begins again.

I look at the clock; it's moved forty seconds since I looked at it the last time. The out-of-town scoreboard shows no score in the Leafs-Flyers game. The shot clock says I've had three shots—one from forty feet by Libett, another by Hamel from almost the centerline, the other I don't remember. At times, I've felt involved in the game, but too often it's distant, and each time I lose it. And whenever we get a penalty, whenever I see them come this way, I get the same unnerving twinge of panic, my mind nagging the same doubts, my body finding the same phony ready posture. I can't get comfortable. I'm not bored, but I'm not enjoying this very much.

When a game gets close to me, or threatens to get close, my conscious mind goes blank. I feel nothing, I hear nothing, my eyes watch the puck, my body moves—like a goalie moves, like I move; I don't tell it to move or how to move or where, I don't know it's moving, I don't feel it move—yet it moves. And when my eyes watch the puck, I see things I don't know I'm seeing. I see Larson and Nedomansky as they come on the ice, I see them away from the puck unthreatening and uninvolved. I see something in the way a shooter holds his stick, in the way his body angles and turns, in the way he's being checked, in what he's done before that tells me what he'll do—and my body moves. I let it move. I trust it and the unconscious mind that moves it.

Once I didn't. Once, as I was told I should, I kept a "book" on all the players I knew, with notes about wrist shots, slap shots, backhands, quick releases or slow, glove side or stick side, high or low; about forehand dekes or backhand dekes, and before a game, I would memorize and rehearse all that was there. But when my body prepared for Thompson's backhand before I knew it was Thompson, I realized that what was in my book, and more, was stored away in my mind and muscles as nerve impulses, ready, able to move my body before I could.

And once when I couldn't see a shot, yet felt my body move, I resisted its move, unwilling to move foolishly for something I couldn't see. Then, as I noticed pucks I couldn't see go by me where I was about to move, but didn't, I let myself go and stopped them. It's what others call *anticipation* or *instinct*, and while both may be accurate, to me neither suggests the mysterious certitude I feel. It's the feeling I get when I use a pocket calculator—pushing buttons, given no trail of figures, no hints to let me know how I got to where I did; no handwriting I can recognize as mine to let me know it was me who did it. I get only the right answer.

It's why I work all day to blank my mind. It's why I want a game to get close enough to absorb me. I don't want my eyes distracted by clocks and out-of-town scores. I don't want my mind divided by fear, my body interrupted with instructions telling it what it should do. I want eyes, mind, body, and puck to make their quickest, surest connection.

Lafleur comes onto the ice more than twenty-five times a game, and when he does, fans nudge and point and talk into a buzz, and sometimes they applaud. And when he gets the puck, there's the sudden escalating roar of a scoring chance though he's barely to center. And when he scores, which is often, he gets a sound reserved for no one else.

Lemaire loses the faceoff, but Shutt gets the puck to Robinson, who sends it to Lafleur at the blueline. Helmetless, he starts with a suddenness that sends his hair flipping up in back, in three or four strides pulling away at his temples, streaming out behind him like a flag in a breeze. Stooped and coiled, an ascetic, blade-like figure, he moves without the elegant smoothness of Gilbert Perreault or Mike Bossy, instead cutting and chopping at the ice with exciting effort. He crosses center. Shutt and Lemaire scramble to catch up; Hamel, Harper, and Polonich, abandoning all else, turn tail in desperate chase. But since his early disappointing seasons, Lafleur has learned what Muhammad Ali learned before him—that if you're quick enough, you can play a hitting game and rarely get hit. It was a crucial discovery. Confidence, he called it, simple comfort knowing that he could play with dazzling abandon, using all his special skills, undistracted, undeterred by intimidation, protected by nothing but his legs.

Crossing the Wings' blueline, suddenly he swirls clockwise, sending Hamel and Polonich hurtling by. Surprised, the crowd laughs: our swashbuckling hero toying with two bumpkin cops, having fun. He cuts for the middle. The laughing stops. Harper and Polonich come at him again. As they reach out, slashing him with their sticks, he sees Shutt uncovered at the edge of the crease. A quick pass, Shutt tips it in.

The game goes on. Fans, players, wait for whistles, talk, shake their heads, and laugh. When the puck drops, they keep talking. Some goals create the mood for other goals; this one belongs only to Lafleur.

Late in the period, Lupien and Polonich nudge along the

boards and decide to fight. It's a comic sight, the spidery-tall Lupien, the grizzled, gnome-like Polonich, taunting each other, swinging awkwardly, wrestling, the linesmen on top, all writhing on the ice in a pile. The crowd roars its excited approval, laughing at the same time. To the side, we watch, reacting to any sudden shift of fortune, otherwise waiting out its end. Other nights, when a fight flares from the escalating feeling of a game, when it shares its same ferocity, we stand passionately rooting, pretending the mood of the game, perhaps the game itself, is at stake. But this is a ritual fight. Each is a goon/player, each has a role he understands, doing what he thinks is expected of him. So if it seems a little like slapstick to others, to them it is not. It is more a duel than a showdown, more eastern than western. Though they both will fight again, it means satisfaction or a dangerous loss of face; in front of fans, in front of teammates suddenly less comfortable and less secure. It is a short, hard life. Like Hollywood starlets, their bodies open the door, giving them a chance they would never have, giving them the cushion of time to learn their craft; but few make it. A few years later, when they are slightly worn out, someone stronger and tougher, a few years younger and more eager, arrives, and they're gone.

The NHL theory of violence goes something like this: Hockey is by its nature a violent game. Played in an area confined by boards and unbreakable glass, by players carrying sticks travelling at speeds approaching 30 miles per hour, collisions occur, and because they occur, the rules specifically permit them, with only some exceptions. But whether legal or illegal, accidental or not, such collisions can cause violent feelings, and violent feelings with a stick in your hands are dangerous, potentially lethal feelings. It is crucial, therefore, that these feelings be vented quickly before anger and frustration explode into savage overreaction, channelled towards, if not desirable, at least more tolerable, directions. In essence, this is Freud's "drive-discharge" theory of human aggression.

The NHL offers two possible channels for this discharge: fighting, which on ice is little more than a harmless burlesque of threats, sweater-pulling, and off-balance punches, leaving the loser often unmarked, the winner's hands cut and swollen; and stick-swinging. Neither is desirable, one is necessary, so it is a matter of choice. With its worst abuses—mass brawling, goonery— now largely eliminated, fighting becomes the tolerated channel; stick-swinging, infinitely more dangerous, is more severely dealt with, by expulsions, fines, and suspensions. And for those who cite European hockey as evidence disproving the inevitability of hockey fighting, in fact European hockey only reinforces the point. For, playing in the same (albeit slightly larger) confined area, also carrying sticks and travelling nearly 30 miles per hour, colliding (though less often), and *not* permitted to fight, its players resort instead to dangerous stick-swinging. The result, as related to NHL President John Ziegler by his scouts and by Ziegler to us, is that at game's end their bodies are covered in welts.

The NHL is wrong. The reports of Ziegler's scouts notwithstanding, there is much visual evidence to the contrary. But more to the point, the NHL is wrong because if Freud was right, anthropologist Desmond Morris is also right. As Morris believes, anger released, though sometimes therapeutic, is sometimes inflammatory; that is, by fighting, two players may get violent feelings out of their systems, or, by fighting they may create new violent feelings to make further release (more fighting) necessary. If Freud was right, the NHL is also wrong believing as it does that fighting and stick-swinging represent the only channels by which violent feelings can be released. Anger and frustration can be released *within* the rules, by skating faster, by shooting harder, by doing relentless, dogged violence on an opponent's mind, as Bjorn Borg, Pete Rose, and Bob Gainey do. If Freud was right and anger released is anger spent, then a right hook given is a body-check missed, and by permitting fighting, the NHL discourages determined, inspired play as retaliation.

But Freud might be wrong. Anthropologist Richard Sipes thinks so. He has written that violence, instead of being a human potential requiring release, once released is *learned and repeated*, not cathartically purged away—in other words, violence feeds violence, fighting encourages more fighting. If Freud was wrong and Sipes right, the NHL is still wrong.

The NHL theory of violence is nothing more than original violence tolerated and accepted, in time turned into custom, into spectacle, into tactic, and finally into theory. For years the league has argued the wrong-headedness of its critics, and for years it has missed the point. Surely it matters little any more whether hockey fighting is violence or vaudeville, release or just good practice. What matters is that fighting degrades, turning sport to dubious spectacle, bringing into question hockey's very legitimacy, confining it forever to the fringes of sports respectability.

In a TV interview, Dick Cavett once asked John Cleese of England's *Monty Python's Flying Circus* the connection between his training as a lawyer and the group's outrageous, nonsensical humor. It was intended only as a set-up for a quick, witty reply; but Cleese answered that there *was* a connection, indeed a close one.

For though appearing random and nonsensical, he said, the group's humor in fact derived from an outrageous initial premise, but a premise then logically followed, step by step as a lawyer might, to its outrageous but logical end. So if, as in *Monty Python and the Holy Grail*, a knight, both arms cut off in a duel, continues to duel, it follows he must do so by either kicking or biting his opponent. The result, if nonsensical, is only because the original premise made it so.

Often criticized for lenience in dealing with league violence, Ziegler and NHL executive vice-president Brian O'Neill in fact have acted entirely consistently with the league's own understanding of violence. Unfortunately, trapped in their own myth and intending no humor, they too begin with an outrageous premise.

"That's it guys. Got the lead. That's all we wanted," a voice shouts coming in the door.

The door opens again. "Jesus Christ, we're fuckin' dead out there. C'mon!"

I sit down to see if Bowman has anything to say, but when he continues through the room to his office, I get up and leave. I don't like it in the dressing room between periods: nineteen wound-up bodies, together with nothing to do; for fifteen minutes, no equipment to put on, no sticks to tape, with nothing we want to say, quiet, then self-consciously quiet, then anxiously loud, then quiet again, exploding, imploding, uneasy, uncomfortable. We want only to relax. Bowman leaves so we *can* relax. But if I relax and do nothing, I think of other things, quickly unrelaxing; and if we relax, if something seems funny, if someone laughs, we panic.

"C'mon, c'mon, we're too loose in here!"

So I go to the video room.

Though I come here every intermission, Fred, the videotape operator, seems surprised to see me. "I don't have much this period," he apologizes, though not quite sure why. During the game, he notes goals, near-goals, and difficult saves he thinks I might want to see, the first retrieved and ready by the time I arrive. He pushes a button and a picture flickers onto the screen—it looks like random action from any game, then here and there is a pattern I recognize, then nothing. Finally, a tiny figure shoots from a bad angle and my stick swings across, deflecting the puck to the corner. I keep watching, waiting for the moment he has set aside. He stops the machine and asks if I'd like to see it again.

I go back to the room.

For a team or a player, each game, each period, is arguably different from the last. In two days, in fifteen minutes, things can change—a rest, a change of mood or strategy, a deep breath, a second chance, and everything *seems* different, and will again until it seems the same. So at the start of a period or a game, those who need another chance get it; and those who don't must prove themselves again.

The game starts up, and this time builds. Savard gets the puck at our blueline, waits for Libett to come on him, then, spinning counterclockwise, with a powerful but graceful leap, sheds him and starts up ice. Spotting an opening quickly, Gainey breaks, then Jarvis, but no pass comes and, slowing down, they angle back and wait. Savard moves to center. Thompson and McCourt come at him. Like a big stallion, feinting with fluid crossing strides, he prances languorously right, then left, swinging his body to shield the puck, easing by them. Recovering, Libett tries again, running at him, with Larson and Miller crowding him at the blueline. The puck rolls off his stick and trickles to the corner. The game stops.

Every game is *not* different. If not exactly the same, most are predictable, many at least uniform in mood and rhythm, in the types of problems they pose. When asked, I've always said what others have, that each game offers its own exciting and unique challenge. But if I ever really believed it, I don't any more. Maybe it's that I never wanted to shake others' expectations, or my own, or go to the trouble of explaining, risking that it might be misinterpreted; or maybe I've simply reached the age where I see sameness in things I always saw as different.

I see patterns now where I once saw mostly details: in games and seasons, in several seasons, in goals, in saves, in words I hear, in others, in me, everything like something from before, each new something slotted, added to the old, itself disappearing. More than fifty games a season, more than a hundred goals and a thousand saves, many vivid and important, many painful or satisfying, in days, weeks, they are gone. Like yesterday's newspaper, they are discardables, bundled together, forgotten, leaving only a sweep of intense, moderated feelings, and a handful of moments as reminders. Recently, a journalist asked me what were the most memorable saves in my career. Quickly I mentioned three or four to him, paused, waiting for others to come to mind; a few minutes later there was another, but that was all. A little embarrassed and determined to find more, that evening I sat in my office thinking back on nearly twenty-five years of playing goal, writing down each save as I remembered it. When I could think of no others, I counted them—fifteen—the most recent nearly two years ago.

Mostly they were odd saves, more different than special or important. Against Harvard, there was a short, quick shot that hit my skate and disappeared, the puck lodging behind my pad, undiscovered for many seconds. Once I split to my left in "butter-fly" position for a Darryl Sittler shot, never having moved that way before, or since; another time in Minnesota as I lay on the ice in the midst of a scramble, my glove reached blindly around in back of my head, and a tap-in to an open net from the North Stars' J. P. Parise disappeared into my glove.

Whole seasons are now gone for a litter of random, quirky moments. Quarter-final and semi-final series are removed from whole playoffs. Yet I remember each season and each playoffs vividly. Games with the Wings, the Islanders, and the Hawks, with the Kings and the North Stars, I remember what each was like— first periods, third periods, home games, away; players, styles, us, me, and them. All of it is organized, classified, stored away in a trail of feelings, in a pigeonhole mind, in *patterns*, and those that don't fit, I remember. Few don't fit.

For me, a game, a season, has become a series of moods and rhythms which, as a goalie, I must both support and counterbalance, rising as they rise, falling less far when they fall. Games or seasons, even great ones, don't skip from highlight to highlight, triumph to triumph, but come in widely varying moments of good play and bad. They are distinguished only by an inescapable sense of commitment, what some call "intensity," that its players and fans can feel at every moment, assuring them at bad moments that good ones are never far away. Tonight, for more than twenty-five minutes, the game has staggered without rhythm or commitment; it's a game I've played before.

I look at the clock; the next time, it's six minutes later. Like driving hour after hour of highway, suddenly realizing I remember nothing from along the way, I wonder if I was asleep, and scare myself.

"C'mon, c'mon, guys, pick it up. Gotta get goin'. C'mon, c'mon...."

I'm shaking my legs, bouncing around the crease in an exaggerated way, talking to myself, yelling. But penetrating the words and movement as it often does, there is a sudden thought—*we can only lose if I lose it for us*—and I feel another twinge.

Shutt curls lazily one way, then another, the puck fifty feet away, changing hands at each touch. Finally, it is surrounded by skates; bodies sag awaiting a whistle. It jumps loose. Before Lafleur gets it, Shutt bursts through center. From his defense position,

Miller watches him. Small enough as a defenseman to appear small, though he's not, stocky, modestly skilled, in his better games Perry Miller goes unnoticed but for one thing: he is one of the league's few remaining body-checkers. As Shutt takes the pass, he looks up and sees Miller, dead ahead, throw out his hip. Panicked, Shutt dances to his right, glancing off him, skipping by, catching up to the puck on the other side. Stranded at the blueline, Miller turns to watch. Shutt snaps a quick low shot. Vachon kicks out his pad and stops him.

Delivered mid-ice with shoulder or hip, a body-check is the universal symbol of Canadian hockey. Hard, clean, elemental, a punishing man-to-man contest, as it fades from our game it is more and more symbolic of glories themselves past. A lost art it is called, its practitioners—Ching Johnson, Red Horner, Bingo Kampman, Bill Ezinicki, Bill Gadsby, Leo Boivin, Bobby Baun, Doug Jarrett, Gilles Marotte—quickly dying out, their quality dying before them. But while coaches, general managers, journalists, fans, and ex-players all lament its passing, in fact, each generation since the 1930s has done the same, blaming each subsequent generation for its loss. For the body-check, like its obverse skill, stickhandling, began its (remarkably) slow decline as a victim of the forward pass. It is now a lost art whose time is past.

When Vachon stopped Shutt, I silently cheered. It was a cheer for a brilliant save, a fellow goalie, a beleaguered underdog, also for a friend. Then, moments later, remembering it's a 1-0 game we might lose, I admonish myself for cheering.

I don't like playing against friends. My loyalties divide, ultimately in favor of teammates, but that division distracts me, leaving me without the one-dimensional commitment a game requires. Against Vachon or Wayne Thomas, another goalie and former teammate, I want only for the game to end 1-0; against my brother, there is no satisfactory result. But a 1-0 game, hoped for, is easily 1-1, or 1-2, so whenever I think of it, angrily I lecture myself to stop, that Vachon is on his own.

Six players and the boards push in an isometric stalemate. The puck pops loose, Labraaten breaks with it. Swinging wide of Savard, over the blueline he is hammered into the boards, this time by Chartraw. Labraaten is a Swede, and Swedes, we are told, don't like to get hit, so they get hit often. It's a test, and long after non-Swedes have passed and been left alone, a Swede faces it again. You test him as you test anything you think might be weak and broken—you bang him, you bend him, you look for cracks, you bang him again, you bend him some more. He may be strong, he may not be broken; if you test him enough, he'll break.

Slowly the Wings enter the game. For thirty minutes they've been the unseen part of our show. Playing Abbott to Costello, the Washington Generals to our Globetrotters, they are our straight man and our victim, here only to make us look good, nothing more. But letting them stay close, we've made them feel like partners in the game, and now they want something more.

The game moves to our zone. Thompson beats Robinson to the puck, McCourt hooks it away from Savard; they bang it off the boards to Larson and Huber at the point. In front, Polonich, Libett, and Woods high-stick, cross-check, slash with Lupien, Lapointe, and Robinson. Eyes on the puck, referee Harris pretends not to see. Larson, then Huber, slap the puck towards the maze with "Go to the front of the net," "Tie up the defenseman," "Screen the goalie," "Let it hit ya" goals in mind. Ricocheting around, the puck finally shoots to the corner, pursued by a scrambling, flailing pack.

At the bench, Bowman is transformed. Angry, he pounds the boards with his fist, bellowing at Harris. Angrier, his body jerks into fast-forward, jumping up on the bench, down again, racing to the penalty box, yelling, his rich baritone now a whiny falsetto. It is more than the moment demands, like a three-year-old's tantrum, and we watch both amused and embarrassed. In the first period, stuttering to find a rhythm, Bowman quietly orchestrated what he wanted. Now, with the game in an unconcerned drift—ahead 1-0, in Montreal, against the Wings—with nearly thirty minutes to play, he wants to slap us out of one mood into one more urgent. He knows it's his job to give a game, to give us, the mood we're missing.

Before Bowman and the crowd can settle, Shutt, with a half-step but going nowhere, feels Larson's stick tug at him, hooking him off balance, allowing Larson to catch up. At his next tug, Shutt launches himself in a head-first dive, skimming across the ice on his belly, content to slide as long and far as he can. When he comes to a stop, still on his belly, leaving a twenty-foot trail of freshly dusted ice behind him, on cue Harris shakes his head vigorously—no penalty. The crowd boos.

Shutt dives often and well, as often and as well as Bill Barber of the Flyers, as the Leafs' Borje Salming. Occasionally, when the mood is right and a referee reacts too quickly, he draws a penalty. But growing too predictable, more often now he draws nothing but some scattered boos and in-joke chuckles from those who watched and felt privy to it. The irony, of course, is that Larson deserved a penalty. Not from Shutt's dive, which was self-inflicted, but from the hooking and hindering that stopped Shutt just as surely. Indeed, airlifted into North American hockey from soccer by way of European hockey to dramatize undetected fouls, gradually the dive has come to dramatize only itself. So far as all those who watched Shutt and Larson are concerned, what happened a moment ago was that Shutt took a dive.

Yet if the score was not 1-0, if the Wings were not deservedly competitive in the game, if their presence was not so fragile that a penalty and a goal might take them out of it, if this wasn't the Forum, if our power play was not so productive, if we weren't so superior that a non-call would hurt our chances, if this was the first period, or earlier in the second, if Lapointe had not gone uncalled in a borderline decision moments before, if Harris was not the referee, if someone else was, it might have been called differently. It is called discretion, and for an NHL referee, *it* is the rule.

NHL refereeing is an impressionistic exercise. A referee finds the mood of the teams, the direction they're going, and applies the rule book, a penalty here, several uncalled penalties there, letting the game find its natural rhythm, hoping in the end it looks like the game it should. For a hockey game is filled with infractions, more than can be called consistent with the other values of the game. So some penalties are called, most are not. Our only guide is a referee's reputation, the standard he imposes early in a game, certain basic refereeing principles—a scoring chance created or denied, the likelihood of injury—and the kind of "scenario officiating" all of us understand. It is refereeing by the clock, by the score, by what's come before, so that at any moment we can all sense who will be penalized next, and flagrant/cheap, what it will take.

Beyond this obvious inadequate consistency is a much deeper problem. Because a penalty disturbs a game, changing its rhythm, often (more than twenty percent of the time) its score, only a limited number of penalties can be called without infringing on the referee's credo—*Don't interrupt the "flow" of the game.* So though a game may have fights and brawls, and its players may be heavily penalized, only four or five times does a team hook or hold or slash enough to play shorthanded. Any more and that critical flow becomes disjointed; or worse, a game gets decided on power plays (directly), or by a referee (indirectly).

No doubt it's an important principle, but its side effects can be worse. Because of the self-imposed ceiling, the greater the number of infractions committed, the greater the proportion that go uncalled. Larson tugs once, twice, a third time—it's a penalty. So he stops, but so does Shutt. A permissible foul. No penalty. A staccato of hacks to arms and legs, a quick grab, and the black and white turns gray and the gray gets darker; and the players understand. It's not what's a penalty, it's what the game allows. And the more it allows, the more it gets, and the more it gets, the more it allows. It becomes a player's game just as it should be. Who pays to watch a referee? But hooked, held, and muscled back, what kind of game is it?

Hockey is the most difficult of professional sports to officiate well. There is just one referee, whereas in basketball there are two, in baseball four (sometimes six), in football one, though he is assisted by several others. A hockey referee is required to move with the play, changing and rechanging direction as he does, often out of position, his vision usually at least partly obscured. As in basketball, it's refereeing on the run; in football, officials take up strategic, mostly stationary positions; in baseball, the action comes to the officials. Yet though the game is more difficult and less precise to referee, a penalty in a hockey game is more important than it is in other games. One goal in every four is scored on a power play, two goals a game, and unlike basketball, where points resulting from infractions are scored in tiny increments, a penalty (and a goal) in hockey can swing the mood and momentum of a game.

But mostly it is the extent of a referee's discretion that makes hockey so difficult to officiate. In baseball, the best-officiated sport (if replay cameras are any judge), there is virtually none. It is ball-strike, safe-out, fair-foul, and except for balks, doctored balls, brushbacks, and a few other rarely called infractions (each a cause of great controversy), there are no non-calls. In hockey, officiating is like doing spot-checks on New Year's Eve. Anything signalled is bound to be an infraction, but sensing the randomness, those stopped ask angrily, "Why me?" And so good calls can seem like bad ones, everything becomes arguable, and no one is happy.

In the mid-1970s, the Flyers figured out the system, played it to cynical perfection, and won two consecutive Stanley Cups. Penalized more than anyone else but far less than they might be, with the league as unintended co-conspirator, they benefited hugely from the informal penalty ceiling and the league's commitment not to appear to intervene in a game's outcome. Some years later, the abuses of the Flyers largely gone, more subtle abuses increase. What the league never understood about the Flyers, what it doesn't understand now, is that it cannot be the passive actor it wishes to be. That like any *laissez-faire*, non-interventionist approach, there are consequences predictable and certain that follow for which it is responsible, and by deciding not to intervene it is in fact intervening just as surely on behalf of those consequences. A league, through its referees, sends messages to the game, the players react, the game takes on its form. But what is the message, and what is the form? And what would it be like if the message was different?

Woods has the puck in the corner; Robinson winds around him, but the puck dribbles out in front. I bob and weave, searching for the player I can't see but I know is there. *Whaack.* A shot speeds for the net. My eyes hack at legs and torsos in front of me, but it's no use. I see nothing. Unaware, my arm moves, my legs split to either side, my fingers pull away, then snap back tightly closed. From a crush of noise, there's profound silence, then suddenly a roar. I look in my glove—a good save, maybe better.

My chin, my backbone, tighten and set; arms, shoulders, thighs flex; fingers clench, teeth bare, nostrils flare, burning/chilling, bursting, I feel ten feet wide. I do not pace my crease like a duck in a shooting gallery, or sweep at ice shavings no longer there; *free*, my nagging doubts are gone. The Wings change; we change. New players come onto the ice to slap my pads. Unmoved, I say nothing. The clapping goes on.

I'm not sure when I began leaning on my stick. Perhaps at Cornell, perhaps sooner; it was a resting position at first, a habit, in time a personal trademark of sorts, and though I'm never conscious of doing it, after a good save or a bad goal I always hold the pose a little longer, as if wanting to deliver a message. Wishing to appear crushingly within myself—"A great save?" it says, with curious indifference, "Not even a test. You might as well give up." A bad goal? In a quietly defiant way it reminds fans and opponents, "You'll never get to me."

Slowly losing its energy, the applause continues none the less. It is too much praise, and suddenly uneasy I begin to pace, turning away from the sound again and again. *Stop*, I say to myself. *C'mon, get on with it. Drop the puck, make it stop.* But like the performer who holds up one hand for silence, with the other, off camera, I motion it on. Just once I'd like for a game to stop. For a referee to say, "Take your time, Ken. Ready when you are," and with everyone fading to the side, to look up at the crowd, eyes closed, and listen— to live the moment fully and completely through, to feel the sound and the save *together*, as long as they both shall last. Forgetting messages to fans and opponents, forgetting phony invincibility and what comes next. For them to get to me, just once.

I lean on my stick; the noise stops.

I get cocky. "Hey Wally, Wally," I yell to Harris, "how're ya doin'?" but what I say doesn't matter. I'm acting out a feeling, the first imperious moment of command.

"Bird!" I yell, interrupting the faceoff. "Hey Bird, c'mere. Bird," I say, repeating his name, "gotta wipe that guy out in the corner. C'mon, we need it," and Robinson nods. About to skate away, I ease up. "Hey Bird, ya see anybody shoot like that Larson?" I ask, then too quick with my own set-up, "'Cept maybe Reggie, eh? Heh heh heh."

I look at the clock, the shot-clock, the scoreboard, and invincible intoxicating thoughts fill my mind—shutouts, goal average ($\ldots 38^2\!/_3$ games, 84 goals; two times $38^2\!/_3$, $77^1\!/_3$; from 84, $6^2\!/_3$; $38^2\!/_3$ is the same as $^{116}\!/_3$; $6^2\!/_3$ is $^{20}\!/_3$; so $^{20}\!/_3$ divided by $^{116}\!/_3$, cross out the 3s, $^{20}\!/_{116}$, $^{10}\!/_{58}$, $^5\!/_{29}$; 29 into 50, 1,$\ldots$), Vézina Trophies, the Flyers, Islanders, North Stars, Kings, parade by me in my moment of triumph; it is some time before I'm back to the game.

A fan, seeing the save, watching me with Harris, then Robinson, seeing Robinson smile, is impressed.

It doesn't take long. Terry Harper, a former teammate, has the puck at the point. Tall, stiff, he slaps at it torqueless and two-dimensional like a table-hockey player. Thompson and Libett are in the corners with Robinson and Jarvis, Gainey and Chartraw are at the points, Savard is on the ice near the faceoff circle, the front of the net is clear except for McCourt. Standing about ten feet away, he sets himself for an easy deflection. Harper's shot approaches in a slow, unconcerned way. I shift my weight to the right, to the puck's new direction. McCourt angles the blade of his stick, and waits. He misses. The puck races undisturbed to my left. I lurch back, feeling nothing against my pad or skate, nothing against my stick, my glove. Nothing. No! Maybe it missed the net, maybe it hit the post or one of their players or one of ours. I throw my head around, listening for the boards; the glass; the post; the near-miss gasp of the crowd, the yell of further play. Instead, I hear two or three quiet, penetrating shouts; then eloquent silence.

I shoot, throw, kick the puck out of my net.

My father used to comment on how goalies reacted to goals scored against them, whether they showed disgust or resolution, whether they got up quickly or lingered prone in theatrical disappointment. He preferred, of course, that they get up and show resolution, and always made sure to tell me. Then, when I was about ten years old, and an overtime goal eliminated his Bruins team from the playoffs, I saw Harry Lumley break his goalie stick over the top bar of his net. Knowing I should be upset at his poor sportsmanship, I could only admire his honesty.

Pacing, sweeping, caged in my crease, I scream at myself. Then slowly, as anger turns to self-pity and finally embarrassment, suddenly weak, I feel an immense nausea that won't go away. *C'mon, give me another chance, two out of three, three out of five, anything. Please.* But the hope I can't quite feel tells me something is different and will never be the same. Before I lean on my stick, bent over, my hands on my knees, I stare at the ice.

I've always envied the *chutzpah* of Bruins goalie Gerry Cheevers. After a bad goal, he would look so inappropriately cocky that he challenged the crowd's memory of what they'd seen. Second-guessing themselves, quickly they decided a goal was screened or deflected and not his fault at all. But staring at the ice, I deliver another message, and the crowd knows what it knew all along.

Robinson skates back, tapping me on the pads, telling me lies I don't want to hear. When finally he goes away, and there's no one around, I hear the crowd, this time a loud grumbling buzz. I've lost them.

I had them once, in the beginning. When I was new and different, when the team was good but only good, when there were teams that were better. I had them in 1971, in 1972 and 1973, when Béliveau was gone and Lafleur was timorously arriving, when the team needed a goalie to *win* games in Montreal, not just a goalie not to *lose* them. But as the team improved, and there were none better, saves that became less frequent became less important, and goals against me, occasionally odd, inexplicable goals that might lose games (but didn't), stood out. And slowly, with each game and each goal, the goodwill that seemed inexhaustible was stripped away.

It's what happens to all Canadiens goalies. It happened to Vachon and Gump Worsley, to Plante and Bill Durnan before them, now to Larocque. After a few generous, exciting years of support, the support taken away, we become uneasy, sometimes fearful of playing in the Forum, preferring instead the road, where we can just play, where no matter how good the team is, it needs us to win. So little by little, a newer face takes over at the Forum— once Vachon, once me, once Larocque, soon someone else, excited, happy, made better for the support. But if a goalie survives long enough in Montreal, he can change again, if never completely. Though I prefer the road, no longer surprised by any reaction I get and less able to be hurt, the Forum doesn't bother me as it once did. Still, undeniably, I wish it were different.

It's not supposed to be that way. I am a professional, paid to do my job no matter the circumstances. Paying their money, my salary, the fans have the right to do as they please. It makes no difference to me. I can't control them, I can't depend on them; so I ignore them. They mean nothing to me. But of course they do. Being professional or not has nothing to do with it, I do only what I can. And by buying a ticket, does a fan acquire a right that a fan in the street has not? Opportunity, yes; access, yes; but any greater right? Does he acquire license to abuse me any way he likes, to say what he won't say to anyone else, anywhere else? Is that what I'm paid for, like a lightning rod, to stand in the place of *everyman* and attract and purge the resentments from his life? Am I supposed to take it and feel nothing? Is that all part of the game? I hear it all: every "On veut Larocque," every angry buzz, the tone in words I don't understand, the meanness in bitter, mocking applause. And the louder and longer they yell, the longer and straighter I lean on my stick.

I get them back for the start of each game and lose them with the first goal. Too many things have gone before, too many memories are too willingly recalled. The white gloves off, the Mulligans all played, they just wait, and so do I.

Okay, over and done with, can't do anything about it now. Still got a period to go. That's what's important. Gotta work at it, now. That's it, here we go. Here we go.

I'm not listening.

A bouncer from center, a penalty to Hamel, a penalty to Risebrough, a goal by Lambert, a save by Vachon; the period ends.

"That's it, guys. That's it."

"Jesus Christ, we're horseshit out there!"

We are of two minds: unhappy the way we played; ahead 2-1, scoring a late goal, playing in the Forum, worried silent that we're overreacting, gradually not so unhappy.

Behind, but close, after forty minutes it's the only way the Wings can beat us.

When a game takes off, you can hear it. Sounds rush at you, cramming your head, squeezing it louder and louder, driving your mind away, and driving your legs mindlessly on. Urgent, staccato sounds: skates that bite and crunch and get back in the play; pucks clickety-clacking from stick to stick; voices screaming sounds when words arrive as echoes. And over the boards, roaring, rising, swelling sounds that empty your stomach and run up and down your spine—the martial Muzak of the crowd as it rollercoasts the game.

The game has changed. For most of forty minutes, the Wings were afraid: of losing as badly as they might lose; of being embarrassed in front of 17,000 fans and two million television spectators; of what a crushing loss might do to proud parents and friends who have talked of this game for days. Afraid of getting ahead and hoping foolish hopes, of getting close enough to think they might have a chance. For what would you do if you were the Detroit Red Wings and you led the Montreal Canadiens at the Forum with forty minutes to play? or thirty-five? or thirty? First you would celebrate, then you would just feel good, better than you've felt in a long time, thinking, hoping, no dammit, *thinking*—tonight's the night, confident, excited, feeling like you feel when a game is over and won. Then the puck is dropped. Scrambles, penalties—twenty-seven minutes to go. Goalposts, missed open nets—twenty-five minutes. More goalposts—please let it be over. Please!—twenty-four minutes, eighteen seconds. Feeling it slip away. Afraid of the joy you feel. Afraid of what joy feels like when it's played with and mocked, and finally crushed. Afraid of driving on lemming-like, punch line to your own Big Joke. *Hey, you guys didn't really think you were going to beat the Canadiens, did ya? Hah hah hah. That's the best I've heard yet.*

But now, down 2-1 and only twenty minutes to play, the Wings have no time to be embarrassed. There's nothing left to be afraid of. We've made a terrible mistake. When you let an underdog think he can play with you, he forgets how bad he is and how good you are and is swept along on the moment. Like a cartoon character running off a cliff, when he forgets where he is, he can do remarkable things. We've made it into a game we can't be sure of winning.

It warmed up in the dressing room and started in the middle. Seven minutes later, it's in a sprint. We are twelve rats in a box, changing on the go, in a 45-second relay race. The whistle blows. The game goes on, too fast to stop, too fast for anything but a penetrating burn of feeling that later, with time, will explain itself. Its smile has disappeared. It has lost its professional cool; it is *fun*. Desperate, twisting, thrilling fun that hurts so much you want it to stop; and need it to go on.

"On him! On him! Two on ya, Bird. 'Round the boards! Get it out. Get it out! That's it. That's it. . . . Shoot it in, Sharty. Shoot it—look out! Back! Back! Two-on-two! Stand up! Stand up! Offside. C'mon, offside! They're changin'. They're changin'. Go with it, Pointu, go! Move it up. Move it up! Stay back, Pointu. Back! . . .

Stand up! Stand up! Right on ya! Freeze it! It's loose! It's loose! In front! It's loose! Ice it! Ice it!..."

The puck moves from stick to stick and team to team. More than six times a minute, more than 120 times a period, it changes possession. Physically contested all over the ice, the game is in constant transition. Patterns disrupt and break apart, moods skip, unsettled in one, on to the next, spiralling higher. Three quick strides, coast and turn, and turn again, and stop; three more quick strides, a pass, checked, and three quick strides the other way. Fragments, hundreds of them, each looking the same, some going somewhere, most not, and as player or fan you can never be sure which it will be.

Gradually as the period builds, as time gets shorter, there is a moment, one we can all sense, when a game will be won or lost. It is now. For fifteen minutes, the Wings have done what they were sure they couldn't do, and with nothing more to give, can slowly feel us getting stronger. With the puck at center, they shoot it into our zone and pile after it. Four, five, six bodies, the puck bouncing between them. The moment drags on.

Then it stops. Lapointe's shot deflects off Tremblay's right knee through Vachon's legs and it's 3-1.

Every minute or two, the Wings test us. Pushing their game a little higher to see if we push back, and when we do, they know it's over. It's like a cycling race, 2½ hours around and around; slowly, we looked over our shoulders, and close behind, they looked back at us. Here and there they speeded up, and we speeded up with them, always ahead. Then, nearing the end, they sprinted and we sprinted back. They pulled up alongside, nearly even, and we both went faster and faster until, finding a little more, or they a little less, we pulled ahead. Now we are looking back and, further behind, they look at us. They slow down; we slow down. They slow some more; we slow some more. Ever slower, in control.

SATURDAY
PART III Montreal

"C'est ça, gang. That's it."

"Another two [points], guys. Another two."

One by one we burst into the room.

"That's it, guys. That's it."

Equipment is thrown to the floor. Drinks are grabbed up and swallowed thirstily. The room goes quiet. Houle looks up, uneasy.

"Hey, good third [period], gang. Good third," he blurts. But no one seems to hear him. Again, "Big four-pointer, gang." Nothing. There is a muffled cheer from the arena. Tremblay charges through the door, the first star of the game. We look up.

"C'est ça, Mario," we yell. A few seconds later, it is Lambert. "C'est ça, Yvon." The noise picks up, then fades. Silence. This time we can all hear it.

"Hey, get 'em any way we can, guys."

"That's right. That's right," Robinson begins earnestly. "Takes a good team to win when uh, uh..." He doesn't finish. There is a longer silence. Lambert, last in the room, explodes.

"*Câlisse*, gang. Mad when we win, mad when we lose. Let's be happy. We won, *tabernac*. We won!"

The mood changes.

"Hey yeah, c'mon we won, guys. We won."

"That's right, guys. That's right."

"We got our two. That's all we wanted."

Lapointe warms up, "Yeah, let's have some noise in here." Instantly there is noise.

"That's it. That's it. Now we're goin'."

The noise begins to die. Robinson jumps in.

"Hey Lambert, 'play that funn-ky music'!" he shouts.

There are more shouts, loud and enthusiastic this time. Lambert disappears around a corner; Lapointe behind a divider across the room. From the stereo, there is a hard, heavy, pulsating beat. Lights strobe on and off in time. The room comes alive. Tremblay starts dancing, then Lambert.

"Aww-right! Aww-right!" we shout happily.

"Hey, that's it, gang. Now we're goin'. That's the old gang."

A few minutes later, the music stops.

Sunday

*"More often than I like, I am saddened by a historical
myth. . . . I can't help thinking of the Venetian Republic in their
last half-century. Like us, they had once been fabulously lucky.
They had become rich, as we did, by accident. . . . They knew, just
as clearly as we know, that the current of history had begun to
flow against them. Many of them gave their minds to working
out ways to keep going. It would have meant breaking the
pattern into which they had crystalised. They were fond of the
pattern, just as we are fond of ours. They never found the will to
break it."*

(C. P. Snow, *The Two Cultures and the Scientific
Revolution*)

PHILADELPHIA

SLOW, RELENTLESS RAIN DRIZZLES DOWN. I CLUTCH THE
curtains around me like a cloak and peer at the soggy outback of
the airport across the road. It is Sunday morning in Philadelphia.
No planes are in sight, no cars streaming off and on the busy
interchange below, nothing but cold, tired, day-long rain. Behind
me Risebrough snores, warm and contented in last night's dark-
ness. I close the curtains and go back to bed.

I don't like the feeling I get in Philadelphia. It is a hollowness,
deep and disturbed, as if something is about to happen that I don't
want to happen but can't stop. Before the day ends, I will feel
threatened and physically afraid. I will hate fiercely (and admire). I
will scream and curse, and get angrier than I ever get. In victory, I
will gloat. Then slowly the hollowness will return, and I will be left
to wonder about feelings I didn't know I had, about the nature of
what I do, about things I never wonder about at other times. Only
the Flyers do that to me.

It used to be it was the way the Flyers played. Now it is them. I
have no room left for tortured ambivalence. I once saw the
admirable and contemptible side by side, the simple, courageous
game they played, their discipline and dedication, Bobby Clarke,
Bernie Parent, their no-name defense, Fred Shero. It was the way
they turned a hockey wasteland into something vibrant and excit-

ing. It wasn't the the brawling and intimidation that finally turned me. It was their sense of impunity. They were bullies. They showed contempt for everyone and everything. They took on the league, its referees and teams; they took on fans, cops, the courts, and politicians. They searched out weakness, found it, trampled it, then preened with their cock-of-the-walk swagger—"C'mon, ya chicken. I dare ya!" For two years, they were kings of the mountain. Not many years from now, those two years will be symbols of the NHL's lost decade. For Clarke, Parent, and a few more, I feel sorry.

It has been a decade of turmoil: expansion, the WHA, the Soviets, the Flyers, the haves and have-nots, money in new and disturbing quantities, violence, the courts, the legislatures. "The sport of the seventies," hockey was called; its decade almost over, it was a promise that was not kept. It was just thirteen years ago that the NHL was a cozy six-team enclave in the northeast, an overnight train ride east and west, north and south. Prosperous, inbred, deeply conservative, like a collection of old-world barons, the Montreal Molsons, the Boston Adamses, the Chicago and Detroit Norrises, the Toronto Smythes, the New York Kilpatricks, held in their contented hands the tight little world of hockey. Four of its teams were highly competitive, the Bruins and the Rangers provided competition for each other, and occasionally for the rest, while the league operated at more than ninety percent of its seating capacity.

But changes were coming, big changes in sports, that were beyond their control. The continent was booming west and south; commercial jets were turning miles and days into comfortable hours, turning regional leagues into anomalies. Everywhere there were new "big league" cities, looking for "big league" status; everywhere local politicians and first-generation money were looking for the same. So franchises moved. The baseball Dodgers and Giants moved west, the Braves south to Atlanta, other teams, other sports, following. But it was too little, too late, too slow for bullish times, and soon rival leagues sprang up—the AFL in football and the ABA in basketball, while baseball expanded by four teams to head off Branch Rickey's proposed Continental League.

In this same environment, the NHL faced the same dilemma—to expand or not? It had expanded forty years before, from four teams to ten, as it moved into the United States for the first time, but the results had not all been good. The league acquired a broader, more substantial base, and new expectations; the Rangers, Bruins, Hawks, and Red Wings (née Cougars, later Falcons) survived, the Pittsburgh Pirates, Philadelphia Quakers, St. Louis Eagles, Montreal Maroons, and New York (later Brooklyn)

Americans did not. It had seemed a lesson—major-league hockey was not for everywhere; without a large indigenous player base in the United States, there was a similar absence of broad-based fan support. A city would need to be in Canada, or proximate to Canada, in a traditional American hockey stronghold, or need to be so large that even a cult-like percentage of followers could attract 15,000 people for a game.

For twenty-five years, through war and emerging prosperity, the league stayed put. When the subject of expansion came up, as it rarely did, it was argued away—*this* city, *that* city, *this* owner, *that* owner always unsuitable, by standards that seemed fortuitously to rise according to the quality of the applicant. In fact, the league didn't expand because it didn't believe it to be in its interests to expand. For why would owners like Conn Smythe or James Norris want expansion? Their arenas were full. It was a gate-receipt league; radio and TV brought them little in revenue. How could teams in Los Angeles or Atlanta possibly help them? Indeed, an expanded league would only mean fewer games with old rivals, teams that had kept those arenas full. Would Los Angeles and Atlanta teams be as good and exciting, would they fill their arenas just as full? These men may have been "hockey enthusiasts," as then-league president Clarence Campbell described them, owners with "one foot on the bench," but first and foremost they were businessmen. They needed fans in Toronto and Chicago, not somewhere else, not later.

But in the 1960s, it changed. With extant rival leagues, the status quo would no longer guarantee them prosperous peace. Moreover, TV had become a factor. Once considered a dangerous leisure-time competitor, TV had emerged as both partner and promoter of sport's new growth. In 1966, CBS and NBC paid $26 million for the rights to NFL and AFL games, NBC $10 million for major-league baseball. For the NHL, playing to near-capacity crowds in barely expandable arenas, its tickets priced to what the market could bear, TV was a new, potentially immense source of revenue where few others existed. This was no pie-in-the-sky dream. Pro football, for decades in the shadows of its college cousin, had boomed in the late 1950s, a phenomenon of TV. Offering a similar recipe of speed, violence, and excitement, hockey could do the same. It has "all the potential of pro football," TV sports-guru Roone Arledge announced to a *Newsweek* reporter in 1966. And so it seemed.

But there were problems. TV in the 1960s meant network TV, and network TV meant shows that could play in Birmingham and Bakersfield as well as in Boston. Hockey would need a national audience. With tens of millions of viewers with no hockey pedigree, where would it come from? The answer, of course, lay in the innate attractiveness of the sport, and in expansion. To get Mahomet to the mountain, it would be necessary to bring the mountain to him. So, in 1967, the league expanded. Midwest to St. Louis and Minnesota, west to Los Angeles and Oakland, again into Pittsburgh and Philadelphia, doubling its size. Three years later, Vancouver and Buffalo were added; in 1972, New York and Atlanta. In only five years, the league had spread to much of the continent. It had done so to thwart the emergence of a rival league, and position itself for the fruits of network TV. In neither case did it succeed.

Yesterday, a brief item appeared in the paper. Coming at the end of a story previewing our game with the Wings, it said that NHL owners will meet in two weeks to discuss merger with the WHA. Further, it said that this time merger was likely. It has been seven years. Seven rancorous years of achievement obscured, of great reward for some, of mess and muddle—lawsuits, antitrust suits, contract wars; teams and players everywhere. There were 6 teams in 1967, 1 league, 120 players, 6 coaches, 6 managers, 6 owners. Eight years later, there were 32 teams, 2 leagues, 640 players, 32 coaches, 32 managers, 32 owners. The quality of play, the style of play, the administration and stability of the game, have been predictably affected. But now the war seems over. The WHA is no longer a serious rival. Each of its teams loses money every year, its lost millions the memory that nags it on; survival its one remaining tactic to achieve merger. And the NHL, bloodied but unbowed, is slowly willing to give up its fight.

Even the players can now sense the tired inevitability of it all. Beneficiaries many times over because two leagues were bidding for our services, our every gain lies precariously at stake, yet the attitude I hear is "Let's get it over with," and no amount of selfish good sense seems able to penetrate it. Today, hockey is a game in desperate search of good news, a "light at the end of the tunnel," as league president John Ziegler puts it, to turn a cynical public momentum that has swung around hard in its face; to build again. There will be a merger this time, because this time there must be a merger.

Tucked into this little corner of February-March is a brief denouement. A quiet, clear-eyed time unconnected to the retrospective mood that comes with such things as decade-endings and career-endings. This is rather a moment of resolution, when many of the themes and directions of the game over many years have come together, and now play themselves out. It is a moment to stop, and see where we stand.

Two weeks ago, the Challenge Cup ended in New York, the

Soviets defeating the NHL all-stars two games to one. It was a much less decisive series than its 6-0 final game score would indicate, yet it seems somehow an appropriate close to the first seven years of open international play, seven years of which I was a part. In 1972, it had begun as a party, a huge national coming-out party, with Canada the not-so-reluctant debutante. Pioneers, unchallenged champions of hockey for all its near century, Canadians had suffered through a decade of humiliating defeats, losing first to the Swedes, then year after year to the Soviets, our amateurs finally and forever outmatched, our professionals ineligible for international games. But what seemed worse, nagging at us like a secret we couldn't tell, was the fear that the man in Nevsky Prospekt or Wenceslas Square didn't know of our incomparable pros, didn't know that *we*, not they, were the true World Champions.

In 1972, we had our chance, in what was called hockey's showdown. And we won, and the party was more glorious than any before it or since. Yet even before it had ended, we knew something was different, never again to be the same. The Soviets had been good, *very good*, much better than we had expected. And our 34-second margin of victory, the cause of such explosive national celebration, became the cause of unforgettable national concern. Our birthright was suddenly at risk. It was like being shot at and missed. We couldn't forget how close it had been, and could only worry that the next time would be different.

And some day it would be different, we were sure. We were up against a country more than ten times our size, sharing our winter climate and our passion for the game, but with a more insistent ideology, a more disciplined and committed system, a more scientific and modern sporting approach. In only twenty-five years, the Soviets had done what had taken us nearly a century. And now, close to our shoulder, they continued at full sprint. It seemed for us a simple, hopeless equation—numbers, climate, commitment, approach. In time, we would surely stand no chance. And to cushion that inevitable day, we pretended that it was nearer than it was, reading in every sign the final evidence of its coming. Never again as a nation would we commit ourselves as we had in 1972. Never again would we put our national psyches so nakedly on the line. If we couldn't be sure of being the best, we would step back. Maybe hockey shouldn't be so important to us after all, a part of each of us decided.

Yet with that hedge safely in place, we have responded—with studies and government inquiries, with clinics, books, films, seminars and symposia, hockey schools and coaching programs, off-ice training and a return to the "2Fs," *fun and fundamentals*. A game that is in our blood was finally put on the couch and examined. And it has changed. Yet after seven years of inconclusive results— the Soviets beating the WHA all-stars in 1974, Team Canada winning the Canada Cup two years later, Soviet club teams winning the majority of games with NHL teams, but often losing to the better teams—the Challenge Cup tells another story: only three games during four days in February, reversible by three other games another year. But this time, there was something different, something definitive and clear: though we have changed, the immense traditions of our game still overwhelm us, and, slaves to our past, we look undeniably the same; and the Soviets, stuttering for a time with problems of their own, now seem to have found an answer.

After the 1972 series, a friend told me of being in London in the early 1950s when Hungary beat England at Wembley, 6-3. Motherland of soccer and long its dominant power, England had never before been beaten at home (except by other teams from the British Isles). My friend likened the reaction that followed to what occurred in Canada after the opening 7-3 loss to the Soviets in Montreal in 1972. Last week, still in a self-pitying daze after the Challenge Cup, I went to a library to read microfilm accounts of that game from English newspapers. I found the parallels astonishing.

"Once again the day will mirror the two styles prevalent in modern football," *The Times* said, previewing the game. "The Hungarians, like the Austrians and South Americans, put their faith in swift short passing, often carried out at a bewildering pace, and with supreme dexterity, a style of game which excludes the hard tackle and shoulder charge so much a part of British football." The English style, it went on, "is none the less artistic in its way. Certainly it may not possess quite the same rhythmic beauty as the other, but it has a more human quality. It is not a cold, precise, almost inhuman mathematical science." It then summed up presciently, "The outcome may not necessarily prove anything conclusively, but may be no more than a pointer to the way things may develop in the second half of the century."

"A New Conception of Football," *The Times* headlined the Hungarian victory the next day, concluding ominously, "English football can be proud of its past. But it must awake to a new future." Articles followed for many weeks, the tone and the message always the same. "The aftermath of the fine Hungarian display...has been as spectacular as the contest itself," an editorial proclaimed more than a week later. "The air is loud with prescriptions for re-educating English footballers and those who train and direct them. Whether they like it or not, a million or more spectators at to-day's League matches have...new standards of quality of performance by which to judge their favourites." It likened the game's effect to that of appearances in London of the Russian ballet and the musical *Oklahoma!* Both had shown the elementary need for imagination and technical perfection, it said, "lessons which...English footballers, resting too much on the pioneer laurels of the past, badly need to learn."

It sounded very familiar; and so too did the prescriptions: improved technique, more imaginative team play, team play based on offense not defense, on ball control and speed, better conditioning and better finishing around the net. And to make it all possible, increased emphasis should be placed on the national team at the expense of "the interminable league program," as one newspaper put it, to give players more time to play together, as the Hungarians and others insisted on. Change a few of the terms, colloquialize the language slightly, and it might have been written in Canada, about hockey, in 1972 or since.

The Canadian and English reactions were similar, perhaps because they came from countries sharing a common culture for many years, and sharing parallel traditions in their respective sports. But that is only part of the story. Everyone, every country, has a watershed moment like this sometime, about something. The point is, what happens next? With all that had been learned, what happened to English soccer in the more than twenty-five years since?

I am told by my friend and others that the stereotype English style remains, that even with its greater pace and stamina, the essence of the game has not changed. Indeed, if anything the gap in global styles has widened. But why? For more than twenty-five years, the English have seen the problem and understood it as well as it can be understood, always with the will to bring about the necessary changes. So what stops them? Why are they so powerless to do anything about it? Why indeed. It is the burden of their soccer history. A whole glorious culture of ideas, beliefs, myths, and traditions preserved, shared, and passed along. They won in the past, they lose in the present; it must be in the past that the answers lie. But there are no answers in the past, only clues as to what went wrong along the way. They know it, yet they can't stop themselves from looking, and hoping.

When I was at Cornell, I was a history major, but I managed to graduate with little sense of history. With most of my courses organized by century or epoch or personality, focusing on political, diplomatic, or military events, I got little hint of the social currents underlying each, which affected each so profoundly. It wasn't until I began uncovering some of the roots of hockey that I discovered my own best metaphor for what history and culture can mean.

For me, it began a few years ago. I was in a friend's house in Ottawa and while he was called to the phone, I picked up a book lying on a table in front of me and began to browse through it. It was called *The Hockey Book*. It had been written in 1953 by a journalist named Bill Roche, who had covered professional hockey from the mid-1920s until 1940. During that time, he had begun collecting stories and reminiscences of players, coaches, managers, and referees from the past, finally putting them together in a book. It was the recurring themes that startled me most: hockey as big business, the decline in interest in the United States, the NHL's pandering to the American fan, the increase in fighting and brawling—all were themes we had been led to believe had begun with our generation. Even more fascinating were references to different styles of play.

Until then, I hadn't known that hockey was once an onside game (where back passing was permitted but forward passing was not), that hockey had been played by seven players a side, that the forward pass was something introduced late to the game, or that there could be any connection between the forward pass and stickhandling, between stickhandling and body-checking. The "dump and chase," for me, had been a feature of expansion, but here it was being vilified in the 1950s in almost the same words as we vilify it today. Later I would realize that anything in one time can be linked to anything in another, that there is always someone who took a slap shot in 1910 or built a car in 1880, even if the recollection is exaggerated and the connection artificial. More important now was the discovery that hockey before my time was more than just tales of "Cyclone" Taylor's goal while skating backwards, George Hainsworth's twenty-two shutouts in forty-four games, Howie Morenz's death from a broken leg and his subsequent funeral in the Montreal Forum. And if there was a connection between the forward pass and stickhandling, maybe there were other connections as well. There suddenly seemed to me a story I had never heard, a link between present and past that might tell us why we play as we do. So I went back to the beginning to find out.

In the early 1870s, a group of Montreal lacrosse players were looking for a winter game. At first, they simply put on skates and tried to adapt lacrosse to ice, but quickly they found that unsatisfactory. One of their group, J. G. A. Creighton, suggested that they use shinny sticks and a ball instead (shinny, an ancient stick-and-ball game, was something like today's field hockey). The experiment proved more successful. But with lacrosse discarded, they would need a new model for their game. As many of them were rugby players as well, they decided to make it English rugby. So a scrum became a "bully" or a faceoff; and hockey became an "onside" game (with no forward passing). Its "first 'public' exhibition" was held on March 3, 1875, in Montreal. The *Gazette* previewed it this way:

> A game of hockey will be played at the Victoria Skating Rink this evening between two nines from among the members. Good fun may be expected, as some of the players are reputed to be exceedingly expert at the game. Some fears have been expressed on the part of the intending spectators that accidents were likely to occur through the ball flying about in a too lively manner, to the imminent danger of lookers-on, but we understand that the game will be played with a flat, circular piece of wood, thus preventing all danger of its leaving the surface of the ice.

Though hockey-like games had been played for centuries, this was the sport's true departure point. Rules were drawn up, and with rules came organization, and with it a continuity and structure that in time would draw to it and gather up all other ad hoc variations.

It was a far different game from any we now know, yet present in it were principles that would affect how we play a century later. Perhaps most obvious was its ponderous, slow pace. There were nine men to a side, later seven, finally six by 1911, and, importantly, no substitutions were permitted except for injury. It was the accepted sporting tradition of the time. Sports were character-building exercise, it was argued, so games were a "test," and suffering, more than efficiency, their noblest characteristic. Football players played "both ways," hockey players all the time at an all-the-time pace, the patterns and skills of the game, the nature of the contest, held back and limited. (Later, when rosters increased and non-injury substitutions were permitted, hockey used all of its available players, rotating them in greater numbers of lines and defense pairs. Other sports kept most substitutes in reserve as injury replacements or "special team" players. It meant that only in hockey would an injury require a team to play undermanned. As a result, the ethic of playing with injury, often painful, dramatic injury, although disappearing from other sports, has remained.)

But there were other reasons for the disappointing pace. Early skates had long, heavy, unrockered blades, like those of today's goalie skates, making turning awkward and difficult. Games were played in thirty-minute halves, the ice, unflooded at intermissions, gradually becoming slow and snowbound. But most important, hockey was an *onside game.* To sportsmen of the time, there seemed something vaguely unethical about a puck (or a ball) being passed forward, as if territory gained this way was somehow unearned, so a forward pass was whistled down as offside. The puck could be advanced only by the puck carrier, invariably the centerman, his wingers left and right and slightly behind, mere secondary figures, watching him, reacting to him, waiting. The defense was out of the offensive play entirely.

It meant a game that moved at the pace of the puck carrier, dependent always on him for its initiative and creativity. Since his options were limited, defenders could defend him in large numbers with little risk. They could skate slowly in front of him to slow his pace, or funnel him helplessly towards their salivating teammates. It was usually with no other play to make, and nearing the blueline, that his wingers came into play: a back pass, a lateral pass left or right, often ahead and offside, more often the puck just taken away.

Yet it was out of this slow and static style that the priority skills of our game emerged, and in many ways have never changed. Offensively, it was skating and stickhandling; defensively, body-checking. Body-checking had not been a feature of the original game, but made its appearance soon after. I have found no explanation for it, yet using other circumstantial evidence, a reasonable hypothesis emerges. It had to do with an often small ice surface (though the Victoria Rink was of contemporary North American dimensions, 200′ x 85′, many early rinks were a curling-size 112′ x 58′), cluttered with eighteen players, then fourteen, many of them out-of-season rugby players used to body contact, their hockey skills new and primitive, their equipment clumsy; the unavoidable result would be frequent if inadvertent collisions. But, inadvertent or not, early players soon discovered that in a puck carrier's game, collisions were effective deterrents. So from accidents emerged our basic defensive strategy. As for skating and stickhandling, with no forward pass there was no other way to advance the puck. Skating was the fundamental skill, of course, but speed (which itself might take a player around or between opponents) was not yet a consistent tactic. Instead, it was by stickhandling that scoring chances were earned.

It took more than fifty years for the forward pass to be introduced. In that time, the tiny, curling-size rinks had more than doubled in size to a nearly contemporary 185′ x 86′, nine-man sides had diminished to six-man sides, rosters growing to twelve, then to fifteen, as non-injury substitutions were permitted; and many of the game's myths and attitudes had become firmly entrenched: its straight-ahead, straight-line playing patterns, body-checking and body contact, the puck carrier as focus and creative man, and the consequent slow, congested attitude of the game.

The game was tied up in lines and rules and ice surfaces, and it had never been allowed the freedom of open ice. (By contrast, Soviet hockey emerged out of soccer and "bandy"—a game something like field hockey on ice—each with large playing surfaces, giving it an open-ice attitude that remains.)

The forward pass should have changed all that. Borrowed from basketball, more recently from football, it was brought in to restore hockey's offense-defense balance, and give it a much-needed aesthetic boost. For defense had taken over the game. NHL teams had averaged nearly five goals a game in 1920. Five years later, it was three, in 1929 fewer than two (Canadiens goalie George Hainsworth recorded twenty-two shutouts in forty-four games that season, and seven of the league's other nine goalies had ten shutouts or more; Ace Bailey of the Leafs won the scoring title with thirty-two points), a figure dangerously low for a league trying to sell itself to a new American audience. The rule was introduced in stages, was tinkered with for a few years, and was finally settled into place for the 1931 season. With no centerline (it was not introduced until the 1943-44 season), two bluelines divided a rink into three parts roughly equal in size—the offensive, defensive, and neutral zones. Under the new rule, the puck could be passed forward in each of the three zones, but not across either blueline. It should have revolutionized the game, but it didn't.

Offensively, it opened up the immense possibilities of team play. Before, the game had been tied to the puck carrier for its pace and initiative, for its creativity. Now the focus could change. It could be on the others, darting ahead into open spaces without the puck, creating the play, pushing the pace of a game to the sprint speed of a pass. Moreover, defensemen could now join in on offense. In the past, playing at the rear had meant a permanent defensive exile for them, as those ahead were offside to any pass. It meant infrequent forward "runs" by the even more rare defenseman who took them, or most commonly, lofting the puck high down the ice while teammates, as if covering a punt, raced beneath it. But with the forward pass, a defenseman could set the game in motion from behind, then move up, adding support, quarterbacking a five-man attack inside the offensive zone.

It should have meant a whole new set of basic skills, for the defenseman and everyone else. Passing, of course, and skating should have become critical, and so too the creative mind that made both work. Stickhandling would no longer be important. A slow, intricate art, like dribbling in basketball or soccer, it was an artistic self-indulgence, out of touch with the themes of speed and team play that had emerged with the new rules.

On the other side, as the offense changed, so too would the

defense. The change of focus from the puck carrier to the rest that would give the game its new variety and pace—and take away the stickhandler—should have taken away the body-check. Needing a slow, static, predictable game to be effective, a body-check should have worked no longer.

This is, of course, what should have happened, but it didn't, and it never really has. Fifty years of history, fifty years of habit and tradition, intervened. There was no revolution, no conquest of styles, no abrupt change, no players suddenly obsolete and extinct. The forward pass became simply part of the game, part of an ancient game played on an ancient grid that was unsuited to it. And because change did come, because more goals were scored and the game was speeded up, it seemed a success, and few wondered what other possible changes were missed. This was the turning point. The limits of the forward pass were never explored. The limits to our game were set. It was from this moment that other nations, with other styles, got their chance.

Why did we not foresee the possibilities of the forward pass as others later would? It was what Clarence Campbell called the "snowbankers" tradition of our game. The boy becomes a man; the player a coach, a manager, a scout, a father; a game is passed on like tribal history, one voice, one mind. There was no bigger picture, no history in like games, in soccer or basketball, no parallel traditions in schools or universities, no critical mind, no oblique other eye to break the relentless continuum; there was simply no other way to play. Our writers and journalists, those outside the game, were experts with no vision, or with vision, no audience. And without external competition, without incentive, there was no chance that this would change. So, locked in our rooms with nothing but our own navels to look at, we saw nothing, and missed our chance.

Since then, for nearly fifty years, the story of hockey has been speed. It was the forward pass that gave speed its chance; later it was the center red line, better ice conditions, better equipment, better training and conditioning of players, and shorter shifts that accelerated its impact. But it was speed unaccommodated, never allowed to work, because the playing patterns, skills, and attitudes of our game were never changed to make it work. As a result, the major developments in our hockey—forechecking, the dump and chase, escalating violence, the slap shot, tactical intimidation, the adrenaline attitude of the game—are all logical implications in a pyramid of implications with unharnessed, undirected speed as their root.

But this is a view in panorama. The story of a game moves much more slowly, one step at a time.

In the 1930s, forechecking appeared. In response to the forward pass, defenses began packing five men together near the defensive blueline, making passing and puck control more difficult, poised to strike in counterattack. Offenses continued to pass ritually into their midst, usually without success, but the new forward momentum of the game carried the players into the offensive zone, often into the vicinity of unclaimed pucks. It was the beginning of forechecking. Nothing so relentless and systematic as that which would come later, yet greatly troublesome for defenders unused to its pressure, and obliged by the rules to *carry* the puck across the blueline, not to pass it. Moreover, forechecking represented an important discovery: offense could be played without the puck. Until then, checking had seemed a strictly defensive skill. But if offense was in part territorial, then checking in the offensive zone—forechecking—could have an offensive purpose. And if speed (without any other accommodations for it) made a puck more difficult to control, then forcing bad plays (turnovers) might become more important than making good ones yourself.

As usual, defenses readjusted, easing their pressure by lofting the puck the length of the ice. As usual, the pendulum returned. This time, the league intervened. To silence fans annoyed by this negative tactic, it brought in an icing rule. And the defensive pressure returned. But out of it had come a new development—from the forward pass and the game's new speed, new skills and styles of play were emerging geared to an out-of-possession game.

In the early 1940s, the offense-defense-aesthetic balance proved unable to right itself, and the league intervened again. Many players had been lost to the war, and those who replaced them had found the styles and tactics they inherited too difficult to play. So teams simplified them. Less skilled passers, unable to penetrate a packed defense, made no pretense of passing, instead shooting the puck ahead of them to the corners, and chasing after it. It was what we later came to disparage as the dump-and-chase style, and it was in these early war years that it had its systematic beginnings. But more troublesome were the problems the defense faced. They were in a box. The rules prevented them from passing the puck over the blueline. Yet the alternative, shooting it out, meant only that it would be shot back in for the struggle to begin again. And it was a struggle. For the attacking team had the blueline behind it as a safety barrier, and could harass with five men unworried by consequences. The defense simply needed help. And help it got.

Frank Boucher, a former great player and coach with the Rangers, then assistant to league president Red Dutton, was asked to recommend changes to the game. He suggested a center red line, and a rule that would permit passing over the blueline as far as the centerline. He wanted a way to force attacking defensemen out of the offensive zone, to break the defensive logjam and make the game faster and more interesting. In fact, his rule worked, though not in the way he intended. The defense got its needed break, the game got faster, but, its patterns unchanged, the lowest-common-denominator dump-and-chase style, explainable by the times, persisted, even as the war ended and the top-class players returned to make it less explainable.

Moreover, an attitude was untouched. For more than seventy years, offense and defense had been kept apart—by traditions, by rules, by the styles and tactics that had emerged from each. There was an offensive zone, a defensive zone, a neutral zone between. In the defensive zone, a team played defense. In the offensive zone, offense. And with no forward passing, or passing over bluelines, there was no way to join them. Boucher's rule should have been the link. It should have brought offense and defense together for the first time. It should have created more open ice, and with it more passing, more speed, more open-ice skills, more attackers and defenders outdistanced from the play, less eleven-man congestion from the bluelines to the nets. It should have turned offense and defense into all-ice activities, each the transition of the other. But old habits and traditions die slowly. The game speeded up; the schizophrenia remained. Offense was still offense; defense, defense.

(At this moment, after the war, after the forward pass and the center red line, after nearly seventy years of tradition had hardened the arteries of our game, Soviet hockey was beginning.)

With the new centerline, the dump-and-chase style only intensified. In a 1947 story, *Time* described it as "high-pressure 'shinny.'" *Saturday Night*, under the headline "It Isn't Hockey," disagreed, certain it could be neither shinny, nor tag, nor wrestling, nor jiujitsu, in the end unsure just what it was. Journalist Bill Roche knew only that he didn't like it. "...[W]hen an entire forward line gets a breakaway against a defence pair," he wrote in *The Hockey Book*, "and the puck-carrier, instead of skating over the blue-line and setting up a clean play for his mates, merely heaves the rubber into a corner to start a free-for-all scramble—well, I feel like walking out of the rink and often do." The dump and chase had come to dramatize all that had changed in hockey, all that was wrong with it, according to many: the absence of great stick-handlers and body-checkers, the great individual players whose skills could be seen and appreciated, the intricate teamwork of the Cooks and Boucher of the Rangers and others like them, the *color* of the game. All gone. Replaced by a shot, a chase, a congested crush of bodies, and speed. But whose bodies, and doing what? Not passing or stickhandling—they were not needed in this game. And how could a defenseman, chasing to the boards for a puck, deliver a body-check? Goals? Mostly they were from ganging attacks, from a strategic clutter of legs and bodies, and blinded goalies behind them. The "screened shot" became a popular phrase at the time, and for fans came its logical companion, the "screened goal."

"On half the goals scored nowadays not ten percent of the fans know who scored," Boucher complained to journalist Trent Frayne in 1953. How then did the fans recognize a goal? "By watching for the...glare of the red light," according to Frayne. (Twenty-five years later, syndicated columnist Jim Murray, claiming to have watched hockey for thirty years without seeing a goal, asked the question, "...what does a goal look like? What color is it? What does it sound like? Is it bigger than a breadbox?") But the dump-and-chase style survived. It was a team game everyone could play. It required no real finesse, just good legs and a willing mind. And as perhaps our first real venture into team play, involving all five men, it showed us how effective five players, working together, can be. As a rueful Boucher admitted, "Any club that doesn't use it will have its brains beaten out." To those who felt the game limited and uninteresting, there were no apologies. This was the modern game. Like everything else in the postwar world, it was based on speed—"speed in cars, speed in sports, speed in ladies," *Saturday Night* wrote in 1951. But it was speed for what purpose, and to what end?

What happens to a game when it speeds up? What happens to its patterns and skills and to those who play it? I once read an article on senility in which the writer said that what many regard in the elderly as a hopeless inability to function is often nothing of the kind. Instead it has to do with the shattering impact of pace. When people age, their minds and bodies slow down, and require more time to do the same things. An old man can walk to the store, he just needs longer to get there. But for most daily functions, we are not allowed additional time. A certain unforgiving pace is expected. It is at this pace, a normal living pace, that the elderly must function. Yet when they try, their minds and bodies get muddled; they appear senile. It is what each of us feels at every age when things move too fast. On a squash court with someone my equal, I play comfortably, the scope of play well-matched to what I can do. But against someone who is clearly superior, my mind and body seize up, and I lose the coordination I had at the slower pace.

It is no different for a game when it speeds up. Simply, it

becomes harder to play. Offense, defense, team skills, individual skills; with less time for each, each must be done more quickly: by practicing skills to perform them faster, by using different skills that take less time, by changing the way skills are used—or, as the game goes faster, probably by all three. And if we don't find enough time, if the game moves too fast for its patterns and skills, it loses its coordination and breaks down. It becomes over-matched, overwhelmed by speed. For speed, like the forward pass and the centerline, like the non-injury substitution, changes the way a game can be played. It gives a game new skills, and takes away others. It requires direction and control.

Yet we have made no accommodation to it. Instead, we have allowed it to dictate our style of play. Speed makes passing more difficult, so we pass less, and do something easier that takes less time. We have not changed our ancient straight-ahead, straight-line patterns, though they were only appropriate to the onside game. To accommodate speed, but also to make passing possible, we could move on diagonals across the ice, to give a better target, to find open ice, to use its width unharassed by offside lines. But we do not. We dump and chase, or shoot from a distance, and the faster the game gets, the less chance there is that we can do anything else. Gradually, speed had created a whole range of new and necessary skills, and a new approach to the game, but after the war, after forechecking and the dump and chase, speed also had another effect.

Hockey was a rough game, and had been very nearly from its start. Its speed, its confined, congested playing area, had almost guaranteed it, and made body-checking accepted defense strategy. But the forward pass, and later the centerline, made body-checking immensely more difficult. Never abandoned, as it might have been, it evolved in part into something else after the war. The sequence was not surprising, for what does a defenseman do when a game speeds up and changes direction on him? When locked in tradition, he continues to do what his coach and his instincts have taught him to do. He body-checks. But more often than not, given the increased speed of the skaters, he misses, but not completely. For just as a well-avoided hip turns into a knee, so a shoulder becomes a high-stick, or a hook, and a punishing ride to the boards.

This was something new. The stick and the boards had never been used so systematically in this way before. But, stuck in old traditions, it was how the defense responded to the game's new speed. And the league allowed it. To the finesse player, it was one more crushing blow. What good was it to skate and stickhandle to gain an advantage so easily wrestled away? Why not just dump and chase like the rest? It was from this simmering frustration that violence emerged. Brawling and stick-swinging became more frequent and vicious than before. Not grim and calculated, goon against goon, as it was decades later; this was human nature boiling over. Often it was the game's biggest stars, Maurice Richard, Gordie Howe, Ted Lindsay, Geoffrion, hooked and high-sticked until they would take no more. The league intervened with fines and suspensions for the worst abuses, but did nothing to penalize its insidious causes, in the end more damaging to the game.

The effect has been profound. The game was pushed far more completely down the dump-and-chase road, its various alternatives plainly discouraged. The game was made more violent. The hockey stick had been allowed a new use. Not just as a tool of offense and defense, but as a weapon as well, a legal weapon to impede and punish. Those with memories of the 1920s or 1930s, or before, will insist there were more serious incidents of violence in other times. Perhaps so. But it was in the late 1940s that a *pattern* of violence entered the game. For the first time, it became part of the regular play. And when it wasn't removed, it only meant it would get worse. The nature of violence, the emerging style of play, guaranteed it.

The 1950s and 1960s brought other changes, yet the direction of the game never varied. Recently, I watched some kinescopes of games of that time. It was hockey's "golden age" as I remembered it: six teams, the Rocket, Howe, Hull, Béliveau, all seen through my childhood eyes. I had wanted to see how we compared, the Canadiens then and now, the best of this time and the best of that. I had grown suspicious of middle-aged recollections and highlight packages that showed Richard always scoring, Béliveau always elegant, Doug Harvey always in quarterback-command. I wanted to watch complete games, games at random, season games, with good teams and bad, for it would tell me far better about the hockey of the time.

I was disappointed. To those used to the thirties and forties, the game may have seemed dizzyingly fast, but to eyes used to the present, it appeared slow. Shifts were two minutes or longer (down from five minutes in the 1930s), the leisurely pace of the game geared to it. Players dumped the puck ahead often enough that Jacques Plante innovated out-of-crease play for goalies, but chased after it less rigorously than they would a decade later. It was a possession game, of sorts (like the Soviets, I had been told), but it involved little passing: the puck brought to center by a centerman or a defenseman, wingers spread suitably wide right and left (how often as a child I heard Foster Hewitt say, "The Leafs are at center, three *abreast*"), the defense stacked up, waiting, the patterns of the game still rigidly intact. To me, it looked like an ancient siege. An army on one side charging, an army on the other waiting; each taking turns.

By the early 1960s, shifts were shorter by thirty seconds or more, the game was faster, the level of skill consistently higher. The slap shot was new, and wonderfully exciting until everyone had one, then badly overused. Goalies rushed for their masks, moved out to cut angles, and gradually got bigger. Yet the slap shot marked no fundamental change to the game. It was in fact only a variation of the dump-and-chase style, born of the same root problem—the inability to penetrate a defense. A player could shoot for the corners of a rink, or take a distant shot on net. The traditional wrist shot, intended for in-close attempts, lost power from a distance, and was of little use. The slap shot took its place. It produced glamorous new stars, most especially Bobby Hull and Frank Mahovlich, and a glamorous new image. This was the league's competitive and commercial zenith. And if the style of play remained basically unchanged, it was clearly well-played. Indeed, watching it, I felt I was seeing players who had taken it about as far as it could go.

The 1967 expansion changed everything. Shading and subtlety left the game; trends, unseen, ignored for many years, were suddenly unmistakable. The stereotypes had come true. There were one hundred and twenty new players, one hundred and twenty old. New teams, old teams, teams in the same league bore little resemblance one to another; and side by side, teammates and linemates the same. It was massive dilution, and produced massive disparity. The march towards the dump-and-chase style, towards stickwork and violence, slowed by the skills of the sixties, accelerated.

The game was caught in a familiar spiral. Shifts got shorter, the game speeded up; the faster it got, the more difficult to play, the fewer alternative styles of play, the more systematic the style, the more time without the puck, the shorter the shifts, the faster it got. And the faster it got, the more players on the puck, the more crashing and bumping, the more violent it got—like punting for field position, trying for a turnover. It was offense based on a defensive skill, forechecking: over center, into the corners, and chase, again, again, again. Goalies passed the puck; defenses banged it around the boards and out; defenses rushed up to keep it in. It was all a matter of who got there first, with how many, and how much punishment you could take.

The game became an immense physical struggle. In corners, along the boards, in front of nets, the puck would be the center of two or three or more players constantly fighting for it. It made for a new range of skills, for players who were bigger, stronger, tougher, by skill and power better able to maneuver in the clutter and emerge with the puck, by temperament loving to hit and be hit; it made for centers better trained for the more frequent faceoffs (in the 1950s, there was an average of about sixty faceoffs a game; today's average is nearly eighty); it made for penalty-killers and power-play specialists, the quid pro quo.

The game had become rougher. If speed and confined space had guaranteed collisions in the first place, more speed, more congested space, and this style of play would guarantee more. If collisions were unavoidable, they would be made calculated: a hit now, a message for the next time, and there would be a next time. The style of play made it so. It was intimidation, an effective tactic in an overexpanded league. Great disparity wouldn't allow competition on the same level, yet teams had to compete. So, if it wasn't with artistry or finesse, it would be with *character*—hard work, discipline, courage—and no little intimidation. Teams could find character even among the lesser players available to them; intimidation was to make a good player worse. And it worked. The league circled and jabbed at the worst abuses; the Flyers won two straight Stanley Cups. Violence had been allowed to make sense.

It had come down to this, one final development many years coming, the Flyers its visible iceberg tip. For what happens to a game when it picks up speed and never learns to use it, when its balance of speed and finesse is disturbed, when finesse turns to power? It becomes a game of energy—an *adrenaline game*. Listen to its language. Listen to a coach talk about a game. He talks of "emotion," of being "up" or "not up"; of "pressure," two men on the puck, defense "pinching" on the boards, "hits," turnovers, shots, all in exquisite volumes; and especially of "momentum," head-shaking, hand-shrugging "turning points" and the irreversible destinies that flow from them. Adrenaline *is* important to a game, but like the batter who chokes a bat too tight, not all the time. It is important to sharpen senses, not to overcome them; to enhance skills, to push them to their high-pitched best, but not to replace them. We have lost the *attitude* of finesse necessary to a game, and now we pay a double price. For adrenaline has its dark side. Fouled or resisted, it turns to anger, frustration, retaliation. And inside a pattern of violence allowed many years before, it sends violence spiralling higher.

It is a hundred years since the original Montreal rules, almost fifty years since the forward pass. For us, it has been like a journey through a maze, one path, then many, and finally coming to where we can go no further, and realizing that we missed a turn along the way. Yet had the Soviets not held up a mirror to our game, first in 1972, and again this year, much of what has happened might have gone unnoticed. We had been the best, we had always been the best. So, however we played, it was the best way. And there could be no other way to play. That the Soviets played differently was well known to us by 1972. That their style would work against the world's best players was not. Nor was it seriously considered. They had taken up hockey only twenty-six years before, in 1946. But playing more months of the year, more hours of the day, they had short-cut time: World Champions in eight years, Olympic champions in ten; their long domination of amateur hockey beginning less than a decade later.

Indeed, their tardy start for them would prove fortuitous. For 1946 was after hockey's great upheavals, after the forward pass, after the center red line, leaving the Soviets no accumulation of obsolete thinking to burden their future. They had, as well, a long tradition in hockey-like games such as soccer and bandy. Soccer, played by most of the world's countries, was much more advanced in strategies and techniques than hockey. To its off-season players, the first coaches and players of Soviet hockey, the common principles of the games were quickly evident. This was of no small importance. It would give the Soviets the necessary confidence and will to develop their own school of hockey, quite distinct from the Canadian game.

In the 1972 series, we dominated those parts of the game to which our style had moved—the corners, the boards, the fronts of both nets, body play, stick play, faceoffs, intimidation, distance shooting, emotion. In the end, it was enough. But disturbingly, the Soviets had been better in the traditional skills—passing, open-ice play, team play, quickness, finishing around the net—skills *we* had developed, that seemed to us the essence of hockey, but that we had abandoned as incompatible with the modern game. The Soviets had showed us otherwise. It would be unfair, perhaps incorrect, to say that nothing has come of it. Yet little has. What we didn't understand, what we don't understand now, is that body play, stick play, faceoffs, intimidation, distance shooting, and the rest have become the fundamentals of our game; that the fundamentals of any game are the basic skills needed to play it, and our present game requires those. To a dump-and-chase game, passing and team play are not fundamental. We may practice them rigorously, we may intend to use them in a game. But unless they fit in a style of play, and are rewarded, it will come to nothing. To change the fundamentals of a game, a style of play must change; to change a style of play, the attitudes and patterns that underlie it must change first.

Yet still there was room for illusion. The pendulum that was swinging away from us seemed to stop for years. They won, we won; they changed a little, so did we. And the more we played, the more their bewildering patterns seemed not bewildering at all. What had seemed to us so unpredictable—the crisscrossing patterns, the breakaway pass through center, the goalmouth pass to an unseen defenseman—was really just surprising. And when it stopped being surprising, it began to seem predictable; and less successful.

The Soviets needed open ice for their open-ice patterns and skills. They wanted a high-tempo game, 4-on-3, 3-on-2, 2-on-1, always outnumbering an opponent, fast-shrinking numbers on a fast-shrinking ice surface. It was this way that their skills worked best. It was up to us to see that it didn't happen. We forechecked when we were sure of not being trapped; peeled back when we weren't. We jammed the middle to interrupt their first pass, which set their game in motion, which created the tempo and the numerical advantage they needed. We checked hard in the center zone, and retreated when we couldn't, always certain of at least three defenders to clutter the defensive zone. On power plays we waited more patiently, watching for the offside defenseman and the offside winger we had ignored before. And it worked, more often than it should have worked against a team of their calibre.

In their intricate, patterned game, there seemed a fatal flaw. A few years ago, a friend working at the Canadian Embassy in Moscow told me he had seen the Soviet soccer team play several times. What had amazed him, he said, were its obvious similarities to the Soviet hockey team, in style and patterns of play, in its very *look*. Yet, on a world scale, it was decidedly mediocre, and the hockey team was not. Why? he wondered.

Later, I asked an international soccer coach the same question. He described the Soviet team much as we might the hockey team—well-conditioned, highly skilled, highly disciplined and organized, its style based on speed and passing. Yet in this patterned style was a basic weakness. For when a team knows what it will do next, soon an opponent knows too, and can defend against it. The Soviet style was *too* patterned, *too* predictable, he said, and in the large, cozy world of soccer, there could be no greater sin. Offense, by its nature, must be unpredictable. It may evolve out of earlier pattern and understanding, but its ultimate act is individual creation. No team can depend on weaving rink-long textbook patterns. They are too easily interrupted and broken. And, as with a memorized speech, when it happens you lose your place and must start again to find it. Except that then everyone is waiting.

It was what I was beginning to feel about the Soviet hockey team. There was also something else. The Soviets were remarkably ineffective as one-on-one players. Since they were quick skaters and excellent puck-handlers, it was a game they should have excelled at, but they didn't. They always needed the extra man. It was basic to their game. Find the open man, and use him. But nearing a net, often there is no open man. A puck-carrier must do it himself. He must use his skills to create an advantage, his will to do the rest. But the Soviets seemed never to make that commitment—looking, always waiting for the open man until the chance was lost. It was a burden from *their* past, on *their* game, one they seemed no better at handling than we did ours. Problems remained for us, of course (facing Goose Gossage, a batter may know what's coming, but he still has to hit it). Still, it was something. And if instinctively I knew the Soviets had found the right direction, if not quite, I hoped, maybe believed, that our high-pressure, high-energy style could interrupt theirs, could break it down and simplify it, just as it had broken down our own; that in our game we possessed the permanent antidote to theirs.

Then came the Challenge Cup. I don't know when it happened. I don't know how. I don't know even if I understand it the same way the Soviets understand it. I am convinced only that it happened—that the Soviets fundamentally changed their approach to the game, that they understand finally that hockey is not a *possession game*, nor can it ever be. Possession was what they were supposed to be about: passing, team play, always searching for the open man, regrouping to start again if their possession seemed threatened. But a puck cannot be physically carried up the ice like a football; and a hockey player is not protected from physical battering as a basketball player is. He can be overpowered, the puck can be wrested from his stick by one or two or more opponents, with little recourse except to pass it on to someone else soon harassed the same way. A possession game is hyperbole. The puck changes teams more than 6 times a minute, more than 120 times a period, more than 400 times a game, and little can be done to prevent it. And when it is not changing possession, the puck is often out of possession, fought after, in no one's control. It is the nature of the game, North American or European. There is sustained possession only on power plays. There is possession involving several seconds at other times only when a team regroups to its own zone to set up a play. If possession is team style, it will be frustrated. Worse, if it is attempted, it will make a game cautious and predictable.

Instead, hockey is a *transition game*: offense to defense, defense to offense, one team to another. Hundreds of tiny fragments of action, some leading somewhere, most going nowhere. Only one thing is clear. A fragmented game must be played in fragments. Grand designs do not work. Offenses regrouping, setting up, meet defenses which have done the same, and lose. But before offense turns to defense, or defense to offense, there is a moment of disequilibrium when a defense is vulnerable, when a game's sudden, unexpected swings can be turned to advantage. It is what you do at this moment, when possession changes, that makes the difference. How fast you can set up. How fast you strike. What instant patterns you can create. How you turn simple advantage into something permanent. It is this the Soviets have learned to do, and the balance has been swung.

In the Challenge Cup, for the first time the Soviets joined in the game. They had always stayed a little separate from it, not adjusting and readjusting opponent by opponent, moment by moment. It was as if they feared that the compromises of a particular game and a particular opponent would distract them from a course they believed in; certain that eventually they would raise the level of their game to whatever was needed so that it wouldn't matter anyway. Then, two weeks ago, they entered our game, found its weaknesses, and exploited them. They chased the puck in the offensive zone and the neutral zone, turning the tables and using the smaller ice surface to *their* advantage. They got the puck, with forty feet of ice, or fifty, or eighty, with two teammates or three, and created something with it; no regrouping, no setting up, a teammate in motion, the defense off-balance, a pass, a 3-on-2, a 2-on-1—instantly. It was all-ice commitment, but always under control. It was *our* game played *their* way, a game exactly suited to their skills. Their smaller bodies were strong enough, tough enough, to stand up to the game, to wrestle for the puck, to get it and move it, if rarely to punish. Their short, choppy, wide-gaited stride was quicker to start up, quicker to change direction, quicker to gain advantage and keep it. And finally they had an opportunist's touch, a model transition game.

It worked spectacularly. It offered no patterns to interrupt, no time for us to organize and prepare. It made the unpredictability of the game seem theirs. We had the puck, then they did, and it was too late. By pressuring us, they took pressure off themselves. And without pressure, our offense couldn't work. So we turned up the adrenaline game higher. Only this time it couldn't go high enough. We couldn't move our bodies fast enough, long enough. The Soviets were too quick. We exhorted and yelled; the robot-like Soviets, annoyingly dispassionate to our eyes, played with no less commitment, but with control. Too often the puck moved past us just as we arrived. Usually it was late in periods, or late in games, when we tired slightly. Then, when we were committed and out of position, the trouble got worse. It was like throwing haymakers at a counterpuncher: the harder we threw, the worse it got. In 1972, the Soviets had seemed intimidated by our frightening will; now they turned it against us. Yet the essence of their style of game did not change. It was the final irony. In countering our game, they discovered they could play theirs more effectively.

So where do we stand? There can be no more illusion now. We have followed the path of our game to its end. We have discovered its limits. They are undeniable. More and better of the same will not work. The Soviets have found the answer to our game and taken it apart. We are left only with wishful thinking. We must go back and find another way.

We have paid an enormous price as originators and developers, as custodians and keepers, as unchallenged champions of the sport. That others coming later, unbound, would take greater, more creative steps is understandable. That we should fail to fight back is not. Yet there is a fatalism about Canadians that extends beyond hockey. To a child of celebrated parents (England and France's progeny), raised in the shadow of a southern colossus (America's neighbor), others have always seemed to do things bigger and better; others always would. So, never precocious, never rebellious, reasonably content, we ride their coattails and do *pretty* well. In hockey, now that we've been caught from behind, we wonder why it took so long.

Except that in sports, it doesn't have to happen that way. The biggest, or richest, or most scientific does not always win. The Yugoslavs beat the Soviets in basketball; the Argentines, the Dutch, and others do the same in soccer. For us, the first and biggest problem is not the Soviets, it is ourselves. If we can do little about our national state of mind, we can do a lot about rethinking our national game. Most of our traditions date back fifty years. Since then, there have been two major rule changes, a revolution in all things *speed*, and the emergence of a new hockey model. But the league never carried through the logical consequences of its own changes, and others got their chance. Now we forget what those consequences were. We must go back and find them, ask ourselves if traditions and myths that once made sense make sense any longer.

Mostly, the answer is no. But the value in tracing a game to its roots is to find out why it is no; to realize that once there were reasons, often good reasons, for why things were as they were; to realize that in time good reasons can become obsolete; to watch those same reasons take on a life of their own; to see what happens when they are enshrined as treasured myths; to see that a game can be changed, and to see what change can do. Then to take a game forward in time, to use those lessons, and look again. Our message is clear: ice surfaces may be enlarged, painted lines removed, nets moved forward, old fundamentals practiced and perfected, but until the patterns of the game change, nothing else will. Simply, speed must be harnessed and directed, the forward pace must be made to work.

The Soviets pass better than we do because their crisscross diagonal patterns allow it, and demand it; because passing is a fundamental of their game, fostered and encouraged by their leadership; because the instincts and skills necessary to it develop naturally from practice and use. We need no less. We must abandon our tethered, straight-ahead style, up and down like table-hockey players. Offensively, it has made no sense for fifty years. Defensively ("picking up our wings"), it makes sense only because the offense is so strangled. We must find open ice, moving on diagonals to present a better target, a target that skates in front of us, not away from us, using the width of the ice for more space, more time, to pick up more speed, to make those unburdened by the puck the creative figures. We must take the focus off the puck-carrier, to turn ours into a team game. We should remove the individualist's instinct to skate several strides with the puck; we must force a pass—one touch—to pick up speed, to create an advantage and press it. We should use more of the ice, make the game less congested. Like big fullbacks running into a line, we skate always anticipating contact, straining against it even when it isn't there. Breaking into the open, we feel naked and clumsy, as if robbed of our skills. We must become more comfortable with open ice, make quickness and creativity seem like more than just flash. And the league must deliver a message, clear and uncompromising: hooking, holding, and high-sticking will be penalized, so that the quick and skilled are not, so that open ice created will not be taken away.

We must develop new fundamental skills, create new positional stereotypes. We must make size less crucial, we must exchange speed for quickness, power for skill, bigness for muscular strength. We should adapt long, graceful quarter-miler strides to a sprinter's game. Defensemen should become both the stopping point *and* the starting point of the action, developing transition game skills. For in a transition game, it is out of defense, resilient and forceful, that offense emerges. Body-checking should remain an inevitable and attractive part of their game, but with a new function: not accident, strategy, or a means of intimidation, but as part of that transition; used as a way to get the puck, to set a game in motion, not to stop it dead in its tracks, to allow a game to hit and run.

We must free the game from the dump and chase, break the congestion of hits, shots, screens, deflections, rebounds, and scrambles. We should make it seem like more than just patternless chance, more than just fury, mayhem, and the law of averages. Let fans follow it. Let them see goals, and goals in the making. In open ice, a puck *can* be seen, it isn't hard to follow. And if collisions cause angry, violent feelings, fewer collisions will cause fewer of them. To break the pattern of violence, we should get the game out of the corners, away from the boards. Get it into open ice.

The violence of our game is not so much the innate violence in us as the absence of intervention in our lives. We let a game follow its intuitive path, pretending to be powerless, then simply live with its results. The game now has more Americans and Europeans who play it, it is trained and developed more often in schools and universities, yet its conservative culture remains.

And if we were to do something, who would decide what is right and wrong for a game? Who decides what is in a *game's* best interests? Who is the keeper of the game? John Ziegler? The NHL owners? They are surely the only ones who can do something. But what are their interests? Why should they want the game to change? They are businessmen. They may love hockey profoundly, but they have an investment to protect. Their arenas are already more than eighty percent full, more than seven hundred times a season. What have they got to gain? And how would fans accept the change? In the United States, it is axiomatic that speed and violence are what sells. It was what new teams sold in the 1920s, it is what new teams sell today. A few years ago, the Tidewater Red Wings of the AHL told fans in southern Virginia that hockey was coming. Billboards went up—one read, "Brutal, fast, brutal, exciting, and brutal"; the other, "If they didn't have rules, they'd call it war."

But if the pattern of gratuitous violence were eliminated, what then? Who would watch? Maybe the axiom is wrong. Maybe it has always been wrong. Maybe its formula only limits the appeal of the game, committing the already hardcore fan, turning away millions of others. Maybe fans really do want change. Maybe it would bring them into arenas in even greater numbers, in front of TV sets in greater numbers still. And maybe not. And who wants to take that risk? Years ago, it was simple. We didn't have to worry about the best way to play because we were the best, and how we played was the best way to play. Then the Soviets came along, and things got complicated.

But what can we do now? This is no public enterprise. Why should we think of hockey as a national possession? Why should we think of the Montreal Canadiens as *ours*? If we buy a car, we don't think of General Motors as ours. So why is hockey any different? But it does seem different. The Canadiens do seem ours. We cheer them as if they are ours, and boo them the same way.

Before every game—"*Accueillons.* Let's welcome. *Nos* Canadiens! *Our* Canadiens!" And we want to believe it. And we do believe it until something happens that reminds us that they aren't, that they really belong to Molson's.

It is our fundamental dilemma. A game we treat as ours isn't ours. It is part of our national heritage, and pride, part of us; but we can't control it. Baseball has no similar problem, nor basketball or football, for there is no external challenge to bind a public together, to turn a league and a sport into a national cause. And there is no sport in the United States that means the same as hockey means to Canada. So what is our future? How can we meet the Soviet challenge, and our challenge? It is to find a coincidence of interests. That point where the interests of the game and of those who own it are the same.

For it is only there that our game can change enough to make a difference. And it can only happen if the NHL makes international hockey the climax to its season, in World Championships, or, more likely, in a year-end series between the Stanley Cup winners and the Soviet league champions. It would give a season a new, never-forgotten goal, because teams gear to win championships. They draft players and plan their teams with that in mind. They focus on last year's winner. How can we beat them? Where must we improve? When the Flyers were champions, teams got bigger and tougher, just for the Flyers. When we took over, teams changed. With the Soviets as each season's ultimate opponent, they would change again. Or should. Players' skills and sizes would change, styles of play, the league's enforcing of its rules; never to become some European facsimile, but something new, ours. It may never happen, but it could. For such an annual series *will* come about. The exponential revenues soon available by cable and pay-TV make it certain. Also certain is that the more competitive and attractive the series is, the higher those revenues will be. There is the coincidence of interests. There is the incentive to compete, and change. It is the chance we need.

"Whom the gods would destroy, they first oversell." The NHL's American dream has come to an end, again. It will be back, years from now when old lessons grow hazy, when enough is different that everything before it seems hopelessly quaint and irrelevant, when optimism returns. For hockey is too appealing a game for the dream to die. Whether it will ever fare any better is less certain. In America, it is a game most of whose fans were never players, and now that the latest minor-hockey boom has busted, it seems they never will be. It changes how a game is watched, and enjoyed, how it is sold to its audience. It becomes a promoter's game, a hard sell of hype and hyperbole—the fastest, the toughest—always pandering to stereotype. It is a game relegated to the fringes, to the not quite respectable line between sport and attraction.

Hockey was not the sport of the 1970s as deadline writers wished it to be, nor was there ever really a chance it could be. An exciting mix of speed and violence, it was simply a game that made sense. And in the irrepressible logic of the time, that seemed enough. Whatever its problems, money and *exposure* would overcome them. But the economy turned down, too few sat by their TVs to be exposed, and it didn't happen. There would be no quick fixes: no network TV contracts, no American superstar messiahs to start an unstoppable ball rolling. So at the end of its decade, hockey is where it was at the start—a minor American sport with major regional appeal. Except that the mood around it has changed. It is sour. The gods that oversold it are bitter. They feel betrayed. It is not the game they said it would be; it's the game's fault, they decide.

The Challenge Cup was the bottom, on the ice, and off— Madison Square Garden, the Waldorf-Astoria, *the Russians*; a week in the *Big Apple*, big corporate clients wined and entertained. It was to be like Super Bowl Week, its model. "...one of the world's most dynamic sports events," columnist Dave Anderson wrote in *The New York Times*, "but no impact....It should be the talk of the town. Instead, it's hardly mentioned except by the hockey community." And finally what should have been clear was clear. It is easy to feel big when you're not, if you surround yourself with others who are smaller. But if you pretend you are big, and surround yourself with others bigger, you feel crushingly small. That is what happened in New York. There was *Ain't Misbehavin'*, *Sweeney Todd*, *The Best Little Whorehouse in Texas*, the New York Philharmonic, the New York City Ballet, the Metropolitan Opera's *Don Carlo* and *Madama Butterfly*, the Knicks and the Celtics, harness racing at Roosevelt Raceway and the Meadowlands, St. John's at Fordham, Queens at Brooklyn College, and us. And if any doubts remained, they disappeared on Saturday. For though Sunday was the final game, Saturday was the bottom. It was the day of the great TV fiasco.

Unable to sell the series to an American network, the NHL put together an ad hoc group of stations for two games, selling the Saturday game to CBS for its afternoon sports program. Highlights would be aired on a delayed basis, sandwiched between coverage of the *Los Angeles Times* track meet, a WBA welterweight championship fight, and the International Pro Surfers Women's

Team Championship. The NHL also sold advertising space on the boards. When CBS found out, they asked the league to remove the advertising. The NHL refused. CBS decided to go ahead with the game anyway, but shifted their camera angles so that the advertising wouldn't show. It would be the only extended network coverage of the season. For the game's allotted minutes, CBS cameras followed the puck, but as it approached the boards, everything taller than a puck got chopped. It was the final humiliation. The league had tried too hard.

But now the trains have passed through the tunnel, and the light remains. What now? It will be a quieter decade for the NHL. Expansion and the WHA behind it, it will be a time to turn inward, to put its unwieldy house in order. Like an aging adolescent having grown too fast, it will get reacquainted with its parts, get them in hand, and do something with them. It will be a time of realism, and stability, for chastened hopes and dreams deferred—except one. Off ice, the whispered word will be "cable." But it will represent a more modest dream this time, and more realizable, if the promised bonanza is only for some. It is time for a deep breath, a pause, a time to return the game to the ice. For that is the real tragedy of the 1970s, and the real opportunity of the 1980s. It is on the ice that its next great challenge lies.

It was an easy win, 7-3, where wins are never easy, but the Flyers are not the team they were. Parent is injured, seriously again, perhaps for the last time. It's his eye. A few years ago, it was his neck. A marvellous goalie at his best, Parent must play untroubled. His goaltending-guru, Jacques Plante, had seemed always able to unburden his mind, but now, in his thirties, Parent's body overcomes him. So too Jimmy Watson, a small, brave defenseman, who plays often when he shouldn't. He played tonight, but didn't play well.

Even Bobby Clarke has changed. The spirit of his team, Clarke could always find a level of commitment no one else was willing to find. But now there seems a different desperation in his game, as if he can't quite feel that same commitment, and he's scared. It's as if he's suddenly come face to face with human weakness—his own. It's different when a body wears out, when legs get tired and slow. It seems an act of nature, unstoppable, beyond control. And it is forgivable. But not so a mind. Then it is weakness, unforgivable weakness. It is *you*. It happens often to those nearing thirty, when the best seems suddenly past, before age is accepted and new goals are found. Still Clarke, being Clarke, fights back, pushing himself to do what once was natural. But tonight he looked tired. He needs a new goal. The Flyers have always depended on him. Now it is his turn. He needs them to be real contenders again.

But they are not. Their points totals may improve, they may move up in the standings, but it's all illusion. They have a fundamental flaw, and can't win. Each year since 1976, since their two-year hold on the NHL was ended, they have been the "new" Flyers. They are faster, more talented, more versatile, less goon-like than their predecessors. But each year, they show they are not. They are simply *the Flyers*. It is an attitude, and a tradition, that will not change. They have the same swagger. They play as if with the same impunity, as if penalties, fines, and suspensions are mere costs of doing business, to be served, paid off, killed without consequence. But things are different now. The costs are too high, the consequences too certain. The style that won them two consecutive Stanley Cups only guarantees that they will win no more. The irony is wonderful.

It changes the mood of our games. It makes each less threatening. Knowing the ending, the rough parts are easier to take. So when Paul Holmgren beats up someone until my stomach turns, when the Spectrum crowd roars its approving roar, when Behn Wilson, Ken Linesman, and other "new" Flyers file by him in tribute, I smile. It is what we never got to feel as kids. What never happened to the bully on the block. For Holmgren, Linesman, Wilson, and the others, there is no more impunity. *They will get theirs*.

The bar is Sunday-evening empty. Suddenly it's full. One game is over; another begins.

"...Aries, right?"

"Huh? Oilers? No, no, no, Canadiens."

"Canadiens?"

"You asked me if I played for the Oilers?"

"No, I asked you your sign."

"Oh, *hah hah hah*, I'm a..."

"You play for the Houston Oilers?"

"No, no the Canadiens. The Montreal Canadiens. The hockey team."

"You're a professional athlete? Oh wow! I mean, I don't know much about hockey, but..."

Games are played, so games are to be won. But they are easy games, soon forgotten. Until the next time. It's a fact of every road trip. Some play, some don't; no one keeps score. At home, wives and girl friends wonder.

It's quiet. The music has stopped. For some, the weekend is over. They gather up cigarettes and coats, say perfunctory good-byes; at a table at the back, no one moves. It is our time. The luckless climb from their bar-stools; more tables are pieced together. Jackets get slung into chairs, ties loosen, talk comes dressing-room easy. It's about goals and goals missed, money, women, cars, golf. Anything. Stories that we've heard before, and some we haven't; and will again. It's my favorite time, when something is done and over, and good, when there's nothing more to do, and no place to go until morning. Everything slows down. Words get softer. We speak of "the game" *this*, "the game" *that*. Sentences trail off, never finished. Things go unsaid. Yet we nod and understand. It is at moments like this that I remember why I play.

Last year, after we had won the Stanley Cup against the Bruins, several journalists asked what it had meant to me. I couldn't really tell them. I heard myself speak of satisfaction and pride, yet I knew that wasn't it, or all of it. I sat in my office a few days later, and tried again. I wrote this to myself:

"I am good, and we are good, and when I do my best and we do our best, we win most of the time. When we win, we receive trophies and plaques, our names go in newspapers; they go on checks alongside numbers with lots of zeros. When people talk, they talk about us a *certain* way. And after a while, everything is inextricably linked—winning, playing our best, money, celebrity. If someone asks us why we play, we're not sure any longer. We might speak ritually of 'loving the game'; then, embarrassed, skip on to winning, money, and the rest. And everyone understands.

"But ask us after a game. After we've played the Bruins or the Islanders; after a playoff game. If you don't understand the excited tumble of words, look at our gray-white faces, at eyes that glitter and pop at you. Look at our sweaty smiles, at hands that won't shut up. An hour later, a day's tension sucked away, look at our bodies. All gangly and weak, so weak we laugh it feels so good. Look at our faces, at smiles distant and content."

I have a picture. It shows nine or ten guys, arms hanging on each other's shoulders, faces dripping with sweat. *Beaming.* Tremblay, Lafleur, Palchak, Nyrop, Jarvis, me. I don't beam; Jarvis doesn't beam. A week before, we had won the Norris Division, Prince of Wales Conference, and $4,500; five weeks later, we would win $15,000 and our second straight Stanley Cup. Pete Mahovlich, our designated captain, held a tiny trophy we had given ourselves for winning a series of week-long intrasquad games. Later, we received $25 a man. It's the happiest picture I have.

Coaches like Vince Lombardi and George Allen have told us

we must play for certain reasons. As children, our parents and coaches told us something else. But after the Bruins series, Chartraw came much closer, "I don't play for money," he laughed, "I play for the party after."

A few years ago, I called Dickie Moore to arrange an interview for a friend. Moore had been a fine player for the Canadiens in the 1950s, and after retiring with knee injuries (later, he returned briefly with the Leafs and the Blues), had built a successful equipment rental company in Montreal. It happened that I called on the first anniversary of his son's death in a car accident. It had been a tough day was all Moore said. More for me than for him, he changed the subject. He asked me how I was, how the team was doing; then he turned reflective. He spoke of "the game." Sometimes excitedly, sometimes with longing, but always it was "the game." Not a game of his time, or mine, something he knew we shared. It sounded almost spell-like the way he put it. I had always thought of it as a phrase interchangeable with "hockey," "baseball," any sport. But when Moore said it, I knew it wasn't. "The game" was different, something that belongs only to those who play it, a code phrase that anyone who has played a sport, any sport, understands. It's a common heritage of parents and backyards, teammates, friends, winning, losing, dressing rooms, road trips, coaches, press, fans, money, celebrity—a life, so long as you live it. Now as I sit here, slouched back, mellow, when I hear others talk of "the game," I know what Moore meant. It is hockey that I'm leaving behind. It's "the game" I'll miss.

Monday

"It's not just a job."

—A Chorus Line

ON THE ROAD

"NEVER AGAIN."

No one laughs. Cowlicks, gray stubbled faces, auras of garlic and beer. Stars of the world's fastest game, on a bus to New York. Yesterday's rain stopped moments ago. It's dull and overcast.

"Jesus, it's bright in here," Chartraw bellows. "Ya got no curtains for this thing, bussy?"

"Hey Sharty, try these," Lapointe says, holding out his sunglasses. "Your eyes are makin' me sick." Chartraw reaches for them. Lapointe puts them back on. There are sunglasses everywhere. Behind them, some are reading, most are sleeping. Shutt is bored. He tells everyone near him his newest theory on drinking—"Don't inhale." He laughs; no one else does. He watches Napier beside him. Napier's head lolls from side to side, bounces to his chest a few times, and finally settles there. He's asleep.

"Hey Napes," Shutt whispers, "you asleep?" Napier stirs. "Oh sorry, Napes. But Napes, I gotta tell ya somethin'. Napes, are ya listenin'?" Napier's head lolls upright, one eye struggles open; he nods. *"Sleep at night, Napes!"*

Behind Shutt, a little black book is being updated: "Ooh, she was a firecracker," the diarist mumbles. "Gotta find her a permanent place. Lemme see, Anne, Anne, what goes with Anne... Ooh, she's a silky little thing." At that, those asleep begin to laugh.

237

He doesn't notice. "What goes with—Sullivan! That's it, Sullivan." Eyes pop open. "Silky Sullivan?" A loud laugh this time. "That's not bad," he says, pleased with himself. "Now what'll I call him?" Awake, now sitting up, others shout their suggestions, "Ed? Naw, too obvious. Red? Hayward? Hey, c'mon. Barry? Yeah, Barry. That's not bad." A final laugh, then those around him go back to sleep. He leafs through his book to "S," takes a pen from his pocket, and writes:

SULLIVAN, Barry (wife, Anne)
Presbyterian Minister
Philadelphia   (215)...

The overcast has burned away. I try to sleep, then read. I look out the windows, at turnpike countryside, mile after mile. It's a day to look out windows, to let energy run down, and feel it trickle back. Then feel it build again. It happens each year at this time. When I feel spring, or the playoffs, I never know which it is. It's an instinct, as sure as the seasons. Something that happens, that cannot be rushed. When it's time, I will know. I lean back in my seat, and close my eyes.

"Ya weren't sleepin', were ya?" It's Shutt.

"Huh? Oh no, Shutty."

"I was brilliant last night, eh?"

"Huh? Oh yeah, Shutty, yeah, you were brilliant."

"I was, wasn't I? Happens every time I drink. Can't understand it. Wish I could remember what I said. I oughta drink more often *hee hee hee*." It comes in a dizzying burst. I can't keep up. He sees a pad of paper on my lap. "Hey, whatcha doin'?"

"Huh? Oh, I was just writing down some things. May use 'em sometime."

"Ya writin' a book? Hey great. Need some help? Want some of my quips? Hey, we could do it together. We'd quip 'em to death. Give 'em quiplash *hee hee hee*." And he's gone.

I feel comfortable on this bus, with this team. I'm not sure anyone else knows that. I'm not sure even my teammates know it. I don't say much. I often like to be alone. My background and interests are different enough to make me *seem* different (being a goalie forgives a lot; being a good goalie, a lot more). Still, by now I think most understand. I have changed in eight years. Before my sabbatical season, 1973-74, I had little time for the team. It was due in part to my dual life as a law student, but only in part. I was young, and, in pre-dynasty times, better than the team. I had standards no one could meet. Those who didn't backcheck as often as I thought they should, those who drank too much, let *me* down. They had seemed more like opponents than teammates, lined up against me, keeping me from being what I wanted to be. And, silently, I raged at them. Early in the 1973 playoffs, Bowman took me aside. He wondered if I felt myself "too big" for the team. I don't remember what had prompted it. It didn't matter. I was hurt, and furious. For the rest of the playoffs, I sulked, desperately sure he was wrong, afraid he wasn't. At the end, I got my revenge. It was Bowman's first Stanley Cup. When the team celebrated on the ice, he hugged me as he did the others. I hung from him like a rag.

When I returned from my year in Toronto, things were different. I was older. My contract squabble had made me seem disagreeably normal. I let in too many goals. I improved as the year went on, and since, yet it's never been the same. I lost something those two years—an illusion of my own perfectibility. I had done many things in a short time. The rest I *could* do, I *would* do. It would only take time. I would read the classics. I would learn more science and economics. I would learn to speak French. Then I had the time, and I didn't. On the ice, I made the same bad passes, fell for the same inexplicable reasons, eased up on long shots and sharp-angled shots with the same results. At the same time, the team was getting better. It became less clear to others, finally to me, who really needed whom.

In 1976, the team and I did something together. There was a great sense of quest that season. We had not won the Stanley Cup for two years. The Flyers were champions, so we chased them— over the summer, in training camp, in every game we played. We left them behind in the standings; we chased what they had been, and still might be. We chased them until May; and caught them. No Stanley Cup had felt so good. I had learned the lesson Gainey had learned when he was twelve years younger.

Yesterday, I did an interview with a Philadelphia journalist. After some minutes, he shook his head and told me I was different from other athletes he had interviewed. His voice then got quiet, as if he thought someone might overhear him (though no one was around). "How do you relate to these guys?" he whispered. I sat quiet and said nothing, and he went on to something else. I think it took me so long to want to be a part of the team because I was afraid of a team. Afraid of always having to do what a team does; afraid of losing my own right to be different. When I realized that I could be part of a team, and still be different, I could then be less different. Then I realized I wasn't very different at all. The Philadelphia journalist didn't understand. I may seem different, as others may seem different from me. But together we have one common passion. It has taken much of our time, and most of our energy. It has shaped us. All of that we share. The rest are details.

I look around the bus. What will happen to this team? There will be changes soon. Cournoyer, Lemaire, Savard, Lapointe, each is now past thirty. Not old, but old enough. Excepting Cournoyer, each may yet play several more years. But maybe they won't. Maybe they can't. Like a man of sixty, each is at an age where there can be no more surprise, no sense of tragedy, if something happens. Who will take their place? Where will the next Cournoyer come from? The next Lemaire and Savard? The next Pollock and Bowman? There has always been someone. In twenty-three years, Plante, Charlie Hodge, Worsley, Vachon, Doug Harvey, Tom Johnson, Talbot, Ted Harris, J. C. Tremblay, Laperrière, Harper, the Rocket, Henri Richard, Bert Olmstead, Floyd Curry, Moore, Claude Provost, Ferguson, Bobby Rousseau, Backstrom, Gilles Tremblay, Donnie Marshall, Dick Duff, Roberts, Béliveau, Geoffrion, Pete and Frank Mahovlich have all been replaced. So have Selke, Blake, and Pollock. In twenty-three years, fourteen Stanley Cups have been won. The team goes on. But what now?

It will be harder. The historical advantages of thirty years are gone, or going. What you see on the ice is very nearly all there is. There is no farm team somewhere "better than most NHL teams." Most importantly, the store of draft picks that nourished the success of the 1970s looks now like everyone else's. But great teams need great players; and great French-Canadian teams need great French-Canadian players. Where will they come from? Who will carry the torch of Richard, Béliveau, and Lafleur? Not Mondou, or Tremblay, or Larouche; they are spear-carriers. No one now on the team; no one in Halifax with the Voyageurs. It will be someone somewhere in Quebec. But who?—and when he grows up, will it be with the Canadiens?

Thirty years ago, the answer would have been yes. NHL teams could sponsor amateur teams; the Canadiens monopolized Quebec. When sponsorship ended in favor of a universal draft in the 1960s, the Canadiens were given a concession. They were allowed two picks prior to the draft for players of French-Canadian parentage (in lieu of their first- and second-round picks). That concession expired for the 1970 draft (and Gilbert Perreault). Yet the answer remained a tentative yes. Pollock had used the fruits of Selke's farm system to rebuild the Canadiens dynasty, its rejects to bargain for the future. Expansion teams, vulnerable at the box office and on the ice, needed players. Pollock had them. In return, he got nameless draft picks, who would turn out to be Lafleur, Robinson, Shutt, Larocque, Nyrop, Connor, Risebrough, Tremblay, Mondou, Chartraw, Engblom, and Napier. A new dynasty was built; the torch was passed. Perreault, Dionne, Potvin, and Bossy got away, almost unnoticed; so did many others. Hangsleben, Micheletti, Hislop, Hunter, and about a score more, all drafted but signed by the WHA. None seemed a great loss. The WHA had become a kind of development league for the Canadiens. If any proved themselves, they could be signed later. Yet they were important. Descendants of Randy Rota, Ernie Hicke, and others, they were the barter that would become the draft picks, that would become the future Lafleurs, Robinsons, and Hangslebens, on which succeeding dynasties would be built. For much of the decade, the Canadiens have had to do without them. The stockpile of draft picks has diminished. When the NHL-WHA merger takes place, most will be gone for good. For the Canadiens, this is a crossroads.

I've often wondered what makes this team so good. It's a question we've all had frequent practice at answering, yet I'm not sure any of us has done very well. We each have our pet theories, the latest and most obscure, the most undeniably our own, the best. Yet, it seems there should be *one* reason, more central than others, on which the others rely. Management perhaps. Certainly the Canadiens are a textbook study: stability (three managers, five coaches in forty years), competence (*professional* managers, whose qualifications aren't goals and assists; who are secure enough to hire the best people; who win), dedication (Pollock, Bowman, Ruel, and others didn't marry until well into their thirties), attitude. They feel it's their "God-given duty to be the best every year," former coach Al MacNeil once said. It's a message we all sense. The team is a business, yet its bottom line seems only to win.

Maybe it's the Montreal environment, that conspiracy of expectations, of fans, press, management, coaches, players, that makes losing intolerable. Or it's the team itself. Its mix of ages, sizes, and styles of play; personalities, attitudes; French and English. There is something distinctly different about Richard, Béliveau, Lafleur, Plante; and about Mahovlich, Moore, Gainey, Dryden—something incompatible, or richly varied and strong. Maybe it's the presence of great players like Béliveau and Lafleur. The attitude of a team depends so much on its best player. A coach and a manager can be neutralized; a best player has followers, and must be a leader. He must have the character and personality to match his skills. It's why the Flyers won and the Sabres didn't; why the Kings and Blues never went far; why the Islanders needed the emergence of Trottier. Or maybe it's talent—the first and easiest explanation; the first forgotten. We would prefer that it be hard work, for hard work seems less a gift, more a reflection on us. But without talent, "hard work doesn't work," as journeyman defense-man Bryan Watson once put it. With talent, bad games and a bad season can still be won.

Really, it is all those things, and more. When a team wins once, it can be for one central reason. When it wins for three consecutive years, nine times in fourteen years, it's for a crush of reasons. Winning brings with it such an immense momentum. Everything fits, everything works. Every new thing is made to fit and work. Everything just *is*. Reasons blur and disappear. It becomes a state of mind, an obligation, an expectation; in the end, an attitude. Excellence. It is that rare chance to play with the best, to be the best. When you have it, you don't give it up.

It's not easy, and not always fun. "Satisfaction for me never came during a season," Jimmy Roberts, a veteran Canadiens player, once told me. "There was always too much pressure. . . . It was so sudden and gone again because there was always another game. Then, when a season was over, I'd realize, 'Jesus Christ, I can't live off this. I gotta do it all again next year.' Then I'd get all worried about next year." But it gives you a range, and depth, of feeling no also-ran can have. "Now I look through the old scrap-book," Roberts went on, "at my trophies on the mantel, and try to remember if they were good days or not. Then I look at what I've got." He smiled. "It was really nice."

But it's a state of mind that can get tired. When you win as often as we do, you earn a right to lose. It's losing to remember what winning feels like. But it's a game of *chicken*. If you let it go too far, you may never get it back. You may find its high-paid, pressureless comfort to your liking. I can feel it happening this year. If we win, next year will be worse. But who's going to stop it? Where are the legendary figures that refuse to fall? Pollock is gone. Bowman may soon leave. Cournoyer, Lemaire, Savard, Lapointe. There had always been someone. It's the Canadiens' tradition. Who now?

Irving Grundman continues the line of professional managers. But he came late to hockey. Competent, decent, he learned its language quickly. Can he learn its idioms? Can he deliver the same palpable message? A year of losing and the spirit will rekindle. But more than spirit is needed. Great players, great coaches and managers, must be replaced in kind. In 1960, the Canadiens won their fifth successive Stanley Cup. Richard retired, Harvey and Plante were later traded, and Geoffrion retired. In due course Selke retired, replaced by Pollock. A new generation rose from the farm system, and, after winning in 1965, won three times in four years. There is no farm system now. Nor is there the stockpile of draft picks that built the next generation of success. With Pollock's departure, management is thinner than it has ever been, and unhappy. It's not 1960 again. It's not the fallow end of a cycle. Like snakes and ladders, when the slide comes this time there's less to stop it, and there's farther to fall.

If dynasties come for a crush of reasons, dynasties die one reason at a time. It starts like a slump. The immense momentum of winning slows; the slump doesn't end. The momentum turns. Everything that fits doesn't fit. Obligation turns cranky; expectation and attitude disappear. It's what each of us has felt at times this year. Slowly the team is joining the pack. It must learn to live, and compete, like everyone else. Except, unlike everyone else it must win; and the French-Canadian character of the team must not be disturbed. The team created the expectations; now it must live with them. Fewer than fifteen percent of the league's players are French-Canadian. Since Lafleur, Perreault, and Dionne in the early 1970s, few of them have been superstars. Now there are more teams, more reluctant to trade draft picks, in the market to compete for them. Lafleur must have his heir; the team must win. Ahead may be a tragic irony. Without the strength of the past, the team may face a choice—to win, *or* to be French-Canadian?

"Hey bussy! Turn up that radio."

As we near New York, the singing begins. Then it stops. From an introductory few bars, we know what's coming. "Hey, Reggie!" we shout. Houle's ready, his voice a pristine monotone.

"You took a fine time to leave me, Lucille..." he wails; we cheer, then go quiet. "Four hungry children..." (dramatic pause, catch in his voice), "...a crop in the field..." We cheer again. His accent strains at the words, turning the song into a touching/hilarious lament. "I've had some bad times, been through some sad times..." Here and there, others join him. But it's Reggie's song, and always will be.

Practice is optional; all but Savard and Lemaire go. It feels good to put on equipment, to sweat, to stop shots when no one tells me to, to feel washed-out, tired-out good at the end. It's a practice that has only to do with us. No one mentions the Islanders. The Islanders don't matter. It's up to us. It's time to feel good about ourselves. Later, Bowman has arranged a team dinner. Afterwards, some are going to the racetrack, others to a movie. Other years, I'd take a train to Manhattan, to the theater. Tonight, I'm going to the movies too.

Tuesday

*"Like an army on ice, we march south every winter,
We return in the spring the conquerors!"*

—Sebastien Dhavernas,
translated by Rick Salutin,
Les Canadiens

NEW YORK

WE DON'T LOSE WHEN WE NEED TO WIN. WE WIN, WE ALWAYS win. We lose when it doesn't matter, when nothing's on the line, when illness, injury, fatigue, boredom, laziness, personal problems, travel—when the law of averages beats us. There's no law of averages in big games. Big games we gear to win. And win. We don't lose when it's *us* on the line, when something must be proved, when we *can't* lose. *We don't lose showdowns. I* don't lose showdowns.

But we lost tonight. To the Islanders.

I don't know what to feel. I've thought about this moment, what it would be like. But it's different. I'm not angry, or even disappointed. I feel a strange peace. Reporters come by, my voice comes out softer and slower, the questions I hear sound the same. Maybe I'm numb. Maybe I'm afraid to feel what I really feel. Maybe I've had enough. Maybe I don't want to fight and struggle and pretend any more. Maybe I want to lose. I feel such a wash of sympathy. So wonderful, cozy and warm. No more nagging voices, no more self-hating words. It's over. There are new targets now. The king is dead; maybe he's not such a bad guy after all.

I pack up my things and go. At the door, I see Bowman. I see Gainey and Lemaire. We look at each other. They look almost serene. But in their eyes, just beginning, is a glint. I can feel it too. This is what Bowman's been waiting for. This is what we've all been waiting for. I walk out the door. Inside, I feel a smile.

Epilogue

*"It was a dream, and everything I dreamed came true.
Now my dream is finished. That's a new life for me.
Because what I do now, what I keep on doing is
something I never dreamed of."*

—Henri Richard

NOTHING HAPPENED THE WAY IT WAS SUPPOSED TO. THE Islanders caught us, then we caught them. In the season's final game, we needed a tie against Detroit for first place, and we lost. The Islanders, waiting to be crowned, lost to the Rangers in the playoffs. And we won again. It was no triumph; we only survived. After the season we had had, we could hardly hope for more.

It was my last playoffs, something that never quite left my mind. I felt no real nostalgia, no sudden paralysis at the brink. Yet I kept looking back, for I needed a guide. Nothing in the present was making sense. I felt like a chess player at a scrambled board. I was playing poorly, and couldn't stop. I searched for answers, and found none; for patterns and precedents that would tell me how it would all end. I discovered the symmetries in my career: the Bruins, Boston Garden; coming in a winner, going out a winner. When nothing else gave comfort, they did. There seemed a kind of perfect destiny.

Then we lost three times in Boston Garden. The Bruins took us to seven games. There were no tidy circles, no symmetries—a cruel punch line at the end. Irony was my pattern. *My* town, *my* team, *my* rink, *my* solid ground, my first and lasting reputation— with less than four minutes left in the seventh game, Rick Middleton scored from behind the net. The Bruins were ahead. Savard was closest to the play. He let out a groan of curdling sadness, as if it was over. The Bruins got a bench penalty. Lafleur scored. Lambert won it in overtime. I felt nothing, as if my strings were being pulled, as if everything was beyond my control. Irony was not my pattern either.

The finals were no different. I was taken out after the second period of the first game, replaced by Larocque. I had played every minute of every playoff game until then (except for the year I was in Toronto), more than one hundred consecutive games. Larocque shut out the Rangers the final period. The Rangers won. Larocque would take over, just as I had taken over from Vachon for the playoffs, eight years before. Irony *was* my pattern. Then, in the warm-up for the second game, Larocque was struck in the mask by Risebrough's shot, and couldn't play. I felt like an observer to my own fate. Yet I knew with blissful certainty what would happen next. It was what always happened at times like that. I laughed and joked before the game because I knew that's what I should do. I put everyone at ease. For me it would be vindication and triumph. The Rangers scored in the first minute, again a few minutes later. I had no more patterns left. The rest was nerve-endings. We won that game, and the next two. In my final game, I had a chance for a shutout, but a long, looping, screened shot beat me. It was just. When it was over, Bowman went to Buffalo, Lemaire to Switzerland; the team retired unbeaten.

A year later, my family and I moved to England. We lived in Cambridge, where there was a soccer team, Cambridge United, in the English league, Second Division. I had watched soccer a few times on TV, excited and intrigued by its spectacle of flags, scarves, and game-long singing, but knew little about the game itself. I asked an English friend to go to a game with me. He explained the rules to me, going over the offside rule more than once, and gradually what I didn't understand seemed less important than what I did. I began to see patterns to the game, to recognize rhythms and moods, to anticipate what might happen next. I found that often I was right. In understanding one game, I discovered that I understood another.

But there was one player I couldn't help watching—number 7 for Cambridge, a short, chunky, hard-trying winger who seemed a great crowd favorite. All through the game, he raced ahead onto long passes ("Good ball, good ball," my friend would mutter), only to shoot wide, or be stopped by the goalie. He seemed undiscouraged by it, as the fans did ("Bad luck," they yelled), cheering his every attempt. Yet there was something very familiar about him. Then it occurred to me: I had seen him before, hundreds of times. He was a player on every team I played on, on every team I played against—the same size, the same style, the same results. It hadn't been "bad luck" at all.

Late in the game, Cambridge was a goal down. Another long pass put number 7 into the clear. The crowd roared. For forty yards it roared. My friend began bouncing up and down. "Here it comes. Here it comes," he shouted. I smiled.

Number 7 missed the net.